Immigration
Made Simple

An Easy-to-Read Guide to the U.S. Immigration Process

8th Edition

By Barbara Brooks Kimmel

and

Alan M Lubiner, Esq.

Published by

 **Next Decade**

books that simplify complex subjects

Chester, New Jersey, USA
www.nextdecade.com

Immigration Made Simple
An Easy-to-Read Guide to the U.S. Immigration Process
Eighth Edition

by Barbara Brooks Kimmel
and Alan M. Lubiner, Esq.

Published by:
Next Decade, Inc.
39 Old Farmstead Road
Chester, NJ 07930 USA
Telephone: (908) 879-6625
Fax: (908) 879-2920
E-mail: info@nextdecade.com

Library of Congress Cataloging- in- Publication

Kimmel, Barbara Brooks.
  Immigration made simple : an easy to read guide to the U.S. Immigration process /
by Barbara Brooks Kimmel and Alan M. Lubiner.
      p. cm.
  Includes index.
  ISBN 978-1-932919-16-5 (alk. paper)
  1. Emigration and immigration law--United States--Popular works. I. Lubiner, Alan M. II. Title.
  KF4819.85.K56 2009
  342.7308'2--dc22

$24.95 Soft cover

Table of Contents

About the Authors

Barbara Kimmel spent over fifteen years employed in the New York area as a relocation consultant to many international corporations and several prominent immigration lawyers. During that time she successfully guided thousands of aliens through the complex immigration process.

In 1990 Barbara began writing and publishing "books that simplify complex subjects". She has written or co-authored eight editions of **Immigration Made Simple,** first published in 1990. Barbara is also the co-author of **Citizenship Made Simple**, first published in 1996. These books have received outstanding professional reviews in *Library Journal* and *Booklist*, and have been Quality Books #1 bestsellers.

Finally, she is the President and Publisher at Next Decade, Inc. in Chester, New Jersey. Barbara's company was named Quality Book's Publisher of the Year at the 1997 Book Exposition in Chicago. For more information, visit our web site at www. nextdecade.com.

Ms. Kimmel was awarded a Bachelor of Arts Degree in International Affairs from Lafayette College in Pennsylvania and an MBA from the Bernard M. Baruch Graduate School of Business of the City University of New York.

✳   ✳   ✳

Alan Lubiner has been practicing Immigration Law since 1975. From 1975 until 1981, the Immigration & Naturalization Service employed him in a number of capacities including assisting in the drafting of legislation for the Select Commission on Immigration in Washington, DC. He also spent time in the United States Attorney's Office in the Southern District of Florida where he served as a Special Assistant United States Attorney assigned to special Immigration prosecutions.

In 1981, Mr. Lubiner opened a private law practice, with headquarters in Cranford, New Jersey and specializing in Immigration law. His practice is heavily concentrated in professionals, and he currently represents major corporations, individuals and universities in the scientific field with emphasis on computer science, electrical engineering, chemical engineering, chemistry and pharmaceutical research. He has successfully handled over 1000 cases for foreign students and other individuals.

Mr. Lubiner's credentials include a Bachelor of Science Degree in Finance from New York University and a Juris Doctorate degree from Brooklyn Law School. He is a member of the American Immigration Lawyers Association, an affiliated organization of the American Bar Association, and served on its Board of Governors. He is also a past Chairman of the New Jersey Chapter of the American Immigration Lawyers Association, and a past chairman of the NJ State Bar Section on Immigration. Mr. Lubiner is a member of the Bar of the States of New Jersey, New York and Pennsylvania and is admitted to practice before the Federal Courts in New Jersey, New York and Pennsylvania, as well as the United States Supreme Court. Finally, he is the co-author of **Immigration Made Simple** and **Citizenship Made Simple.**

*With special thanks to all those who continue to recognize
the importance of this valuable reference book*

✳   ✳   ✳

Disclaimer

The purpose of this book is to provide interested individuals with a basic understanding of the rules and regulations concerning U.S. Immigration procedures. It is sold with the understanding that the publisher and authors are not engaged in rendering legal or other professional services in this book, only in sharing information in regard to the subject matter covered. If legal or other expert assistance is required, the services of a competent professional should be sought.

This book was not written to provide all the information that is available to the authors/and or publisher, but to compliment, amplify and supplement other texts and available information. While every effort has been made to ensure that this book is as complete and accurate as possible, there may be mistakes, either typographical or in content. Therefore, this text should be used as a general guide only, and not as the ultimate source of U.S. Immigration information. Furthermore, this book contains information on U.S. Immigration only up to the printing date. The rules and regulations change frequently.

The authors and Next Decade, Inc. shall not be held liable, nor be responsible to any person or entity with respect to any loss or damage caused, or alleged to be caused, directly or indirectly by the information contained in this book.

**If you do not wish to be bound by the above,
you may return this book to the publisher for a full refund.**

Preface

The authors have assisted thousands of people, from all over the world, process petitions for temporary and permanent U.S. visas. These individuals have included students, trainees, and entry level employees. Others were sophisticated investors and senior executives.

Regardless of their backgrounds, all of the people mentioned above shared one common characteristic. They lacked the necessary knowledge of the U.S. Immigration process. We repeatedly heard the same question. *Isn't there a reference book that I can use as a guide in the future, a simple manual that will provide me with a basic understanding of immigration?* We could not give them a recommendation that really met those needs, and so in 1990 we published the first edition of **Immigration Made Simple**. Thousands of orders were received from every state in the U.S., and many foreign countries as well, and we were finally able to recommend a book that meets this need!

Over the next several years, many administrative and regulatory changes mandated the publication of several more editions of **Immigration Made Simple**. As we go to press, there are many major areas of our immigration law that are undergoing close scrutiny by our government and various public interest groups.

This revised eighth edition has been updated and covers, in detail, more categories of visas and related matters. **Immigration Made Simple** has, once again, been developed as an easy to use reference for foreign nationals who currently live and work in the United States, and for those wishing to do so in the near future. The book should also continue to be valuable to those who work with foreign students; corporate personnel working with foreign employees; business managers; the legal profession and its support staff; and others who have occasion to work with our U.S. Immigration process.

The order of the subject matter is intended to be useful. We start by defining some frequently used terms. The sections that follow describe the most common categories of temporary and permanent immigration categories, give examples, and explain how to go about obtaining these visas. We have tried to make these sections as easy to understand as possible. This has not been an easy task! The last section of the book will provide the reader with answers to some of the most common immigration questions. At the end of the book, is an updated **Directory of Immigration Lawyers and Service Providers** to assist our readers in locating a qualified attorney. There are also several appendices containing information that we think you will find very helpful.

Keep in mind that this book was not written to give legal advice, recommend solutions to complex immigration problems, or to replace the service of immigration lawyers. Many topics are not covered, including exclusion and deportation proceedings, political asylum applications and appeal procedures. Our goal in making **Immigration Made Simple** available to you is simply to provide you with a better understanding of the practical side of our immigration system and the options available to you. I hope that the book will serve as a helpful reference guide in the future.

Barbara Brooks Kimmel
Alan M. Lubiner, Attorney

Introduction

The United States has, for generations, been called a "melting pot", a nation of immigrants. For over two hundred years, people from other countries have come to the United States to find safe haven from religious and political persecution, to seek economic opportunity and to reunite with family members. The ethnic and cultural diversity, the brains and talent, as well as the dreams and hopes that immigrants have brought to our country over the years are what have molded our national character and made the United States the super-power that it is today.

In recent years, our immigration policy and our immigrants have come under attack from groups that would have us believe that immigrants are the root of all evil in our society. Major legislation has been enacted with the intention of sealing our borders, including establishing a huge fence along the US-Mexico border. Various politicians and special interest groups seek a moratorium on immigration. Over the past several years sweeping changes in our immigration laws have been enacted that severely restrict the ability of our residents and citizens to reunite with their loved ones. Backlogs in quotas and harsh penalties have caused the breakup of families. Husbands are being separated from wives, parents from children, all in the name of "immigration reform".

The reality is that less than one million immigrants arrive in the United States each year. Undocumented immigrants constitute only one percent of the total U.S. population. Most immigrants are coming to join immediate family members, while a relatively small number are coming to jobs where the employer has demonstrated the inability to find U.S. workers.

The extremist groups would have us believe that immigrants take jobs away from Americans. Nothing could be further from the truth. Immigrant entrepreneurial spirit has been the backbone of American industry, and today immigrants are likely to be self-employed and start new businesses.

Politicians, calling for welfare reform and for keeping immigrants off public assistance claim immigrants are a drain on the U.S. economy. Again, rhetoric that has no basis in fact. Immigrants must prove that they have the ability to sustain themselves or they will not be allowed in the U.S. They are barred from any means tested programs for at least five years. Their sponsors, who must file an affidavit of support with the U.S. government, are now held to their promise of support by a binding contract.

Immigrants permeate the very fabric of America. They are our parents, grandparents, teachers, friends, doctors, lawyers, sports heroes, actors, cooks, waiters, baby-sitters, merchants, and yes, even our politicians. They are an integral part of America and what makes the United States the greatest country in the world.

Alan Lubiner
Immigration Attorney and Co-Author

1
Definitions

Citizens of other countries who come to the U.S., and individuals, who have occasion to work with the U.S. visa process, should become familiar with immigration "jargon". You will frequently encounter the following terms, so it is best to know what they mean before reading further.

- **AC21:** The American Competitiveness in the 21st Century Act-Signed into law on October 17, 2000, this law greatly affected the H-1B category, increasing the cap and providing additional benefits to alien workers.

- **ACWIA:** American Competitiveness Workforce Improvement Act.

- **Antiterrorism and Effective Death Penalty Act (AEDPA):** The Act signed into law by President Clinton on April 24, 1996 included sweeping new reforms, expanding the definition of aggravated felony and severely restricting the ability of an alien to obtain any form of waiver.

- **Alien:** A person who is not a citizen or a national of the U.S. The term refers to all foreign nationals in the U.S., whether they are here temporarily or with permanent resident status. Although the term may seem strange to you, it is frequently used in the immigration field and therefore in this book.

- **Asylee:** An alien who is in the U.S., or at a port of entry, who is unable or unwilling to return to his own country because of a well-founded fear of persecution.

- **Beneficiary:** An alien who is the recipient of an application or petition filed on his/her behalf by another individual or organization.

- **Citizen:** A person who owes their loyalty to, either through birth or naturalization, the protection of a given country. A permanent resident of the United States is not a United States citizen.

■ **CBP-Customs and Border Patrol:** One of the three agencies created by the breakup of the former Immigration and Nationality Service. CBP is responsible for the protection of our borders, including the control of goods as well as people. It is an agency within the Department of Homeland Security.

■ **CSPA-Child Status Protection Act:** The Act that gives a benefit to children who otherwise would have failed to qualify for benefits or "aged out" due to the delays in processing by USCIS.

■ **Dependent:** The spouse, or unmarried dependent children under age 21.

■ **Employer Sanctions:** The Immigration Reform and Control Act of 1986 prohibits employers from hiring, recruiting, or referring (for a fee) aliens who are known to be unauthorized to work in the U.S.

■ **Fiscal Year:** The fiscal year for the INS covers the twelve-month period from October 1 through September 30.

■ **Form I-9-Employment EligibilityVerification:** An employment form that must be completed by every employer and employee to verify the employee's identity and right to work in the U.S.

■ **Form I-94- Arrival and Departure Record:** A document that is issued to every alien who enters the United States for a temporary stay and who is officially inspected by a U.S. Immigration Officer. This document is stapled in the passport and indicates the amount of time the individual can initially remain in the United States. Form I-94W will be issued to individuals entering the U.S. under the Visa Waiver Pilot Program.

■ **Green Card:** A slang term for the identity document or alien registration receipt card issued to permanent resident (immigrant) aliens. The card includes the alien's photograph, fingerprint and signature. At one time the Form I-551 identity card was green, which is how it derived its name.

■ **Illegal Immigration Reform and Immigrant Responsibility Act of 1996 (IIRAIRA):** The Act signed into law by President Clinton that became effective on April 1, 1997. It made extensive changes to the immigration laws affecting the arrival of aliens, their treatment by the Immigration Court, and available forms of relief.

■ **Immediate Relatives:** Those immigrants who are exempt from the numerical limitations of immigration to the U.S. They are: spouses of U.S. citizens, children (under age 21) of U.S. citizens, and parents of U.S. citizens age 21 or older.

■ **Immigrant:** An alien who comes to the United States to live permanently. (sometimes you will hear the term "illegal immigrant" referring to a person who is in the United States without lawful status.)

■ **Immigration Act of 1990 (IMMACT 90)**: The Act signed into law by President Bush on November 29, 1990. It represents the most extensive change in all areas of immigration in over fifty years.

■ **ICE- Immigration and Customs Enforcement:** One of the three agencies created by the breakup of the former Immigration and Nationality Service. ICE is responsible for enforcement functions for the Department of Homeland Security.

■ **INFOPASS:** The system to get an appointment to speak to an officer of the USCIS at one of the District Offices.

■ **NAFTA:** North American Free Trade Agreement, approved by Congress in 1993. The Agreement liberalizes trade between the United States, Canada and Mexico, and contains immigration provisions.

■ **Nationality:** The country of a person's citizenship.

■ **Naturalization**: A process by which permanent resident aliens can convert their status to U.S. citizenship. Naturalization permits the individual to obtain a U.S. passport and to vote in U.S. elections.

■ **Nonimmigrant**: An alien who comes to the U.S. for a temporary stay.

■ **Passport**: A document issued by a government that identifies the holder and his citizenship, and permits that individual to travel abroad under the protection of that sovereignty.

■ **Patriot Act:** In the wake of the terrorist attacks on the World Trade Center and the Pentagon on September 11, 2001, Congress passed the Uniting and Strengthening America by Providing Appropriate Tools Required to Intercept and Obstruct Terrorism Act of 2001 (USA PATRIOT Act)-This gives law enforcement broad powers to control and monitor the entry and exit of persons to and from the United States and to investigate and prosecute violators in the name of National Security.

■ **PERM:** The new permanent foreign labor certification program that went into effect on March 28, 2005.

■ **Permanent Resident**: A person who has the right to live permanently in the U.S. Individuals are given alien registration cards upon approval of their application for permanent residence and are thereafter called permanent resident aliens. Immigrant is another name for permanent resident alien. A permanent resident is not a U.S. citizen.

■ **Petitioner:** The employer or individual that is filing a petition on behalf of an alien.

■ **Port of Entry:** A port or place where an alien may apply for admission into the U.S.

■ **Preinspection:** Immigration inspections of air travel passengers before departing from the foreign country. This alleviates the need for further immigration inspection upon arrival in the U.S.

■ **Quota Systems:** Established by the U.S. Congress, the system under which a limited number of immigrant visas are issued each year.

■ **Stateless:** A person who has no nationality.

■ **Trusted Traveler Programs:** Programs developed by CBP (Customs and Border Patrol) to expedite travel to the US by certain enrolled individuals considered low risk. These programs include GLOBAL ENTRY, NEXUS and SENTRI.

■ **United States Embassy or Consulate:** U.S. foreign headquarters of the U.S. Ambassador/Consul, and his or her staff. These offices, which are located in most countries, have many departments, including a visa section that processes temporary and permanent visas for foreigners coming to the U.S.

■ **United States Citizenship and Immigration Services (USCIS):** USCIS-U.S. Citizenship and Immigration Services-one of the three agencies created by the breakup of the former Immigration and Nationality Service. USCIS is responsible for adjudication functions within the Department of Homeland Security.

■ **Visa:** The document needed for entry into the U.S. Individuals planning to travel to the U.S. from many countries as nonimmigrants (for a temporary stay) must apply for entry permission at an American Consulate outside the U.S. A stamp (visa) placed in his or her passport permits that individual to board a carrier to the U.S. The stamp contains the visa category, a visa number, the location and date that it was issued, the number of entries into the United States for which it can be used, and the expiration date.

2
Temporary Visas

The U.S. immigration system is divided into nonimmigrant and immigrant categories. Nonimmigrants are individuals who wish to come to the U.S. for a temporary stay, for vacation, to attend school, or for temporary employment. Immigrants are those people who wish to live permanently in the U.S.

This chapter covers temporary or nonimmigrant visa categories. It first explains each nonimmigrant classification, and describes processing procedures, including the documents that are required in order to apply for these visas. The reference chart at the end of the chapter lists all of the nonimmigrant visas.

CATEGORIES OF TEMPORARY OR NONIMMIGRANT VISAS

Nonimmigrant visas are issued to individuals who wish to enter the United States for a temporary period of time ranging from one day to several years. In most cases, an individual must establish that he or she has a residence in his home country that will not be abandoned. Some people may be eligible for many different types of visas, while others may not qualify for any visa. There is a long list of reasons why certain individuals cannot be admitted into the U.S. Examples of such reasons are certain mental or physical disorders, criminal convictions, drug or alcohol addiction, prostitution, etc. Waivers are available in some cases. Further information should be obtained from a knowledgeable professional.

A-1, A-2, A-3. Foreign Government Officials

"A" visas are granted to foreign government officials, their families and servants. This includes ambassadors, public ministers, diplomats or consular officers who are assigned to represent their country in the U.S. The processing of these visas is usually handled directly by the sponsoring organization.

B-1. Temporary Business Visitor

B-1 visas are granted to foreign business people coming to the U.S. for their foreign employer. They are also issued to self-employed individuals who need to conduct business in the U.S., such as attending meetings or conferences, meeting customers, or negotiating contracts. The alien must continue to be paid by the foreign employer, and must maintain a residence abroad that he or she has no intention of abandoning. The B-1 visa holder cannot be employed in the United States or earn money directly from U.S. sources.

In some countries the American Consulate will issue a multiple entry B-1 visa so that the alien may enter the U.S several times using the same visa. In other countries, only a single entry visa will be issued. The validity date of the visa will vary depending upon the country in which the visa is issued. Upon entry into the U.S., the B-1 visitor is usually admitted for the length of time need to complete the purpose of the trip, generally for three months, but not exceeding six months.

The visa application is made to the appropriate American Consulate abroad. It consists of:

Visa Application

1. DS-156-Nonimmigrant Visa Application

2. DS-157-Supplemental Nonimmigrant Visa Application- for all male applicants between the ages of 16 and 45 and for all visa applicants, male or female, with travel documents or passports issued by North Korea, Cuba, Syria, Sudan, Iran, Iraq, and Libya.

3. Passport photograph

4. Letter from foreign employer explaining the reason for the visit to the United States

5. Valid passport or travel document

6. $131.00 nonimmigrant visa application fee

7. Visa issuance fee-consult visa reciprocity table which can be found on the internet at: http://travel.state.gov/visa/reciprocity/index.htm.

B-2. Temporary Visitor for Pleasure

B-2 visas are issued to people coming to the U.S. to visit friends or relatives, to vacation or to accompany a B-1 visa holder as described above.

In most cases, the American Consulate will require evidence of the nature of the trip, as well as proof that the applicant intends to return to the home country. Sometimes an invitation from a friend or relative in the U.S., proof of residence and employment abroad, and other evidence of permanent ties outside the U.S. can help to establish the "intention to return". The applicant should also provide a round-trip airline ticket, and proof that he or she has enough money available for the duration of the trip, such as bank statements or credit cards. The B-2 visa can be issued for multiple trips.

Upon entry to the U.S., the alien is generally admitted for six months.

The application must be made at an American Consulate. It consists of:

1. DS-156-Nonimmigrant Visa Application

2. DS-157-Supplemental Nonimmigrant Visa Application

3. Passport Photograph

4. Valid passport or travel document

5. $131.00 nonimmigrant visa application fee.

Visa issuance fee-consult visa reciprocity table which can be found on the internet at: http://travel.state.gov/visa/reciprocity/index.htm. If the applicant is traveling to the US to obtain medical treatment, they should also present:

1. Medical diagnosis from a local physician, explaining the nature of the ailment and the reason the applicant requires treatment in the United States.

2. Letter from a physician or medical facility in the United States, expressing a willingness to treat this specific ailment and detailing the proposed medical treatment as well as the projected length and

cost of treatment (including doctors' fees, hospitalization fees, and all medical-related expenses).

3. Statement of financial responsibility from the individuals or organization which will pay for the patient's transportation, medical and living expenses. The individuals guaranteeing payment of these expenses must provide proof of ability to do so, often in the form of bank or other statements of income/savings or certified copies of income tax returns.

B-2 visas may also be issued to those persons who intend to be bona fide students in the United States but have not yet selected a school. The Consular Officer must be informed of the prospective student's intent and will mark the visa with the notation: "Prospective Student; school not yet selected." Once the student enters the United States and is accepted into a school, he or she can then make an application to change status. However the student cannot start classes until the application for change of status has been approved. If a visitor can show a good reason for needing to stay in the U.S. beyond the initial six months, the alien can apply for one six month extension. The application is filed with the USCIS Service Center having jurisdiction over the applicant's temporary residence in the U.S. It consists of:

1. Form I-539- Application to Extend/Change Nonimmigrant Status

2. Letter of explanation and any documentation in support of the extension request showing why it is requested

3. Copy of return transportation ticket

4. Proof of ability to maintain oneself financially, or an affidavit of support

4. Copy of Form I-94

5. Filing fee of $300.00.

Chapter 3 covers the "Visa Waiver Program", which allows citizens from many countries to travel to the U.S. as business or pleasure visitors without having to apply for a B-1 or B-2 visa at an American Consulate.

C. Transit Visas and Transit Without Visa

"C" visas are transit visas. People who are traveling through the U.S. to a final destination outside the U.S may be admitted in "C" status and may remain in the U.S. for a maximum of twenty-nine days. A "transit" alien may not apply for change of status to any other nonimmigrant category except "G", and may not apply for an extension of temporary stay.

Some people who are in transit through the U.S. do not have visas. Transit without visa or TWOV is reserved for those who are applying for admission to the U.S. to travel on to another country. Someone flying into the U.S. who has a confirmed reservation, within a specified time period, to catch a connecting flight to another country will be admitted as TWOV. Aliens in TWOV status are not permitted to leave the airline terminal. Application for TWOV status can only be made at certain designated U.S. ports of entry.

Note: Employees of transportation companies are often given C-1D visas. These visas are issued for the purpose of allowing crewmen in transit through the US to join their vessel or aircraft. This is a combined C-1/D-1 visa. See description of D visas below.

D. Crewmen of Aircraft or Sea Vessels

Aliens who are applying for admission into the U.S. as members of a foreign vessel's crew such as flight attendants on foreign owned airlines or crewmen on foreign owned ships use this visa. Usually the foreign vessel personnel will make the arrangements for "D" visa issuance. Many crewmen have both "C" and "D" visas. They use the "C" visas for the purpose of entering the U.S. to "join" their vessel.

There is no derivative classification for the spouse or children of crewmen. Spouses and children are classified as B-2 visitors if coming solely to the U.S. to accompany the principal alien.

E-1 & E-2. Treaty Trader or Investor

E-1 visas are available to Treaty Traders, while E-2 visas are available to Treaty Investors. Both categories require that the United States maintain treaties of commerce and navigation with the foreign country, allowing for trade and/or investment in the United States. Aliens applying for either type of "E" visa must have the same citizenship of the country that maintains the treaty with the United States. The following is a current list of countries that have such treaties. Countries followed by one asterisk (*) have treaty trader provisions, allowing only for issuance of E-1 visas. Countries followed by two asterisks (**) have treaty investor provisions, allowing only for issuance of E-2 visas. Countries with no asterisk(s) maintain both treaty trader and treaty investor provisions, and issue both types of visas.

Albania **	Germany
Argentina	Greece *
Armenia **	Grenada **
Australia	Honduras
Austria	Iran (may be affected by embargo)
Azerbaijan **	Ireland
Bahrain**	Israel *
Bangladesh **	Italy
Belgium	Jamaica**
Bolivia	Japan
Bosnia and Herzegovina **	Jordan
Brunei * (Borneo)	Kazakhstan **
Bulgaria **	Korea (South)
Cameroon **	Kyrgyzstan**
Canada	Latvia
Chile	Liberia
China (Taiwan)	Lithuania**
Colombia	Luxembourg
(Republic of)The Congo (Brazzaville) **	Macedonia
Costa Rica	Mexico
Croatia **	Moldova**
Czech Republic **	Mongolia**
Democratic Republic of Congo (Kinshasa)**	Morocco**
Denmark *	Netherlands
Ecuador**	Norway
Egypt **	Oman
Estonia	Pakistan
Ethiopia	Panama**
Finland	Paraguay
France	Philippines
Georgia**	Poland

Romania**	Switzerland
Senegal**	Thailand
Singapore	Togo
Slovak Republic**	Trinidad & Tobago**
Slovenia	Tunisia**
Spain	Turkey
Suriname	Ukraine**
Sweden	United Kingdom

Bilateral investment treaties may soon authorize E-2 status for nationals of Belarus, Nicaragua, Russia, and Uzbekistan. Once ratified by the U.S. and each country involved, these treaties should take effect about thirty days after the countries exchange instruments of ratification.

1) Treaty Traders

Treaty traders enter the United States for the sole purpose of carrying on substantial trade. Many are self-employed people whose trade with the U.S. accounts for more than 50% of their total volume of trade. The definition of "trade" has been expanded over the years to encompass not only goods and services, but also trade in technology. The treaty trader may also be an employee of a company that qualifies for treaty trader status, but the employment must be in a position that is either executive or supervisory in nature, or one involving essential skills.

2) Treaty Investors

Treaty investors enter the United States to make a substantial investment in a U.S. business, and to direct and develop the business. There is no specific dollar amount needed to qualify for this type of visa. The investment must, however, be substantial in terms of the total investment in the enterprise. The investment must be in a business that generates active income, rather than passive income such as rental property, and the business must be at least 50% owned by nationals of the treaty country, (that being the same country of nationality as the alien investor). Treaty investors may also be employees of a company that qualifies for treaty investor status, but like the treaty trader, the employment must be in a position that is either executive or supervisory, or one that involves essential skills.

Rules involving "E" visas are very complex, and there are ramifications of some treaties, including certain rules under NAFTA (the North American Free Trade Agreement) that affect the procedures for entry into the United States. (See Chapter 6). Those seeking "E" visa status should speak with an experienced immigration practitioner.

F-1. Student

F-1 visas are available to aliens coming temporarily to the United States to attend school. The applicant must plan to pursue a full time program of academic study at an educational institution that is authorized by the USCIS to enroll foreign students. The student must have a home in a foreign country to which he or she will return after completion of studies. In addition, he or she must be proficient in the English language, and have sufficient funds available for his or her support during studies in the U.S.

F-1 status is not available to an alien who seeks to attend a public elementary school or a public adult education program. Entry into the U.S. to attend a public secondary school is also prohibited unless the total period in F-1 status does not exceed one year, and the alien reimburses the school for the costs of providing education. Any alien who violates this provision is barred from admission to the United States for a period of five years.

The visa application consists of:

1. Form 156- Nonimmigrant Visa Application

2. Form 157-Supplemental Nonimmigrant Visa Application

3. SEVIS Form I-20 - Certificate of Eligibility of Nonimmigrant (F-1) Student Status- for Academic and Language Students-issued by the sponsoring school, with proof that the SEVIS fee (Form I-901) has been paid. The SEVIS fee may be paid by credit card at the internet site: www.fmjfee.com.

4. Passport photographs

5. Proof that the applicant has enough money to pay all school related expenses and to support himself or herself during the program,

as indicated on Form I-20. Form I-134, affidavit of support may be submitted.

6. Proof that the applicant has a home abroad that is not being abandoned, and that the student plans to leave the U.S. when the program is completed

7. Valid passport or travel document.

8. Application fee if required.

Note: Students who have not yet made a final decision on the school they wish to attend, and want to come to the U.S. to visit schools in order to make a final selection, may apply for a "B-2" visitor's visa. The applicant must disclose the reason for his/ her trip to the American Consul. The Consular Officer will note "prospective student" on the visa. After entry to the U.S., prospective students must apply to the USCIS for a change of visa status when they have made their final school selection, and have been accepted by the school.

Qualified students who wish to enter the U.S. more than thirty days before their school's starting date, can apply for a B-2 visa with the understanding that they will file with the USCIS to change to F-1 status prior to commencing studies.

Note of caution: In the above instances, after approval of a change of status, the student will not have a student visa, only student status in the U.S. If the student leaves the U.S., he or she must apply for an F-1 visa at an American Consulate before reentering the U.S. as a student.

The visa is usually granted for the period of time in which the student is pursuing a full time course of study, including engaging in practical training, plus sixty days to prepare for departure from the U.S. This is referred to as "duration of status" or "D/S". The American Consular Official will sometimes write the school's name on the visa. The SEVIS I-20 should be returned to the student, who should subsequently present it to the USCIS official at the point of entry into the U.S. The USCIS officer will then issue Form I-94, write the admission number from Form I-94 on Form I-20, and return the SEVIS I-20 identification to the student. The USCIS will then forward the school's copy of Form I-20 to the USCIS processing center, which will then send it back to the school as evidence of the student's admission in F-1 status.

Under normal conditions, the student is not required to apply for extension of stay in the U.S., as long as he or she is a full time student, and will complete the course of study within the time indicated on Form I-20. Spouses and minor children can be granted F-2 visas, which are not valid for employment.

Students who will remain in one educational level for an extended period of time, or remain in student status for eight consecutive years should check with the Designated School Official (DSO) about extending their stay.

A student who is in F-1 status can leave the U.S. for up to five months and be readmitted in student status as long as he or she has:

1. A current valid SEVIS I-20 endorsed by the Designated School Official (DSO), who is often the Foreign Student Adviser, or

2. A new Form I-20A-B if the student's program is changing (such as a change in major, advancement to a higher level of study, or an intended school transfer)

3. A valid student visa and a passport valid for at least six months.

The Student and Exchange Visitor Information System (SEVIS) was implemented after the September, 2001 terrorist attacks as part of the government's effort to restore integrity to the nation's immigration system. SEVIS is a web-based program that maintains information on international students (F/M visas) and exchange visitors (J visas) and their dependents residing in the United States. It is administered by U.S. Immigration and Customs Enforcement's (ICE) Student Exchange and Visitor Program (SEVP) and used by U.S. Customs and Border Protection (CBP) Officers at ports of entry. SEVIS has simplified what was once a manual process, resulting in more accurate and timely data, faster processing and fewer delays.

Prior to SEVIS, school recordkeeping of students was very haphazard. Schools now adhere strictly to requirements, and USCIS will be notified immediately if a student violates his or her status. Regulations require an approved school to keep records containing the following information and documents relating to each F-1 student attending the school

Name; date and place of birth; country of citizenship; current address; status-full or part time; date of commencement of studies; degree program and field of study; whether the student has been certified for practical training, and the beginning and end dates of certification; termination date and reason, if known; the documents required for issuance of a certificate of eligibility; the number of credits completed each semester; a photocopy of the student's I-20 ID copy.

An immigration officer may request any, or all, of the above data on any individual student or class of students upon notice. In addition, the DHS (Division of Homeland Security) periodically (but not more frequently than once a term) sends each approved school a list of all F-1 students shown by government records to be attending the school. The DSO (designated school official) must note the status and current addresses of all listed F-1 students, as well as the names, addresses and identifying information in regard to F-1 students not listed by the DHS. If a student does not have an electronic record in SEVIS, the DHS will notify the school if the student enters the United States to attend their institution. If the student fails to register, the school must notify the government no later than 30 days following the deadline for registering for classes.

The government has created two classes of schools under SEVIS, non-SEVIS schools and SEVIS schools. The difference between these classes is beyond the scope of this book and the school will be able to tell the student under which classification they fall.

Students pursuing a full time course of study may transfer from one school to another within the United States without prior USCIS approval, however, the following rules apply:

■ **Non-SEVIS school to non-SEVIS school** — the student must first notify the school that he or she is currently attending of the intent to transfer, then obtain a Form I-20. Before issuance of any Form I-20, the DSO at the transfer school must verify that the student has been maintaining status. The transfer will be affected only if the student completes the Student Certification portion of the Form I-20 and returns the form to a DSO of the transfer school within 15 days of the program start date listed on Form I-20. Upon receipt of the student's Form I-20 the DSO must note the ``transfer completed'' date in the space provided for DSO's remarks. This acknowledges the student's attendance at the transfer school. The DSO must return Form I-20 to the student and submit the school copy of Form I-20 to the DHS within 30 days of receipt from the student. The DSO must then forward a photocopy of the school copy to the school from which the student transferred.

■ **Non-SEVIS school to SEVIS school** — To transfer from a non-SEVIS school to a SEVIS school, the student must first notify the school he is attending of the intent to transfer, then obtain a SEVIS Form I-20 from the school to which he or she intends to transfer. Before issuance of any Form I-20, the DSO at the transfer school must determine that the student has been maintaining status at his current school and is eligible for transfer to the new school. Once the transfer school has issued the SEVIS Form I-20 to the student indicating a transfer, the transfer school must update and maintain the student's record in SEVIS. The student is then required to notify the DSO at the transfer school within 15 days of the program start date listed on SEVIS Form I-20. Upon notification that the student is enrolled in classes, the DSO of the transfer school must update SEVIS to reflect the student's registration and current address. This acknowledges that the student has completed the transfer process. In the remarks section of the student's SEVIS Form I-20, the DSO must note that the transfer has been completed, including the date, and return the form to the student. The transfer is affected when the transfer school updates SEVIS indicating that the student has registered in classes within 30 days.

■ **SEVIS school to SEVIS school** — The student must first notify his or her current school of the intent to transfer and must indicate the school to which he intends to transfer. Upon notification by the student, the current school will update the student's record in SEVIS as a "transfer out" and indicate the school to which the student intends to transfer, and a release date. The current school will retain control over the student's record in SEVIS until the student completes the current term or reaches the release date. At the request of the student, the DSO of the current school may cancel the transfer request at any time before the release date. As of the release date specified by the current DSO, the transfer school will be granted full access to the student's SEVIS record and then becomes responsible for that student. After the release date, the transfer DSO must complete the transfer of the student's record in SEVIS and may issue a SEVIS Form I-20. The student is then required to contact the DSO at the transfer school within 15 days of the program start date listed on the SEVIS Form I-20. Upon notification that the student is enrolled in classes, the DSO of the transfer school must update SEVIS to reflect the student's registration and current address. This acknowledges that the student has completed the transfer process. The DSO must note on Form I-20 that the transfer has been completed, including the date, and return the form to the student. The transfer is affected when the transfer school notifies SEVIS that the student has enrolled in classes within 30 days.

∎ **SEVIS school to non-SEVIS school** — The student must first notify his or her current school of the intent to transfer and must indicate the school to which he or she intends to transfer. Upon notification by the student, the current school will update the student's status in SEVIS as "a transfer out", enter a "release" or expected transfer date, and update the transfer school as "non-SEVIS." The student must then notify the school to which the he or she intends to transfer of his or her intent to enroll. After the student has completed his or her current term or session, or has reached the expected transfer date, the DSO at the current school will no longer have full access to the student's SEVIS record. At this point, if the student has notified the transfer school of his or her intent to transfer, and the transfer school has determined that the student has been maintaining status at his or her current school, the transfer school may issue the student a Form I-20. The transfer will be affected only if the student completes the student certification portion of the Form I-20 and returns the form to a DSO of the transfer school within 15 days of the program start date listed on Form I-20. Upon receipt of the student's Form I-20 the DSO must note "transfer completed on (date)" in the space provided for the DSO's remarks. This acknowledges the student's attendance. The DSO must return the Form I-20 to the student and submit the school copy of the Form I-20 to the DHS within 30 days of receipt from the student. The DSO must then forward a photocopy of the school copy to the school from which the student transferred.

Generally, foreign students are not allowed to work in the United States. As noted earlier, one of the requirements for a student visa is that the student proves that enough funds are available to pay for his or her education and support for the duration of studies. However, there are five ways that students can work while in F-1 status. They are:

1. On campus employment

2. Practical training- includes curricular practical training and optional practical training before or after completion of studies

3. Off campus employment due to severe economic hardship

4. International organization internships

5. Special student relief.

1. On campus employment- this applies to students who will work in an on-campus establishment such as the cafeteria or bookstore. It may also apply to "off campus" sites which are "affiliated educationally" with the school. The employment must be an "integral part" of the educational program, and cannot exceed twenty hours per week while school is in session. Full time, on campus employment is allowed during summer vacations and holidays when school is not open.

2. Practical training- this is divided into two categories:

A. Curricular Practical Training:
This applies to training as part of an established curriculum during the student's regular course of study. It includes work/study programs, cooperative educational programs, or internships offered by employers through agreements with the school. In order to qualify for curricular practical training, the student must have been lawfully enrolled in school, on a full-time basis, for at least nine consecutive months (exception for students of some graduate study programs who require immediate curricular practical training). The position must be directly related to the student's major field of study.

The application is made as follows:

✓   Student submits request for CPT to the DSO and must follow internal procedures established by the DSO.

Note: Students who have participated in one year or more of full-time curricular practical training may not participate in practical training after completion of their course of study.

B. Optional Practical Training (either before or after completion of studies): Optional practical training can only be authorized in an occupation that is directly related to the student's major. A student may qualify after he or she has been lawfully enrolled in school, on a full time basis, for at least nine consecutive months. The period of optional practical training, both before and after studies, cannot exceed twelve months. Optional practical training is available during the following four periods:

1. During vacation periods while school is not in session, if the student is currently enrolled and intends to register for the next term

2. While school is in session, not to exceed twenty hours per week

3. After completion of all course requirements

4. After completion of the entire course of study.

All optional practical training must be completed within fourteen months after the completion of study. This application is made as follows:

✓ Student submits request for OPT to the DSO. DSO must make recommendation for OPT under SEVIS and must indicate whether it will be part-time or full-time, noting the starting and ending dates. Student will be given the SEVIS Form I-20 and must file the employment page with Form I-765.

The student must apply to the USCIS Service Center with jurisdiction over their residence for an employment authorization document (EAD) by submitting the following:

1. Form I-765-Application for Employment Authorization

2. Employment page of SEVIS I-20

3. Applicable filing fee

4. Copy of Form I-94

5. Two color passport photos.

Once the application for optional practical training has been approved, the USCIS will issue an Employment Authorization Document (EAD). The student cannot commence employment until the EAD is received. The USCIS hopes to be able to approve these applications very quickly.

Note: Students in English language training programs are ineligible for practical training.

On April 4, 2008, USCIS released a new interim regulation making two major changes in OPT. (1) Students with degrees in certain STEM fields (science, technology, engineering and mathematics) may apply for extension of OPT for an additional 17 months if their employers participate in E-verify, the electronic employment verification system. (2) Students with OPT seeking a change of status to H-1B may receive an automatic extension of their status and employment authorization until the effective starting date of their H-1B or until the H-1B application is denied.

In order for students to apply for this extension of OPT, they must request the recommendation of the DSO and the student must agree to report the following to the school within 10 days:

    A.   Any changes to the student's name

    B.   The student's mailing address

    C.   The student's employer

    D.   The address of the student's employer

The student must also check in with the school every six months from the date the STEM extension starts. All information reported to the school must be reported in SEVIS by the DSO.

3) Off-campus employment due to severe economic hardship- A student can apply for part-time (no more than twenty hours per week while school is in session) off-campus employment after having been in good academic standing for at least one year. The request must be based upon severe economic hardship, caused by unforeseen circumstances beyond the student's control. Examples include: loss of financial aid, loss of on-campus employment, substantial fluctuations in the value of currency, inordinate increases in tuition and/or living expenses, unexpected changes in the financial condition of the student's source of support, or unexpected medical bills.

The student must request work authorization from the DSO and the DSO will make the determination.

✓ Student submits Form I-765, the employment form of the SEVIS I-20, Form I-94, two photographs, the required fee, and evidence in support of the application to the USCIS service center having jurisdiction over his place of residence

✓ If granted, the Employment Authorization Document will be issued for one-year intervals up to the date the student is expected to complete studies, as long as the student maintains status, and is in good academic standing

✓ The student may not begin work until the EAD has been issued.

4) International Organization Internships- International organizations falling under the International Organizations Immunities Act can employ full-time F-1 students. The procedure is as follows:

✓ Student files Form I-765 with the USCIS Service Center having jurisdiction over the student's place of residence. The appropriate filing fee must accompany the application. The application must include a SEVIS I-20ID endorsed by the DSO within the last 30 days preceding the filing of the application.The International Organization must certify that the proposed employment is within the scope of the organization's sponsorship.

5) Special Student Relief- In 1998, the USCIS gave itself the authority to suspend its employment authorization requirements in emergencies. The USCIS applied this rule to certain students who were in F-1 status as of June 10, 1998, and whose financial support came from Indonesia, South Korea, Malaysia, Thailand or the Philippines, and who faced severe economic hardship due to rapid currency devaluation. If the economic crises in these countries had caused severe economic hardship, these students were authorized to work either on or off- campus.

This "special student relief" program is in effect indefinitely. Eligibility depends on the source of financial support, not the student's citizenship. The regulations apply only to undergraduate and graduate students. F-1 students in non-degree or language programs are not eligible. The twenty-hour per week limit for on-campus employment does not apply. Please note that the USCIS has not yet announced the procedures with which F-1 students must comply, once the relief program is rescinded.

Note: Those who qualify for "special student relief" and plan to travel outside the U.S. may have a problem obtaining a new F-1 visa.

There are two other types of visas for students, the M-1 and the J-1, which are discussed in this chapter. The requirements and regulations are different for each one. Make sure you choose the student status that will offer you the most benefits.

G-1 thru G-5. Representatives of International Organizations

Similar to "A" visas, "G" visas are issued to representatives of international organizations like the United Nations and World Bank, as well as missions. Family members, staff and servants are also eligible for this category. The application is usually handled directly by the sponsoring organization.

H. Temporary Worker

This is a very broad visa category and covers several different types of temporary workers including: aliens in specialty occupations; farm workers and other temporary nonagricultural workers; trainees; and family members of "H" visa holders. The categories will be described in numerical order.

H-1A. This category, formerly for nurses, is no longer available.

H-1B. Aliens in Specialty Occupations

"Aliens in specialty occupations" (professionals) who have a temporary job offer in the U.S. may be eligible for H-1B classification. Note that artists and entertainers were removed from this category under the Immigration Act of 1990. There is a numerical ceiling of 65,000 annual H-1B petitions, although there are some exceptions to this cap.

The maximum period of stay in H-1B status is six years. However, under AC21, certain H-1B status holders reaching the six year limit, who are the beneficiaries of pending or approved Labor Certifications or I-140's (for permanent residence) may receive extensions of H-1B status beyond the six year limit. It is important to consult with an Immigration lawyer well in advance of the expiration of your status to see what options for extension might be available.

The USCIS definition of "specialty occupation" is: "one that requires theoretical and practical application of a body of highly specialized knowledge; and the attainment of a bachelor's degree or higher in the specific specialty as the minimum for entry into the occupation in the U.S."

As indicated above, prospective H-1B employers are required to file Form ETA-9035 "Labor Condition Application for H-1B Nonimmigrants", with the Employment and Training Administration of the U.S. Department of Labor.

The USCIS regulations require the employer to prove the following:

✓ That H-1B nonimmigrants and other workers in similar jobs will be paid the actual wage for the occupation at the place of employment, or the prevailing wage level for the occupation in that geographic area, whichever is higher. The employer must use either a State Employment Service (SESA) determination or a wage survey, and indicate the source of the prevailing wage information

✓ That the employment of H-1B workers will not impact adversely on the working conditions of other people similarly employed in that geographic area

✓ That there is no strike, lockout or work stoppage in the occupation at the place of intended employment

✓ That notice of the filing of the H-1B application has been given to workers at the place of intended employment through a bargaining representative, or if not applicable, through a posted notice of the filing at the place of intended employment.

The company that is offering the temporary employment must first file a visa petition with the Regional USCIS Service Center in the U.S. The application consists of:

1. An approved Labor Condition Application from the Department of Labor

2. Form I-129-Petition for a Nonimmigrant Worker

3. Form I-129H and Form I-129W (supplements to Form I-129)

4. Proof of the alien's academic qualifications and professional experience—university degrees, letters of reference, etc.

5. A letter from the company describing the company, the temporary job to be filled, including why it requires at least a bachelor's degree, and why the alien is particularly qualified, as well as a statement that the employer will pay for the alien's return trip abroad if the employment is terminated before the authorized stay expires

6. Filing fee of $320.00

7. ACWIA fee of $1500.00 or $750.00

8. Fraud Fee of $500.00.

Note: AC 21 also created an additional fee to fund education, training and scholarship programs for U.S. workers (the American Competitive and Workforce Improvement Act fee- ACWIA). Employers are responsible for paying this fee, and cannot request payment or seek reimbursement from employees. The ACWIA fee is currently $1500.00 for employers of 25 or more full-time employees and $750.00 for those who employ less than 25. Some petitioners are exempt from the ACWIA fee. There is also a new Fraud Prevention and Detection Fee of $500.00 which must be paid by employers who are seeking a beneficiary's initial grant of H-1B status, or seeking to change a beneficiary's employer. It is best to consult with an experienced Immigration professional to determine the proper fees that must be paid.

The USCIS will review the application and issue an approval notice to the company. The USCIS should also cable notice of approval to the American Consulate where the alien will apply for the visa. Approval can be granted for an initial period of three years. Extensions of H-1 status can routinely be obtained for an additional three years (maximum stay in H-1 status is six years). The USCIS processing time for H-1 petitions varies, but is usually not more than two to three months.

Note: An employer may request "premium processing" by completing Form I-907 and submitting an additional fee of $1000.00. This insures that the case will be considered within 15 days, although it does not guarantee approval within that time.

Once the company receives the approval notice, the bottom half should be forwarded to the alien so that visa application can be made at the American Consulate. This consists of:

1. DS-156- Nonimmigrant Visa Application

2. Passport photograph

3. Original H-1B approval notice receipt issued by the USCIS

4. Form DS-157 if applicable.

The alien should obtain a complete copy of the H-1 application prior to applying for the visa. When the application is made, the alien should be able to affirm that he or she will remain in the U.S. temporarily. The visa is normally granted for three years. Spouses and minor children are issued H-4 visas, which are not valid for employment in the U.S.

Note: AC21 also provides for "portability" for those in H-1B status, allowing individuals in H-1B status to immediately change jobs upon filing of a new petition by a new employer, subject to final approval of the petition. If the petition is denied, work authorization ceases. Prior to this, an individual had to have a new petition approved on his behalf before being authorized to start new employment. In order to be eligible for this provision, the individual must have:

1. Been lawfully admitted to the US.

2. The new petition must have been filed before the expiration of the person's authorized stay.

3. The person must not have accepted unauthorized employment before the petition was filed.

H-2. Temporary Worker in Field Where U.S. Workers are in Short Supply

This category is divided into two groups:

H-2A. Temporary agricultural service workers

H-2B. Other workers who will be performing temporary services of labor in which U.S. workers are not available, including some seasonal jobs, certain child care situations, and individuals who will be training U.S. workers. The new immigration regulations include a 66,000 annual ceiling on issuance of H-2B visas.

Processing of H-2 applications is complex.

✓ The employer must first file a request with the local office of the State Employment Service (using Form ETA 750, Part A) for a temporary labor certification

✓ The State Employment Service will then issue instructions to the prospective employer regarding attempts to recruit U.S. workers, including advertising the job opening in a newspaper or trade publication, depending on the nature of the job

✓ Assuming approval after complying with the requirements, the Department of Labor will issue a certification.

An application is then filed with the USCIS, consisting of:

1. Department of Labor Certification

2. Form I-129-Petition for Nonimmigrant Worker

3. Form I-129H Supplement

4. A letter from the prospective employer describing the job and including a statement that the employer will pay for the alien's return transportation abroad

4. Evidence of the alien's qualifications

5. Filing fee of $320.00.

Once the application is approved, the process for obtaining the visa is similar to that for the H-1B, and families can be granted H-4 visas. H-2B visas are issued in one-year increments, with maximum duration of three years.

On May 22, 2008, the Department of Labor, Employment and Training Administration published a proposed rule to amend the regulations regarding H-2B to modernize the program. It is likely that the procedures for H-2B will be changed in the near future.

H-3. Temporary Trainee

The H-3 visa is available to individuals employed by a business in the US, who will participate in a formal training program that does not involve productive work (productive work can only be incidental to the training). The procedure for applying to the USCIS is similar to the H-1 process described above; however, a Labor Condition Application is not required. The prospective employer's petition to the USCIS must be accompanied by a written description of the formal training program, including details such as: the duration of the different phases of the training including classroom work; the instructors who will provide the training; reading and course work required during the training; why the training is not available in the alien's own country; and the position that the alien will fill abroad at the end of the training in the U.S.

The visa is usually granted for the duration of the training program, or for up to two years. Accompanying family members are issued H-4 visas.

USCIS regulations also allow for an H-3 "Special Education Exchange Visitor Program" for nonimmigrants coming to the U.S. to participate in a special education training program that provides practical training and experience in the education of children with physical, mental or emotional handicaps. Only fifty people per year are eligible, with a limit of stay of eighteen months.

I. Representatives of Information Media

This visa category is reserved for aliens who are coming to the U.S. temporarily to work on behalf of a foreign information media such as a foreign newspaper or television station. "I" visa holders are admitted to the U.S. for the duration of their employment. There are very limited visas issued in this category, so it will not be discussed further in this book.

J-1. Exchange Visitor

J-1 visas are available to aliens who will be participating in an Exchange Visitor Program including experts, foreign students, industrial and business trainees, "international visitors", medical interns and residents, and scholars. Exchange Visitor Programs are approved and administered by the United States Department of State (DOS). Previously, the function was handled by the United States Information Agency (USIA).

The Exchange Visitor Program was developed, in part, to allow aliens to pursue education, training or research, or to teach in the U.S. The types of visitors under the J-1 program may include, but are not limited to: Students, professors and research scholars, short-term scholars, trainees, specialists, foreign medical graduates, international and government visitors, teachers, camp counselors, and au pairs.

Many large companies and educational institutions participate. Foreign medical graduates who wish to study further or train in the U.S. may want to first contact the Educational Commission for Foreign Medical Graduates (ECFMG) located in Philadelphia, Pennsylvania.

Sponsors of J-1 programs can be:

❏ An existing U.S. agency or organization

❏ A recognized international agency or organization having U.S. membership and offices

❏ A reputable organization that is a citizen of the United States.

Citizen of the United States is defined as either:

1. An individual U.S. citizen

2. A partnership of which a majority of the partners are U.S. citizens

3. A corporation or other legal entity, which has its principal place of business in the United States, and either its shares are publicly traded on a U.S. stock exchange or a majority of its officers, directors and shareholders are U.S. citizens.

4. A non-profit legal entity in the U.S. which is qualified as tax-exempt,

has its principal place of business in the U.S. and a majority of its officers and directors are U.S. citizens or

5. An accredited college, university or other institution of higher learning created under U.S. law.

Foreign nationals who wish to apply for J-1 visas should proceed with caution, because many aliens must return to their home country for two years after they complete their stay in J-1 status. These include:

1. Individuals who receive any sort of government funding to participate in the J-1 program in the U.S.

2. Aliens receiving graduate medical training in the U.S., such as residents and interns

3. Aliens who are nationals of a country in which a skills list exists.

The skills list indicates occupations for which the foreign country's local workers are in short supply. The Department of State has compiled this list in cooperation with each foreign government. For example, the Brazilian government may have concluded that not enough Brazilians are qualified engineers. Therefore, if a Brazilian citizen comes to the United States with a J-1 visa to pursue a course of study in engineering, he or she is required to return to Brazil for two years after completing the J-1 program in the U.S. This is known as the "two year foreign residence requirement." In some cases this two year requirement can be waived at the end of the program, but it is a difficult procedure, and with no guarantees of approval.

When the alien has been accepted into a J-1 program, the sponsoring organization will issue Form DS-2019- Certificate of Eligibility for Exchange Visitor J-1 Status to the foreign national. The visa application to the American Consulate consists of:

1. Form DS 156- Nonimmigrant Visa Application

2. Passport photograph

3. Form DS-2019

4. Valid passport or travel document

5. Form DS-157 if applicable.

The J-1 visa is usually issued to coincide with the length of the J-1 program. Some J-1 visas can be renewed while others are limited to fixed periods of stay. Spouses and minor children are granted J-2 visas. They may accept employment by applying to the USCIS for permission to work on Form I-765. Employment permission can be granted for up to four years, or the duration of the J-1's DS-2019/I-94, whichever is shorter.

SEVIS (see F-1 visa category) also applies to J-1 visitors. J-1 visa holders must be sure to provide their Program sponsors with any change of address within 10 days as Program Sponsors must ensure that the U.S. addresses of all sponsored J program participants that are reported to SEVIS are actual and current. A program sponsor must update address changes within 21 days of the change notification.

The sponsor must also verify within 30 days of a J visitor's start date, that the participant has indeed begun his or her program. In addition, sponsors will continue to submit annual reports to the Department of State.

K. Fiancé or Fiancee of U.S. Citizen

This category is available to aliens who are outside the U.S. and are engaged to be married to a U.S. citizen. The petitioner and the beneficiary must have met in person within the past two years. The U.S. citizen must file the following documents with the USCIS Regional Service Center having jurisdiction over the US citizen's place of residence:

1. Form I-129F-Petition for Alien Fiancé

2. Proof of U.S. citizenship of petitioner

3. Proof of termination of prior marriages for both parties, if applicable

4. Evidence that the two parties have physically met within the past two years

5. Statements from both parties that they plan to marry within 90 days of the alien's admission to the U.S. and evidence as to this intent

6. Two color photos of the U.S. citizen, and two of the fiancé (e) taken within 30 days

7. Filing fee of $455.00.

The USCIS will approve the petition and forward it to the U.S. Consulate where the fiancé(e) will apply for the visa, after complying with the instructions of the Consul. Once the alien is granted the K-1 visa and enters the U.S., the marriage must occur within 90 days. After the marriage, the alien can file Form I-485- Application to Register Permanent Residence with the USCIS to convert from K-1 to conditional residence (See Chapter 7 for procedures on filing Form I-485). Unmarried minor children can accompany the fiancé(e) to the U.S. in "K" status.

K-3 and K-4- Spouses of US citizens and their children

In 2001 a new nonimmigrant classification for the spouses of U.S. citizens and their children was created by the LIFE Act. Previously, spouses of U.S. citizens and their children who were the beneficiaries of pending or approved petitions could enter the United States only with immigrant visas. Following the enactment of LIFE, spouses of U.S. citizens and their children who are the beneficiaries of pending or approved visa petitions can be admitted initially as nonimmigrants in K-3 or K-4 classification and adjust to immigrant status later while in the United States.

The eligibility criteria for the K-3 are as follows:

a)   The U.S. citizen (USC) spouse must have filed the I-130 immigrant petition.

b)   The USC must have also filed the I-129F petition, and the USCIS must approve it.

c)   After arrival in the U.S., the K-3 holder must continue with the permanent immigration process.

The K-4 requirements are:

a)   The applicant must be the unmarried child (under 21) of a person who qualifies for the K-3 visa. The K-4 child can be listed on the same I-129F as the K-3 spouse.

b)   After arrival in the U.S., the I-130 petition must be filed for the K-4 child, usually together with an I-485 application.

Note that if the K-4 is the stepchild of the USC, the USC cannot file the I-130 petition unless the couple married before the child's 18th birthday. In such case, the K-3 parent will have to file for the child, who will be subject to the long waiting list for relatives of permanent residents. In the meantime, there may also be a status problem and the child may have to wait abroad.

Application Process

The I-129F petition is filed with the new USCIS, PO Box 7218, Chicago, Illinois 60680-7218, which, upon approval, forwards the petition to the National Visa Center (NVC). NVC notifies the consulate by email, sending a scanned version of the I-129F. The consulate will then send a letter to the K-3/K-4 applicants with instructions regarding the medical exam, a list of documents needed, and instructions for notifying the Consulate that all needed documents have been gathered. The Consulate will determine whether applicants will require personal interviews.

The K-3/K-4 visa is issued as a nonimmigrant visa, similar to the K-1. In addition, a packet of documents is given to the K-3/K-4 visa holder, to be presented to the USCIS Inspector at the Port of Entry.

Required Documents

The visa application at the American Consulate consists of:

Form DS-156 in duplicate

Form DS-157 if applicable

Visa application form.

Police certificates (as applicable when required for the particular country).

Birth certificates for both K-3s and K-4s.

Marriage certificate for K-3s as well as proof of termination of prior marriages, if any.

Medical exam for K-3's and K-4's, but the vaccination requirement does not apply.

Valid passport for each applicant. (minor children can have their own passport, or be included in their parent's passport.

> Some proof of financial support is needed for the K-3/K-4 visa and the consulate has the discretion to determine the types of documents acceptable for this purpose.
>
> Filing fee (check with US Embassy in your country).

Consular processing for the K-3 visa will take place in the country where the couple got married.

L-1. Intracompany Transferee

L-1 visas are granted to aliens who have worked for a company abroad, as executives, managers, or in a specialized knowledge capacity, for a total of one year within the immediately preceding three years. The USCIS has very strict definitions of "managerial, executive and specialized knowledge". The alien must be transferred, for a temporary assignment, to a branch office, subsidiary or affiliate company in the U.S. in an executive, managerial or specialized knowledge capacity. The employer in the U.S. must initiate a petition with the USCIS.

The L-1 petition consists of:

1. Form I-129- Petition for A Nonimmigrant Worker and "L" classification supplement

2. A letter describing the alien's current job, held for the past year abroad, and the anticipated job in the U.S. It should include details of the executive, managerial or specialized knowledge features of both positions

3. Proof that the alien has been employed abroad by the foreign company for at least one year

4. Proof that the foreign and U.S. companies are related

5. Filing fee of $320.00

6. Fraud Fee of $500.00

The USCIS will issue a notice of approval to the prospective U.S. employer, usually within thirty days. The visa application process from this point forward is the same as that described for the H-1B.

The initial petition can be approved for up to three years with extensions granted in two-year increments, up to seven years in total for executives and managers. Specialized knowledge L-1 aliens are only eligible for a total of five years in this visa category. Spouses and minor children are granted L-2 visas, which are not valid for work purposes.

If the U.S. company has just started operating, the application rules are different. The USCIS may ask to see more documents, the petition may only be approved for one year, and the subsequent visa will only be issued for one year. Should the employer need to renew the status of the L-1 alien at the end of the first year, the U.S. company will be required to prove to the USCIS that the new operation is growing. If this proof is available, extensions of stay can also be granted, as described above.

Employers are also entitled to apply to the USCIS for approval of an L-1 "blanket" petition, which eases the application process each time the employer wants to transfer an alien. In order to qualify for this program, the employer must be able to meet certain criteria. Included in these are:

1. That the employer must have had at least ten L-1 approvals within the past twelve months or

2. Have sales of over $25 million or

3. Employ at least 1000 people.

4. Have proof of affiliation between the U.S. and foreign branches of the company and

5. Have proof that the U.S. company has been doing business for at least a year.

The documentation that is required for L-1 blanket approval is extensive but can benefit the employer in saving time on international transfer paperwork.

M-1. Student

M-1 status is similar to F-1 status. This visa category has been in effect since 1982 and is designed for students who wish to pursue vocational or other recognized nonacademic educational programs. This does not include English language programs. The application process is similar to that for F-1 students in that the school issues SEVIS Form I-20 to the student. The visa application at the American Consulate consists of:

1. Form DS-156- Nonimmigrant Visa Application

2. Form DS-157 if applicable

3. SEVIS Form I-20Certificate of Eligibility for Nonimmigrant (M-1) Student Status- completed by the student and the DSO (Consular Officers must verify the SEVIS I-20 and the data in the SEVIS system before issuing a visa. Student must pay the SEVIS fee and must generally meet the same criteria as an F-1 student.

4. Passport photographs

5. Proof that the applicant has enough money to pay school related expenses and to support himself or herself during the program

6. Valid passport or travel document.

The visa may be granted for the length of the course of study shown on SEVIS Form I-20. The SEVIS I-20 identification should be returned to the student by the Consular official. The student should present it to the USCIS official when entering the U.S. The USCIS officer will return the student's part of the Form and issue Form I-94. Aliens holding M-1 visas are not permitted to work. Spouses and minor children can be granted M-2 visas, which are not valid for employment. Students can transfer from one school to another within the U.S. only in the first six months and must get DHS permission to transfer on Form I-539.

Students can also qualify for paid practical training upon completion of their program. The alien may only be employed in an occupation or vocation directly related to his or her course of study, as recommended by the DSO. The maximum amount of time for training will be one month for each four months of full time study, but not to exceed six months, plus thirty days to depart the U.S. The application consists of:

1. Form I-765

2. Copy of Form I-94

3. Photos

4. Form I-20ID endorsed for practical training by the DSO

5. Applicable filing fee.

The application must be submitted before the student's authorized stay expires and not more than sixty days before completing the course of study, nor more than thirty days after. The student cannot begin practical training until the USCIS issues the EAD to the student.

Note: The SEVIS reporting rules that apply to F-1 students also apply to M-1 students.

N. NATO

NATO visas are granted to representatives of countries that are members of the North Atlantic Treaty Organization (NATO). They are primarily under the control of the State Department, with little USCIS involvement, and are therefore, not covered in this book.

O. Extraordinary Aliens

"O" aliens are those who have extraordinary ability in the sciences, arts, education, business or athletics. This includes those in the motion picture or television industries. The alien must have sustained national or international acclaim, or with regard to motion picture and television productions, have a demonstrated record of achievement.

The "O" alien must be entering the United States to continue work in the area of extraordinary ability, or for the purpose of accompanying and assisting in the artistic or athletic performance for a specific event. The alien must be an integral part of the actual performance, and possess skills and experience that cannot be duplicated by other individuals.

In the case of motion picture or television productions, the "O" applicant must have skills and experience that are critical, based on either a preexisting long-standing working relationship with the principal performer, or with respect to the specific production. This must be due to the fact that the significant production will take place both inside and outside the U.S., and the continuing participation of the alien is essential to the successful completion of the production.

Aliens of extraordinary ability, or extraordinary achievement in the motion picture or television industries are designated O-1. Aliens who accompany and assist O-1 aliens are classified O-2. This category is only available, however, for aliens who accompany or assist an O-1 alien in a specific athletic or artistic event. It is not available in the fields of education, science or business.

The spouse and children of O-1 or O-2 aliens are designated O-3. O-1 aliens do not need to have a residence abroad that they have no intention of abandoning, but O-2 aliens do have to maintain a residence abroad.

The standards for this visa category are very high. Television and movie artists must prove that they have a very high level of accomplishment, and that they have been recognized as outstanding, notable or leading. To show extraordinary ability in the sciences, business, education and athletics, applicants must document their recognition, with quality outweighing quantity.

"O" visas require a petition (Form I-129 with appropriate supplement) to be filed with the USCIS Regional Service Center having jurisdiction over the area in which the alien will be employed. The procedure is similar to that in H-1B cases. Established agents may file petitions (in lieu of employers) for an alien who is traditionally self-employed or who plans to arrange short-term employment with numerous employers. There are strict rules that agents must follow. Consult a professional for more information in this area.

The maximum period of validity of an approved "O" petition is three years. A petitioner may seek an extension in one-year increments.

P. Outstanding Athletes, Artists and Entertainers

"P" visas are reserved for athletes, artists and certain entertainers who have achieved national or international recognition as outstanding in their field. The standard is somewhat less than for "O" visas but the scope of eligible services is more limited.

There are three subcategories:

P-1. Members of entertainment groups, or individual athletes and members of athletic teams

P-2. Artists or entertainers who are part of reciprocal international exchanges

P-3. Artists or entertainers coming to perform in programs that are culturally unique.

Teachers and coaches, as well as performers are now eligible for P-3 status, to encourage them to disseminate their knowledge. Aliens may also now be admitted for commercial or non-commercial performances. It is interesting to note that individual entertainers are not eligible for "P" visas, except for those participating in reciprocal exchanges, or performing in culturally unique shows.

Prior to the Immigration Act of 1990, athletes were admitted as visitors under a variety of situations. Now USCIS regulations grant P-1 status to professional athletes, while amateur athletes may still be granted B-1 status.

Like the "O" category, a petition is required. Family members are eligible for P-4 classification. All "P" nonimmigrants must seek to enter the United States temporarily, and are required to have a residence abroad that they do not intend to abandon. As with "O" petitions, an agent may file the petition. Individual athletes may be admitted for up to five years, and their stay may be extended for up to five years. The total period of stay for an individual athlete may not exceed ten years. All other "P" aliens can be admitted for up to one year, and their stay may be extended in increments of one year.

Q. International Cultural Exchange

This category was created to allow employer's like Disney to bring foreigners to the U.S. for temporary periods to work in places such as Epcot in Florida. This visa category applies to aliens coming to the U.S. for no more than fifteen months to participate in an international cultural exchange program. To qualify, the prospective employer must have been conducting business in the U.S. for at least two years, have at least five full-time U.S. workers, and offer working conditions and wages that are the same as those given to local workers.

The "Q" applicant must be at least eighteen years old and be able to communicate about their home country. Application is made on Form I-129.

R. Religious Workers

This category was created for religious workers coming to the U.S. to perform temporary services. The alien must have been a member of a religious organization for at least the immediately preceding two years. Three groups of religious workers can qualify: ministers of religion, professional workers in religious vocations and occupations, and other religious workers who are employed by a religious nonprofit organization, or a related tax exempt entity, under IRS definition. Religious workers can be admitted to the U.S. for an initial period of three years. Total stay is limited to five years. Aliens can apply directly at the American Consulate for the R-1 visa. They must present:

1. Proof that the sponsoring organization is non-profit

2. A letter from the sponsoring organization including the salary for the position; the required two years of membership in the denomination; qualifications as a minister, religious professional, or as an alien in a religious vocation; the affiliation between the religious organization in the U.S. and abroad, and the location where the alien would be working.

The spouse and minor children of religious workers are eligible for R-2 classification, which does not allow for employment.

S. Alien Informants

This classification was created for aliens who assist law enforcement agencies in supplying critical information about criminal enterprises and terrorism. It is not covered in this book.

T. Visas

The "T" classification was created under the Trafficking Victims Protection Act of 2000 (TVPA). This status is designed to assist individuals who are in the U.S., American Samoa or the Commonwealth of the Northern Mariana Islands as a result of being victims of severe forms of trafficking in humans, commonly known as slavery. Subject to some limitations, immediate family members of these persons will also benefit from the "T" category.

The T visa is limited to those victims of trafficking who are willing to cooperate with law enforcement actions against human traffickers. An applicant must establish that he or she would suffer extreme hardship involving unusual and severe harm, if removed from the U.S., and that he or she has complied with any reasonable request for assistance in the investigation and prosecution of acts of human trafficking.

A victim files his or her own petition for T status, using Form I-914.

After three years in T status, one is allowed to apply for permanent resident status. Thus, the T visa ultimately provides a long-term solution for the victims of human trafficking.

TN. NAFTA Professionals

This category is covered in Chapter 6.

U Visas

These are visas issued to victims of certain crimes. This category is not covered in this book.

V Visas-Spouses and children of lawful permanent residents

The V visa was created in order to provide an interim solution for the spouses and children of lawful permanent residents, who have to wait many years for a visa to become available to them because of the backlogs in quota availability.

In order to qualify, applications for immigration status must have:

been pending for at least three years

OR

if immigration petitions on their behalf have been approved, 3 years or more have elapsed since the filing date and an immigrant visa is not immediately available to the applicant because of a backlog in the quota.

To be eligible for a V visa, the applicant must be the beneficiary of an application for an immediate relative (under the family based second preference category (F2A)) that was filed on or before December 21, 2000. The petition must have been pending for three years at the time the V visa application is made. However, if the petition has been approved, the person can still obtain a V visa, if the petition was filed more than three years ago and there is no immediately available immigrant visa, a pending application for an immigrant visa, or a pending application for adjustment of status.

A person eligible for V visa status may apply for it at a consular office abroad, or if already in the U.S., may apply to the USCIS.

V visa holders may also obtain employment authorization by filing Form I-765, and the appropriate filing fee, with the USCIS.

V visa holders are eligible to apply for adjustment of status when an immigrant visa becomes available, if the applicant was physically present in the U.S. at any time between July 1, 2000 and October 1, 2000. However, if after obtaining the V visa, its holder ever falls out of valid status (other than through no fault of the holder or for technical reasons), they will not be allowed to apply for adjustment of status unless eligible under section 245(i).

Those living in the U.S. who wish to apply for the V visa are required to submit the following documentation:

- A completed Application to Extend/Change Nonimmigrant Status (Form I-539) along with its Supplement A and required documentation and fees

- A completed Medical Examination (Form I-693)

- Biometrics fee of $80.00

The USCIS will give V status holders (or applicants that changed to the V status) a maximum 2-year period of admission. The period of the V status may be extended, if the applicant continues to remain eligible for V status.

If an eligible spouse or child has an immigrant visa number available, but has not yet applied for an immigrant visa abroad, or for adjustment of status to lawful permanent residence, the USCIS will grant a one-time 6 month extension of the V status in order to provide them time to file the appropriate application when their V status is expiring.

PREMIUM PROCESSING:

As of June 1, 2001, the USCIS began a program of "premium processing" of certain nonimmigrant visa petitions (Form I-129). Currently, premium processing is available for applicants seeking E-1, E-2, H-1B, H-2A, H-2B, H-3, L-1A, L-1B, O-1, O-2, P-1, P-2, P-3, Q-1, R-1, TN-1 and TN-2. The USCIS will also expedite the forms of dependents seeking extensions of stay or change of status based on the principal alien's form I-129. The request for premium processing must be made on Form I-907 and can either be filed concurrently with the I-129 or subsequently for a pending I-129. Premium processing guarantees that the USCIS will process the petition within 15 days or it will refund the fee and continue to process the petition on an expedited basis. The premium-processing fee is $1,000.00 and must be paid with a separate check or money order. Please note that premium processing does not guarantee an approval in 15 days, only that USCIS will process the petition. A special address for Premium Processing has been designated for each of the Service Centers:

California Service Center
Jurisdiction over AK, AZ, CA, CO, GU, HI, ID, IL, IN, IA, KS, MI, MN, MO, MT, NE, NV, ND, OH, OR, SD, UT, WA, WI and WY.

Email inquiries: CSC-Premium.Processing@dhs.gov
Phone to request information about PENDING applications only: 949-831-9670

Mailing Address
USCIS, California Service Center
P.O. Box 10825
Laguna Niguel, CA 92607

Express Mail Address
USCIS, California Service Center
24000 Avila Road, 2nd Floor, Room 2312
Laguna Niguel, CA 92677

Vermont Service Center

Jurisdiction over: AL, AR, CT, DE, DC, FL, GA, KY, LA,ME,ME,MA,MS,NH,NJ,NM,NY,NC,OK,PA,PR,RI,SC,TN,TX,VT,VA,VI and WV.

Email inquiries: VSC-Premium.Processing@dhs.gov
Phone to request information about PENDING applications only: 802-527-4828

Premium Processing
Vermont Service Center
30 Houghton Street
St. Albans, VT 05478-2399

NONIMMIGRANT VISA REFERENCE CHART

A-1, A-2, A-3	Ambassadors, public ministers, diplomats or consular officers assigned to represent their country in the U.S., their immediate families and servants
B-1	Temporary business visitors
B-2	Temporary visitors for pleasure
C-1	Aliens in transit through the U.S. to a third country
C-1D	Combined transit and crewman visa
C-2	Alien in transit to UN headquarters
C-3	Foreign government official, members of immediate family, attendant, servant, or personal employee in transit
D-1	Crewmen of aircraft or sea vessels departing on same vessel of arrival
D-2	Crewmember departing by means other than vessel of arrival
E-1	Treaty trader, spouse and minor children
E-2	Treaty investor, spouse and minor children
F-1	Students pursing academic courses of study
F-2	Spouse and minor children of F-1
G-1 thru 5	Representatives of international organizations like the United Nations and the World Bank, their family, staff and servants
H-1B	Specialty occupations
H-2A	Agricultural temporary workers
H-2B	Non-agricultural temporary workers
H-3	Temporary trainees, special education
H-4	Spouse and minor children of H-1, H- 2 and H-3 visa holders
I	Representatives of foreign information media, and their family
J-1	Exchange visitors
J-2	Spouse and minor children of J-1 visa holders
K-1	Alien fiancé or fiancee of U.S. citizen and minor children
K-2	Minor child of K-1
K-3	Spouse of a US citizen under LIFE Act
K-4	Child of K-3
L-1A	Executive or managerial intracompany transferee
L-1B	Specialized knowledge intracompany transferee L-2 Spouse and minor children of L-1 visa holder
M-1	Students enrolled in vocational educational programs
M-2	Spouse and minor children of M-1 visa holders

N-8	Parent of alien classified SK-3, special immigrant
N-9	Child of N-8, SK-1, SK-2 or SK-4 special immigrant
NATO-1	Principal permanent representative of Member State to NATO and resident members of official staff or immediate family
NATO-2	Other representatives of member State
NATO-3	Official clerical staff accompanying Representative
NATO-4	Official of NATO other than NATO-1
NATO-5	Expert other than NATO officials qualified under NATO-4
NATO-6	Member of civilian component
NATO-7	Servant of personal employee of above NATO 1-6
O-1	Extraordinary ability alien
O-2	Alien's (support) accompanying O-1
O-3	Spouse or child of O-1 or O-2
P-1	Athletes and entertainment groups
P-2	Artists and entertainers in reciprocal exchange programs
P-3	Artists and entertainers in culturally unique programs
P-4	Spouse or child of P-1, 2 or 3
Q-1	International Cultural Exchange visitors
Q-2	Irish Peace Process Cultural and Training Program
Q-3	Spouse or child of Q-2
R-1	Religious workers
R-2	Spouse and minor children of religious workers
S-5	Informants relating to criminal enterprises
S-6	Informants related to terrorism
T-1	Victim of a severe form of trafficking in persons
T-2	Spouse of T-1
T-3	Child of T-1
T-4	Parent of T-1 if T-1 victim is under 21 years of age
TN	NAFTA Professionals
TD	Dependents of NAFTA Professionals
TWOV	Transit without visa
U-1	Victim of certain criminal activity
U-2	Spouse of U-1
U-3	Child of U-1
U-4	Parent of U-1 if U-1 is under 21 years of age
V-1	Spouse of an LPR who is the principal beneficiary of an I-130 filed prior to Dec. 21, 2000 and has been pending for at least 3 years

V-2   Child of a Lawful Permanent Resident who is the principal beneficiary of an I-130 filed prior to Dec. 21, 2000 and has been pending for at least 3 years

V-3   Derivative child of V-1 or V-2

TPS   Temporarty protected status.

3
Visa Waiver Program

Two additional categories of nonimmigrant status exist in which visas are not required for admission into the U.S. The first is the Visa Waiver Program (VWP), covered in this chapter, and the second is the North American Free Trade Agreement, covered in Chapter 6.

On November 6, 1986 the USCIS established a Visa Waiver Pilot Program (VWPP), on an experimental basis, for citizens of certain countries who wish to travel to the U.S. as visitors. It is now a permanent program.

Starting August 1, 2008, The Department of Homeland Security or DHS will accept voluntary applications under the Electronic System for Travel Authorization (ESTA). These applications will become mandatory on January 12, 2009. ESTA is a new fully automated, electronic system for screening passengers before they begin travel to the United States under the Visa Waiver Program. ESTA applications may be submitted at any time prior to travel to the United States, and VWP travelers are encouraged to apply for authorization as soon as they begin to plan a trip to the United States.

All VWP travelers, regardless of age or type of passport used, must present a machine-readable passport. In addition, depending on when VWP travelers' passports were issued, other passport requirements apply:

- Machine-readable passports issued or renewed/extended on or after 10/26/06 – requires integrated chip with information from the data page (e-Passport).

- Machine-readable passports issued or renewed/extended between 10/26/05 and 10/25/06 – requires digital photograph printed on the data page or integrated chip with information from the data page.

- Machine-readable passports issued or renewed/extended before 10/26/05 – no further requirements.

Temporary, emergency, official and diplomatic passports are exempted from biometric digital photo and chip requirements, but must be machine-readable. Note that German temporary or emergency passports are not included in this biometric e-passport exemption. Therefore, holders of German temporary or emergency passports must either obtain a valid, machine-readable regular German passport for VWP travel or apply for a U.S. visa to travel to or through the United States. If a traveler cannot meet all of the requirements, he/she must obtain a visa for entry to the United States, and cannot travel without a visa on VWP.

Citizens of the United Kingdom were the first to be granted a benefit under this program. It has now been extended to include citizens of the following countries:

Andorra	Luxembourg
Australia	Monaco
Austria	The Netherlands
Belgium	New Zealand
Brunei	Norway
Denmark	Portugal
Finland	San Marino
France	Singapore
Germany	Slovenia
Iceland	Spain
Ireland	Sweden
Italy	Switzerland
Japan	United Kingdom
Liechtenstein	

Citizens of the countries listed above can be admitted to the U.S. for up to ninety days as B-1 or B-2 visitors. Extensions of stay or change of visa status are not permitted. Individuals who wish to participate in the program are required to complete Form I-94W, supplied by the transportation carrier, prior to inspection by a USCIS officer, and the carrier must be one that is participating in the program. The visitor must also:

1. Have a valid passport

2. Have a valid round trip airline ticket that has been signed by a carrier participating in the program, and be arriving on that carrier

3. Have proof of the ability to support himself or herself while in the U.S.

4. Be willing to waive any appeal rights if the immigration officer finds them inadmissible (except for asylum)

5. Be prepared to be screened by the USCIS upon arrival in the U.S.

Individuals taking advantage of this program are also now permitted to enter the U.S. at land border crossing points, such as Canada or Mexico.

4

US– VISIT Program

U.S. Visitor and Immigration Status Indication Technology (US-VISIT) system is designed to keep track of visitors to the United States. It was placed into effect on January 5, 2004 at 115 airports in the U.S, Canada, Caribbean and Europe, and at 15 seaports in the U.S and Canada.   The program applies only to foreign nationals entering the US on temporary visas, including those participating in the Visa Waiver Program. It does not screen diplomats, children under 14, and adults over age 79.

The US-Visit Program is, in essence a "check-in" and "checkout" system that allows the Department of Homeland Security to collect biometric identifiers as part of their inspection process. Biometric data (fingerprint and digital photo) is collected on visitors when they check in and out of the United States, and scanned against law enforcement and national security data bases. The Arrival/Departure Information System (ADIS) will electronically show whether they have complied with the departure terms of their admission. Their personal data will also be checked against electronic lookout lists for law enforcement and security purposes. The government will store the images and other information in its data systems for such future use as intelligence, security, criminal investigation, or confirming visa compliance. Therefore, while the data will be used primarily by DHS and DOS (Department of State) officers, it may be made available for law enforcement purposes to other government agencies, U.S. and foreign.

On arrival, individuals will provide two fingerprints on an inkless device, and a digital photograph will be taken. This information, combined with the normal document review, will determine whether the individual will be admitted into the U.S. and issued a Form I-94. When the individual leaves, their travel documents are scanned, the photographs are compared and new fingerprints are taken.

A person who fails to comply with the departure requirements may be found in violation of his admission, parole, or other immigration status. Such failure may also be considered in deciding whether that individual is eligible for a nonimmigrant visa or admission in the future. Failure to comply can also result in a finding of overstay where the visitor has failed to depart when his authorized stay has ended. Thus, the days when government inefficiency failed to keep track of those overstaying their authorized period of stay appear to be over. Overstaying one's period of authorized stay has serious implications for future visits, including the cancellation of one's visa and subjecting the violator to possible long-term bars against re-entry to the United States, even if eligible to immigrate.

5
Trusted Traveler Programs

Global Entry Program

U.S. citizens and U.S. Lawful Permanent Residents aged 14-years and older may apply to this program.

Global Entry is a new pilot program managed by U.S. Customs and Border Protection which allows pre-approved, low-risk travelers expedited clearance upon arrival into the United States. Participants will enter the United States by utilizing automated kiosks currently located at Terminal 4 - John F. Kennedy International Airport, Washington-Dulles International Airport, and George Bush Intercontinental Airport. The process will require participants to present their machine-readable U.S. passport or permanent residency card, submit their fingerprints for biometric verification, and make a customs declaration at the kiosk's touch-screen. Upon successful completion of the Global Entry process at the kiosk, the traveler will be issued a transaction receipt and directed to baggage claim and the exit, unless chosen for a selective or random secondary referral.

THE NEXUS PROGRAM

The NEXUS alternative inspection program has been completely harmonized and integrated into a single program. NEXUS members now have crossing privileges at any air, land, and marine ports of entry. Under the Western Hemisphere Travel Initiative, the NEXUS card has been approved as an alternative to the passport for air travel into the United States for US and Canadian citizens.

The NEXUS program allows pre-screened, low risk travelers to be processed with little or no delay by United States and Canadian officials at designated highway lanes at high volume border crossing locations, at a NEXUS kiosk at the Canadian Pre-clearance airports, and at certain marine reporting locations in the Great Lakes and Seattle, Washington regions. Approved applicants are issued a photo-identification/

proximity card. Participants use the three modes of passage where they will present their NEXUS card and make a declaration. They are then released, unless chosen for a selective or random secondary referral.

The U.S. Customs and Border Protection (CBP), the Canada Border Services Agency (CBSA) is cooperating in this venture to simplify passage for pre-approved, low-risk travelers.

Individuals may qualify to participate in NEXUS if they are a citizen or permanent resident of the United States or Canada, residing in either country, or if they are a citizen of a country other than Canada or the United States who plans to temporarily reside lawfully in Canada or the United States for the term of their NEXUS membership and who pass criminal history and law enforcement checks.

However, individuals may not qualify if they:

- Are inadmissible to the United States or Canada under applicable immigration laws;

- Provide false or incomplete information on their application;

- Have been convicted of a criminal offense in any country for which they have not received a pardon;

- Have been found in violation of customs or immigration law;

- Will not lawfully reside in either Canada or the United States for the term of their NEXUS membership; or

- Fail to meet other requirements of the NEXUS program.

To participate, both the United States and Canada must approve an individual's application. Denial of an application by either country will keep an individual from participating in the NEXUS program.

SENTRI PROGRAM

SENTRI provides expedited CBP processing for pre-approved, low-risk travelers. Applicants must voluntarily undergo a thorough biographical background check against criminal, law enforcement, customs, immigration, and terrorist indices; a 10-finger-print law enforcement check; and a personal interview with a CBP Officer.

Once an applicant is approved they are issued a Radio Frequency Identification Card (RFID) that will identify their record and status in the CBP database upon arrival at the U.S. port of entry. An RFID decal is also issued to the applicant's vehicle or motorcycle. SENTRI users have access to specific, dedicated primary lanes into the United States.

SENTRI was first implemented at the Otay Mesa, California port of entry on November 1, 1995. SENTRI Dedicated Commuter Lanes also exist in El Paso, TX; San Ysidro, CA; Calexico, CA; Nogales, AZ; Hidalgo, TX; Brownsville, TX; and Laredo, TX.

A SENTRI applicant must not have any penalties, violations, arrests, convictions or pending law enforcement investigations in their backgrounds. Any positive encounters with state, federal and local law enforcement, border agencies, military authorities, etc would render an applicant inadmissible to the SENTRI program. In the case of dismissed charges, certified court records will be required before membership consideration into the SENTRI program.

Reasons for Ineligibility

Applicants will not qualify for participation in the SENTRI program if they:

- Provide false or incomplete information on the application;

- Have been convicted of any criminal offense or have pending criminal charges or outstanding warrants;

- Have been found in violation of any customs, immigration or agriculture regulations or laws in any country;

- Are subjects of an ongoing investigation by any federal, state or local law enforcement agency;

- Are inadmissible to the United States under immigration regulation, including applicants with approved waivers of inadmissibility or parole documentation;

- Cannot satisfy CBP of their low-risk status (i.e. CBP has intelligence that indicates that the applicant is not low risk; CBP cannot determine an applicant's criminal, residence or employment history.); and/or,

- Are subject to National Security Entry Exit Registration System (NSEERS) or other special registration programs.

6

The North American Free Trade Agreement (NAFTA)

In November 1993, Congress approved the North American Free Trade Agreement, commonly known as NAFTA. It became effective on January 1, 1994. NAFTA facilitates trade and investment by liberalizing the rules for entry of temporary business people among the three countries in the agreement: the United States, Mexico and Canada. While NAFTA covers many subjects, this book is concerned only with its immigration aspects.

NAFTA affects four categories of business people; equivalent to the USCIS non-immigrant categories of B-1, "E", L-1 and H-1B discussed previously. There is no limit to the number of Canadians that can enter the U.S. annually. However, no more than 5,500 citizens of Mexico can be classified as TN (Trade NAFTA) nonimmigrants each year.

1. Business Visitors

This is equivalent to our nonimmigrant B-1 category. It requires the United States, Canada and Mexico to temporarily allow a business person from another NAFTA party into the host country to engage in an occupation or profession from one of several categories of business activities: research and design; growth, manufacture and production; marketing; sales; distribution; after-sales service; and general service.

The business activity must be international in scope, and the business visitor must not be "employed" in the United States, e.g. be seeking to enter the local labor market. The primary source of compensation for the proposed business activity, as well as the actual place where profits are made, must be outside the U.S.

Applicants may apply for admission to the United States at a Port of Entry. Canadian citizens are exempt from visa requirements, but Mexican citizens must still present a valid passport with a B-1 visa, or a border-crossing card. Canadian business people do not need a Form I-94, but may request one to facilitate subsequent entries into the United States. Forms I-94 will be endorsed for "multiple entry". Mexican business people, admitted under NAFTA, will be issued a Form I-94 for a period not to exceed one year.

If an extension is needed, it may be filed with the USCIS on Form I-539 at least fifteen, but not more than sixty days before the expiration of stay. Derivative status for the spouse and minor unmarried children of entrants in this category does not exist, although they may be eligible to enter the U.S. as B-2 visitors.

2. Traders and Investors

This classification is similar to our E-1 and E-2 categories. It is offered to Mexican citizens for the first time. Under NAFTA, the investor category has also been broadened to include entry of Canadians and Mexicans into the U.S to: "establish, develop, administer, or provide advice or key technical services to the operation of an investment to which the business person or the business person's enterprise has committed, or is in the process of committing, a substantial amount of capital". The alien must be entering the United States in a position that is supervisory, executive or involves essential skills. Applicants for this category must obtain a visa. The American Consulates in Canada have a standard "E" visa questionnaire. The American Consulates in Mexico use an "E" visa form for Mexican citizens.

The initial approval period for an "E" visa is at least five years for Canadian citizens and six months for Mexican citizens. The actual initial period of admission into the U.S. is one year for both Canadian and Mexican citizens. Extensions of stay can be filed on Form I-129 with the USCIS Regional Service Center having jurisdiction over the applicant's residence.

If a trader or investor wants to change employers, they may only do so after a written request has been approved by the USCIS office having jurisdiction over their residence in the U.S. After the request is granted, the applicant's Form I-94 will be endorsed on the back "employment by (name of new employer) authorized", date. Extensions may be granted in increments of not more than two years. However, when the "E" visa alien departs the U.S., he or she will only be granted a one-year stay upon reentry. The spouse and minor, unmarried children of traders and investors are entitled to the same classification as the principal applicant, and are admitted into the U.S. for one year.

3. Intracompany Transferees

This category is similar to our L-1 classification for intracompany transferees. Canadian and Mexican managers, executives and people with specialized knowledge can enter the U.S. if they continue to provide services that are managerial, executive or specialized knowledge in nature. They must also be working for the same company, its affiliate or subsidiary. An L-1 petition is required of all applicants, and the applicant must establish at least one year of continuous experience abroad. See Chapter 2 for complete L-1 petition requirements.

Canadian employers can file the petition at the same time that the alien applies for admission at the U.S.-Canadian border, e.g. at Ports of Entry or PFI (pre-flight inspection stations), located in Canada. If the petition is approved, the USCIS inspector will give the alien a receipt for the fee collected, and send one copy of the petition to the appropriate USCIS Regional Service Center for final action, and issuance of an approval notice, Form I-797. The USCIS inspector will then inspect the alien and issue Form I-94.

Mexican employers must file the petition with an USCIS Regional Service Center having jurisdiction over the alien's prospective place of employment in the U.S., and the applicant must receive an L-1 visa before being allowed entry into the U.S. The visa requirement has been waived for Canadian citizens, but not Mexican citizens.

If an extension is needed, either for Canadian or Mexican citizens, it can be made on Form I-129, with L supplement, to the appropriate USCIS Regional Service Center. The spouse and unmarried minor children of intracompany transferees are entitled to L-2 status. Mexican citizen spouse and children must obtain L-2 visas before they can enter the United States.

4. Professionals

This is similar to our H-1B category. NAFTA established a category for TN (Trade NAFTA) professionals. Canadians are allowed to apply for TN status at the port of entry, without any prior petition or visa approval, but Mexicans are subject to the same requirements as all professionals applying for H-1B status, including LCA and petition requirements. Self-employment in the U.S. is not permitted in TN status. TN status is available to the following listed professionals:

Accountants
Actuaries,
Agriculturists
Agronomists
Animal breeders
Animal scientists
Apiculturists
Architects
Astronomers
Biochemists
Biologists
Chemists
College teachers
   (seminary or university teachers)
Computer systems analysts
Dairy scientists
Dentists
Dietitians
Disaster relief insurance claims adjusters
Economists
Engineers
Entomologists
Epidemiologists
Foresters
Geneticists
Geologists
Geochemists
Geophysicists
Graphic designers
Horticulturists
Hotel managers
Industrial designers
Interior designers
Land surveyors

Landscape architects
Lawyers
Librarians
Management consultants
Mathematicians
   (including statisticians)
Medical technologists
Meteorologists
Nutritionists
Occupational therapists
Pharmacists
Pharmacologists
Physicians (teaching or research only)
Physicists
Physio/Physical therapists
Plant breeders
Poultry scientists
Psychologists
Range managers
Recreational therapists
Registered nurses
Research assistants
   (for post-secondary ed. institution)
Scientific technicians/ Technologists
Social workers
Soil scientists
Sylviculturists
Teachers
Technical publications writers
Urban planners
Vocational counselors
Veterinarians
Zoologists

The various requirements of degrees, credentials in lieu of degrees, and licenses for certain professions are confusing and beyond the scope of this book. If you believe you may be qualified under NAFTA, you should seek the advice of a qualified immigration professional.

Extensions for TN professionals are filed on Form I-129. Applications may be made at the USCIS Nebraska Service Center. Canadians may also apply for readmission at the border. Extensions of stay are granted for up to one year. There is no set limit on the total amount of time one may remain in the U.S. in TN status.

Spouses and unmarried minor children of TN professionals are granted TD status.

7

Change of Nonimmigrant Status and Extension of Temporary Stay

Before concluding our discussion of nonimmigrant visas, two additional types of applications need to be mentioned that apply to aliens who are currently in the U.S.: the application for change of nonimmigrant status and the extension of temporary stay.

APPLICATION FOR CHANGE OF NONIMMIGRANT STATUS

Aliens who are in the U.S. with certain types of temporary visas, and wish to change to a different visa classification, can file an application for change of nonimmigrant status. For example, an alien is in the U.S. in student (F-1) status, completes his course of study and is awarded a Master's degree in Chemical Engineering. He is then offered a temporary job as a Chemical Engineer with a U.S company. Since the alien seems to be qualified for H-1B classification, the employer could file an H-1B petition with the USCIS as described in Chapter 2. Another example would be that of a spouse who comes to the U.S. in L-2 status and then receives an offer of temporary professional employment. If that person is a professional under the definition of H-1B, he or she could also change status from L-2 to H-1B. The alien must file the application prior to the expiration of Form I-94, have a passport valid for the entire stay, and cannot work in the new visa status while the Application for Change of Nonimmigrant Status is pending with the USCIS.

The approval notice will usually be valid for the same period of time as the approved petition. The alien can remain in the U.S. as long as Form I-94 remains valid. There is no requirement that the alien travel abroad to apply for the temporary visa at an American Consulate. Applications to change status to "E", "H", "L", "O", "P" or "R" are filed on Form I-129. Applications to change status to other nonimmigrant categories are filed on Form I-539.

A change of status application cannot be filed for aliens in certain visa categories, including aliens admitted to the U.S. under the Visa Waiver Pilot Program, "C", "D", "K" and "S" aliens and certain J-1 aliens. Also an M-1 visa holder cannot change to F-1 status, nor can an M-1 student change to "H" classification, if the "M" training helped to qualify for the "H" position.

Application to Extend Time of Temporary Stay

If an alien is in the United States in B-1 or B-2 status and wants to extend his or her temporary stay, the alien can file an application with the USCIS on Form I-539. If a petition was originally required, as in the case of the "E", "H", "L", "O", "P" and "R", the employer must file for these extensions on Form I-129. For example, if an individual has been in the U.S. in L-1 status for three years and wishes to extend that status for an additional two years, he or she can apply to extend the status. A passport valid for the entire stay is required. The basic application consists of:

1. Form I-129-Petition for a Nonimmigrant Worker (and applicable supplement depending on temporary visa status)

2. Forms I-94 of the employee

3. Letter from the employer explaining reasons for requesting the extension

4. Form I-539 for family members and their Forms I-94

5. Applicable filing fee.

For H-1B extensions an approved labor condition application is required. If the extension is for H-2A or H-2B, a labor certification valid for the new dates must be submitted in most cases.

When the application is approved, the USCIS will issue a new notice of approval. The bottom half will consist of a receipt and a new Form I-94. The application must be filed prior to the expiration of Forms I-94. The alien is permitted to remain in the U.S. during the processing of the extension request, and once the application is approved, he or she can remain in the U.S. for as long as Form I-94 remains valid. Individuals in TN status may also file extension of stay requests in the U.S.

Note: aliens who are attempting to extend B-1 or B-2 status must provide the USCIS with a reasonable explanation as to why they were unable to complete their visit within the time period originally authorized. The alien must also prove that he or she is really still a visitor. It is always a good idea to file a copy of a return trip airline ticket with the application as proof that the stay is, indeed, temporary.

Individuals who are in the U.S. in "C", "D", "K" or "S" status, and those who have entered the U.S. in B-1 or B-2 status under the Visa Waiver Pilot Program described earlier, are not eligible for extensions of temporary stay.

Immigrant Visas and Adjustment of Status

The terms "immigrant visa", "permanent resident", "resident alien" and "green card" status all imply the same thing. They represent the right of a foreign national to permanently live and work in the United States. This chapter explains how the U.S. Government uses quotas and a preference system to allocate immigrant visas. Some exceptions, such as the concept of "cross-chargeability" are also discussed. Each of the immigrant visa categories is then explained, including procedures for applying, and the documents required to do so.

If you do not qualify for one of the nonimmigrant categories described in earlier chapters, you may only be able to apply under an immigrant category. The procedure for obtaining an immigrant visa is a lengthy one and can be extremely confusing and frustrating to applicants. One reason for the frustration stems from the inability to predict the actual time it will take to complete the application process.

Timing depends on a variety of factors, such as following the correct filing procedures for each type of application, the extent of processing backlogs in the government offices, which varies from state to state, and the availability of the quota. In some cases, the procedure can be completed in as little as a few months while in other circumstances; applicants from certain countries can wait for ten years or longer! Why is there such a variation in timing for immigrant visa processing?

THE QUOTA

The United States Congress established a very complicated system for issuing immigrant visas. Each month the Department of State in Washington, DC prints a visa bulletin, which lists the availability of visas for every country for that particular month. Only a limited number of immigrant visas are generally issued each year. This limitation is called the "quota" and is based on an alien's country of birth.

An individual born in India is eligible for one of the visas allocated to that country. If that same Indian citizen has become a citizen of another country, for example Canada, he or she is still subject to the Indian quota. This is because our quota system is based on the alien's country of birth, not the country of citizenship. The country quota under which an applicant must apply for an immigrant visa is commonly referred to as the alien's "chargeability". There are four exceptions to chargeability by place of birth. These exceptions are known as "cross-chargeability".

1. If the alien is married to another alien who is a citizen of a different country, the couple can apply under the more favorable quota. For example, if a woman born in the Philippines is married to a man born in Canada, the application for permanent residence can be made under either the Philippine or Canadian quota. In this case, the Canadian quota would be more favorable than that for the Philippines.

2. If the alien was accidentally born in a different country from the place of birth of his or her parents, and the parents were not firmly settled in the country where the child was born, the alien can be charged to the place of birth of either parent. For example, a Venezuelan couple on vacation in Mexico gives birth to a baby. Subsequently, the family immigrates to the U.S. The baby will be charged to the Venezuelan rather than the Mexican quota.

    If the parents never immigrated to the U.S., but this child later immigrated as an adult, he or she could still be charged to the Venezuelan quota, as long as there was proof that the child's place of birth was, indeed, an accident.

3. Minor children can be charged to either parent's place of birth. For example, a Canadian executive of an international company is sent to work in Taiwan for two years. His British born wife accompanies him. During the couple's stay in Taiwan, the wife gives birth to a child. At the end of the two years, the family is transferred to the U.S. in L-1 status. They subsequently apply for permanent residence. The Taiwan born child could be charged either to the Canadian or British quota.

4. Former U.S. citizens can be charged to their country of last residence or country of citizenship.

Why are these cross-chargeability categories important? Because many countries have more than their maximum allowable number of citizens applying for permanent residence in the U.S. each year. This results in long delays in obtaining green cards. When an applicant benefits from cross-chargeability, the processing time can be significantly shortened.

THE PREFERENCE SYSTEM

Immigrant visas are currently grouped into two general categories:

1. Family sponsored preferences

2. Employment based preferences.

This is known as the preference system.

Family Based Preferences

The preference categories assigned to relatives of U.S. citizens or permanent residents. The number of visas issued annually in each category are as follows:

■ Family first preference: Unmarried sons and daughters (over 21 years of age) of U.S. citizens: 23,400 plus any numbers not used in fourth preference.

■ Family second preference: Spouses, children and unmarried sons and daughters of permanent residents: 114,200 plus the number by which the worldwide family preference allocation exceeds 226,000, and any numbers not used in first preference.

■ Family 2A- Spouses and children (unmarried, under age 21) are granted 77% of the second preference numbers, and 75% of these are exempt from the "per country limitation".

■ Family 2B-Adult unmarried sons and daughters of permanent residents are entitled to the remaining 23% of the second preference allocation.

■ Family third preference: married sons and daughters of U.S. citizens: 23,400 plus any numbers not used in first and second preference.

■ Family fourth preference: brothers and sisters of adult U.S. citizens: 65,000 plus any numbers not used in family first, second or third preference.

In each category defined above, the U.S. citizen or permanent resident files a petition with the USCIS. It consists of:

1. Form I-130- Petition for Alien Relative

2. Documentary proof that the petitioner is a U.S. citizen or permanent resident

3. Documentary proof that the petitioner and the alien are related

4. Applicable filing fee.

Note: Second preference spouse cases also require separate photos of petitioner and beneficiary and biographic data forms.

When the USCIS receives the petition, it is date stamped. This date becomes the alien's "priority date" on the waiting list for permanent residence.

As soon as USCIS approves the petition, it forwards the approval notice to the National Visa Center (NVC) which handles the preliminary administration of the visa issuing process for the various Embassies and Consulates. The NVC mails out a "fee bill" to the applicant and after the applicant remits the appropriate fees, the NVC sends out an information packet. Once the applicant completes and returns the information packet and advises that they have all of the documents required for the visa interview, the applicant will be scheduled for a visa interview when the quota becomes available, and when security checks have been completed. The interview will be held at the Embassy or Consulate designated by the NVC based on the applicant's place of residence.

If the immigrant visa application is approved at the interview, the applicant will be given either a sealed envelope to take to the U.S. and present at the port of entry, or a visa will be placed in the applicant's passport. Eventually all applicants will have a visa placed in their passport. The first entry into the United States must be made within four months of visa issuance. With the advent of biometrics processing, the issuance of the permanent resident card or "green card" should be within 90 to 120 days of entry. Under the old system the applicant may have received a "stamp" in his or her passport signifying that the card was in production. Travel while the card production is pending is allowed providing the applicant has some proof that the card is in process.

If the beneficiary is in the U.S., it may be possible to complete the application process in the U.S. When the priority date is reached, the alien files an Application for Adjustment of Status at the following address, regardless of his or her place of residence in the U.S.:

U.S. Citizenship and Immigration Services
PO Box 805887
Chicago, IL 60680-4120

If the applicant is in the United States in legal immigration status, has not accepted unauthorized employment, and has never violated his or her status, the applicant can apply with the following documents:

1. I-130 approval notice

2. Form I-485-Application to Register Permanent Resident or Adjust Status

3. Form G-325A -Biographic Information- for each family member age fourteen or over

4. Passport type Photographs for each family member

5. $1010.00 filing fee for each application, which includes the filing fee for an I-765 and I-131 if applicable

6. Copy of Form I-94 for each applicant

7. Copy of any evidence showing continuous lawful status

8. Copy of passport

9. Form I-864 Affidavit of support with supporting documentation for each beneficiary: a letter verifying employment, copies of income tax returns for the past three years

10. Birth and marriage certificates-see note below

11. Proof of termination of prior marriages if applicable

12. Medical examination report.

Note: The USCIS requires that birth certificates be "long form", showing names of parents. All personal documents must be accompanied by certified English translations. In some jurisdictions, the USCIS office routinely requests other documents that are not listed above.

The following groups of aliens were previously able to adjust status under a law that expired on September 30, 1997 but are no longer able to do so unless "grandfathered". This immigration law is known as Section 245(i). Aliens who are the beneficiaries of visa petitions and labor certification applications filed on or before April 30, 2001 will be "grandfathered" provided they meet certain criteria. This means that the following groups of aliens may be allowed to continue to adjust status under Section 245(i).

1. Aliens who entered the U.S. illegally

2. Aliens who have remained in the U.S. beyond their authorized stay

3. Aliens who have accepted unauthorized employment.

Applicants under the three categories shown above need to submit all documents shown in the previous box. In addition, a Form I-485A supplement must be filed along with a $1000.00 penalty fee for each applicant and evidence that they meet the requirements for grandfathering under 245(i). The fee is waived for the following categories of applicants:

1. Children under age seventeen

2. An alien who is the spouse or unmarried child of an individual who was legalized under the Immigration Reform and Control Act of 1986 and who was:

   a. The spouse or unmarried child of the legalized alien as of May 5, 1988;

   b. Entered the United States before May 5, 1988 and resided here on that date;

   c. Applied for family unity benefits under the Immigration Act of 1990.

In addition, under Section 245 (K) of the Immigration & Nationality Act, employment-based visa applicants may adjust status if they are currently maintaining lawful status and have not previously been out status for more than an aggregate of 180 days. This provision is distinct from the grandfathering provision and does not require the applicant to pay a penalty fee.

Although the application forms that need to be filed with the USCIS may differ somewhat from office to office, the events leading up to the final interview are essentially the same as attending a final interview at an American Consulate. At the final interview the applicants must present the following:

1. Valid passports

2. Original birth certificates, marriage certificate and proof of the termination of prior marriages, if applicable

3. Form I-864 Affidavit of Support for the beneficiary and accompanying family members.

6. Letter of employment for petitioner and tax returns for the past three years.

The applicant's passport, and those of accompanying family members, will be stamped with the temporary green card upon approval of the case. The USCIS will then forward the required documents to the Immigration Card Facility in Vermont for processing of the green cards.

Applicants, who are eligible to complete their immigrant visa applications in the United States but choose not to, may complete their applications at an American Consulate abroad. See previous discussion on applying for an immigrant visa at an American Consulate.

Applicants with Permanent Offers of Employment

The Immigration Act of 1990 allows for 140,000 immigrant visas to be issued each year for employment based petitions. The preference categories assigned to applicants who have permanent offers of employment in the U.S., and the number of visas issued in each category are as follows:

- **Employment Based First Preference:** Priority Workers: 40,000 plus those numbers not used for fourth and fifth preference. Priority workers include aliens of extraordinary ability in the arts, sciences, business, education and athletics; managers and executives of international companies being transferred permanently to the U.S.; and outstanding professors and researchers. Labor certification is not required for employment based first preference (see explanation in Chapter 8). Please note those priority workers of "extraordinary ability" do not require an offer of employment as long as they will continue to work in their area of expertise. This only applies to extraordinary ability.

- **Employment Based Second Preference:** Members of the professions holding advanced degrees (any degree above a bachelors) and people of exceptional merit and ability in the sciences, arts or business: 40,000 plus those numbers not used in first preference. Labor certification is required.

- **Employment Based Third Preference:** Skilled workers (must be filling a position that requires two years of training and experience), professionals with bachelors degrees and unskilled workers: 40,000 plus those numbers not used in first and second preference. Labor certification is required. Please note that only 10,000 of the 40,000 visas in this category will be allocated to unskilled workers.

- **Employment Based Fourth Preference:** Certain "special" immigrants: 10,000. This category includes juveniles under Court protection; employees of the American Consulate in Hong Kong; and religious workers, such as ministers, who have at least a bachelor's degree. Please note that not more than 5,000 of these visas will be issued to religious workers. (Application to be filed on Form I-360).

- **Employment Based Fifth Preference:** Employment creation (investors): 10,000, with not less than 3000 reserved for investors who invest in a targeted rural or high-unemployment area in the U.S. There is no labor certification requirement in this category, however, there are other strict criteria, which must be met such as the dollar amount of the investment and the number of jobs the investment will create for U.S. workers. See Chapter 11.

Before an application for permanent residence can be made based on an offer of employment in the employment based second and third preference categories, a basis of eligibility for filing the petition must be established. This usually requires that the sponsoring employer file an Application for Alien Employment Certification with the U.S. Department of Labor. This application should eventually result in the issuance of a Labor Certification. Other aliens may establish a basis of eligibility under a category called "Schedule A", and still others, under another employment based category. In these cases, the U.S. Department of Labor has determined that it is not necessary for a sponsoring employer to obtain Labor Certification. The Labor Certification process, Schedule A, and other employment-based categories are discussed in Chapter 10.

Once the alien has established a basis for eligibility, and a visa number becomes available based on the priority date, the procedure for completing the application is similar to the procedure for relatives of U.S. citizens or permanent residents discussed earlier in this chapter. However, the application is made to one of the four Regional Service Centers, depending on where the petition was filed or where the beneficiary resides.

INDIVIDUALS NOT SUBJECT TO QUOTA LIMITATIONS

Two common categories of individuals who are not subject to the numerical limitations of the quota described above are:

1) **Applicants who are Immediate Relatives of U.S. Citizens:** Citizenship may be on the basis of birth in the U.S. or through naturalization. Immediate relatives include spouses, unmarried sons and daughters under the age of twenty-one, and parents of adult citizens (over the age of 21). This category also includes spouses of deceased U.S. citizens, in certain cases. (This last application is made on Form I-360-Petition for Amerasian, Widow or Special Immigrant.)

   Although the quota system does not apply, the sponsor is still required to file an I-130 petition with the USCIS before the relative can immigrate to America. If the relative is in the U.S. in legal status, the entire application process can be completed within a few months. If the relative applies at an American Consulate overseas, the processing time will vary according to the administrative backlogs at the USCIS and at the Consulate abroad.

In the case of husbands or wives, an applicant who has been married for less than two years will be granted a conditional green card. After two years, the applicant will be required to file another application with the USCIS on Form I-751 (Petition to Remove the Conditions of Residence). The couple will be required to prove that they entered into the marriage in good faith and are still married to each other. At that point, the conditional status will be removed and the applicant will be issued a permanent green card.

Note: There are waivers available for battered spouses and in cases of divorce. You should seek the advice of a professional if you fall into either of these categories.

2) **Refugees:** Refugees are those who are unwilling to, or cannot, return to their country of origin because they fear persecution based on race, religion, nationality, political views or membership in a particular group. Each year the President of the United States, together with Congress, decides on the number of applicants who will be admitted to the U.S. as refugees or asylees. The refugee application processes are complex and are not covered in this book.

9
Child Status Protection Act

The Child Status Protection Act (CSPA) was signed into law on August 6, 2002. Prior to the CSPA, if a child was eligible for an immigrant visa or adjustment of status through derivative status, but was not issued the visa or adjustment of status before age 21, the individual lost their eligibility. CSPA finally gives a benefit to children who otherwise would have been "aged out" due to USCIS processing delays.

Children of US Citizens: CSPA accomplishes this for the children of U.S. citizens who seek to qualify as an ``immediate relative" by freezing their age as of the date that the petition is filed on their behalf.

Family-sponsored second preference: The petition for the child of a lawful permanent resident (FS-2A) is converted to an immediate relative petition when the parent is naturalized. Under the CSPA, the child's age is frozen as of the date of the naturalization. However, to benefit as an immediate relative, the child would need an additional petition filed on his or her behalf by the U.S. citizen parent (because, unlike a derivative relative of a preference petition, a child requires a separate petition to be classified as an immediate relative). But if the child had not yet turned 21 when the naturalization occurred, the immediate relative petition would succeed even if it were filed after her 21st birthday.

Family-sponsored third preference: For a married son or daughter of a U.S. citizen, the petition is converted to an immediate relative petition if the beneficiary's marriage ends and the beneficiary is then under 21, or to the first preference if the beneficiary has by then turned 21. The CSPA preserves the beneficiary's age as of the date of the death, divorce, or other act that terminated the marriage.

The CSPA also offers age-out protection to a child who is the beneficiary of a family-sponsored second-preference or who is a derivative beneficiary under any of the family-sponsored or employment-based (EB) preferences or under the diversity lottery. It does so by preserving the child's age as of the date a visa number becomes available to him or her, less the time the petition was pending. (In the case of a derivative beneficiary, the measuring date is the date a visa number becomes available to the principal beneficiary.) For example, an EB third-preference petition filed on January 2, 2002 and approved a year later (a visa number thereby becoming available to the principal beneficiary). Although the beneficiary's son turned 21 on July 1, 2002, his derivative status as a child is preserved because a year is deducted from the age he reached on January 2, 2003. In the case of a beneficiary whose age, under the calculation, is 21 or more, the petition is converted to the appropriate category, if any, with its original priority date.

To retain the benefit, however, the CSPA requires that the child, whether as a direct beneficiary or derivative, have ``sought to acquire the status of lawful permanent residence within one year of such availability....", meaning, that they have applied for either adjustment of status or the immigrant visa.

The children of asylum applicants also enjoy aging-out benefits. They may be granted asylum when accompanying or following to join a parent granted asylum. And if they qualified as a ``child" when the parent's application was filed, they continue to be eligible for asylum if they are not married when they themselves apply and accompany or follow to join the parent, even if they have meanwhile reached the age of 21. Similarly, the noncitizen who was under the age of 21 when his or her parent applied for refugee status, continues to be classified as a child for purposes of accompanying or following to join the parent granted refugee status even if he or she turned 21 while the application was pending.

CSPA is not only prospective but also covers any petition approved before its enactment, if there was no final decision on the beneficiary's application for adjustment of status or for an immigrant visa.

10

Labor Certification (Perm), Schedule A and Other Exemptions

As explained in Chapter 8, aliens who are offered permanent employment in the U.S. must establish a basis of eligibility for filing an employment based preference petition, either through

1. Labor certification (employment based preference Category 2 and 3)

2. Exemption from labor certification (employment based Categories 1, 4 and 5) or

3. Under a Schedule A category.

This chapter describes the various stages involved in obtaining general labor certification for employment based preference Categories 2 and 3, and exemptions from labor certification.

THE LABOR CERTIFICATION PROCESS-PERM

Aliens who have been offered permanent employment in the U.S., and who do not meet the criteria for exemption from labor certification, must obtain Alien Employment Certification, commonly referred to as labor certification from the U.S. Department of Labor (DOL). The DOL must be satisfied that there are no qualified U.S. workers available to fill the permanent job offered to the alien, and that the working conditions and wages offered for the position will not have an adverse effect on the U.S. labor market. Once the labor certification is approved, it serves as the basis for filing an employment based 2nd or 3rd preference petition with the USCIS. (Appendix C contains Regional Department of Labor office addresses, and the jurisdictions that they cover.)

To obtain labor certification, the employer must demonstrate that he or she has followed a precise program of recruitment that tests the local labor market for qualified and available U.S. workers in the geographic area where the job will be filled.

The PERM process requires that all recruitment be conducted prior to filing the application and recruitment must be conducted within 6 months of filing. Each filing requires the following recruitment:

1. a job order must be placed with the State Workforce Agency serving the area of intended employment

2. ads on two different Sundays in a newspaper of general circulation (if the job requires experience and an advanced degree, a professional journal may be substituted for one of the Sunday newspaper ads).

3. three forms of additional recruitment must be conducted out of the following list of ten: (a) job fairs (b) employer's web site (c) job search web site other than employers (d) on-campus recruiting (e) trade or professional organizations (f) private employment firms (g) employee referral program with incentives (h) campus placement offices (i) local and ethnic newspapers (j) radio and tv ads. In addition, there must be an internal posting for 10 consecutive business days, as was previously done for regular or RIR labor certification applications.

The application can be filed either electronically or by mail on Form ETA 9089, describing the job in detail, indicating the salary offered and describing the minimum qualifications for the position, including minimum education and experience and any special requirements. The Labor Department will either approve the application or select the application for audit. The routine processing time for non-audited cases is expected to be about 60 days.

Once the case is certified by the Labor Department, the applicant's employer can file an I-140 petition with the USCIS and if the applicant is eligible to adjust status, the applicant can simultaneously file an application for adjustment of status. Employment based petitions are filed at one of the four Regional Service Centers.

Note: The American Competitiveness in the 21ˢᵗ Century Act of 2000 also provided, for the first time, some flexibility in the ability to change jobs or employers, for those whose adjustment of status applications had been pending for more than 180 days. The new job must be in the same or similar occupational classification as the one for which the petition was originally filed.

Previously, one had to remain with the same employer, and in the same position, until the application for adjustment of status had been approved.

Schedule A Categories

In some cases, known as Schedule A, the U.S. Department of Labor has determined that the sponsoring employer need not obtain labor certification. There are presently two Schedule A categories:

■ Schedule A Group I: Applies to professional nurses and physical therapists. In each case, the alien must have very specific credentials, including licenses, and must have passed certain exams required by each state to practice their vocation in the United States. Labor certifications are not available to professional nurses and physical therapists, even if their Schedule A Group I applications are denied.

   Note: A nurse or physical therapist must provide a CGFNS (Commission on Graduates of Foreign Nursing Schools) Certificate dated after October 1, 1998 in order to obtain permanent residence.

■ Schedule A Group II: Applies to aliens who have exceptional ability in the arts and sciences and may not qualify under employment based first preference. This category is primarily reserved for individuals who have received widespread international acclaim in their specific field, such as scientists, professors, and authors. Aliens of exceptional ability in the performing arts may also qualify under certain circumstances. The USCIS has very stringent documentary requirements for Schedule A Group II classification, including testimonial letters from experts in the alien's field of endeavor, published works by or about the alien, invitations extended to the alien to speak at international conferences, and awards.

Schedule A applications are filed directly with the USCIS Regional Service Center. Once the application is approved, and the priority date becomes current, the permanent residence application can be completed through adjustment of status, or by visa processing at an American Consulate. The procedures are the same as for aliens who have approved labor certifications, described above.

National Interest Waiver

An alien may seek a waiver of the offer of employment by establishing that his admission to permanent residence would be in the "national interest". There is no hard and fast rule, nor any statutory standards as to what will qualify an alien for a National Interest Waiver. The USCIS considers each case on an individual basis. The procedure is to file Form I-140 together with evidence to establish that the alien's admission to the United States for permanent residence would be in the national interest. Factors that have been considered in successful cases include:

■ The alien's admission will improve the U.S. economy.

■ The alien's admission will improve wages and working conditions of U.S. workers.

■ The alien's admission will improve educational and training programs for U.S. children and underqualified workers.

■ The alien's admission will provide more affordable housing for young, aged, or poor U.S. residents.

■ The alien's admission will improve the U.S. environment and lead to more productive use of the national resources.

■ The alien's admission is requested by an interested U.S. government agency.

Many of the cases in which national interest waivers have been approved were supported by affidavits from well-known, established and influential people or organizations. For example, an application being submitted for a scientist should contain affidavits from leading scientists, representatives of scientific institutions, and from other organizations associated with the type of research to be pursued. Documenting past achievements, as well as proof that the alien has already created jobs, turned around a business or created an increase in exports or other economic improvements should prove instrumental in gaining approval.

Other Employment Based Categories

Aliens applying for permanent residence in employment based preference Categories 1, 4 and 5 do not require labor certification. Aliens in employment based preference categories 2 & 3, who can establish that their admission is in the "National Interest", also do not require labor certification. Application is made directly to the USCIS on Form I-140- Immigrant Petition for Alien Worker in employment based preference Categories 1, 2 & 3, on Form I-360- Petition for Amerasian, Widow or Special Immigrant in employment based preference Category 4, and on Form I-526- Immigrant Petition by Alien Entrepreneur in employment based preference Category 5. Supporting documentation varies depending on the category in which the alien is applying.

11

Immigrant Visas for Alien Investors

The Immigration Act of 1990 created a new preference category for immigrants who are able to invest at least $1 million in the United States.

Immigrant visas are available, subject to quota limitations (approximately 10,000 annually), for immigrants seeking to enter the United States to engage in a new commercial enterprise. This new business must benefit the U.S. economy and create at least ten full-time jobs for U.S. citizens or permanent residents, other than the applicant or his or her immediate family.

The minimum amount of the investment is $1 million, although the USCIS may consider less if the investment is in a "targeted employment" area, i.e., and one where the unemployment rate is 150% of the national average. The investment must have been made after November 29, 1990.

Under this category, the term "investment" generally means that the alien must place his or her capital at risk for the purpose of generating a profit. The company must have been formed for the "ongoing conduct of lawful business". The investment must be in a commercial enterprise that generates active income. Apartment buildings, for example, would not qualify, since the income they generate is considered passive. The term "capital" is defined as "cash, equipment, inventory, tangible property, cash equivalents and indebtedness secured by the investor's assets, provided he or she is personally liable".

The enterprise may be a sole proprietorship, a partnership, a holding company, a joint venture, a corporation or other entity publicly or privately owned. The investment does not have to be completed, but the investor must be "in the process" of investing, showing an actual commitment of funds.

Generally, the investment must be in either:

- A newly created business

- The purchase of an existing business and simultaneous or subsequent restructuring or reorganization such that a new commercial enterprise results

- The expansion of an existing business so long as there is a substantial change of at least 140% in either net worth or in the number of employees of the company.

Debt can be used to secure capital, provided that the alien is personally and primarily liable, and the debt is not secured against the assets of the enterprise. Capital may come from abroad, but ownership of the capital must be established.

The investor will also have to show that he will be actively engaged in the management of the enterprise. Any assets or capital derived from illegal means or criminal activity will not be considered.

Generally, the documents for the immigrant investor are those that would establish the investment, that is, proof of the capital invested, proof of the creation of new jobs, proof of the alien's management position and evidence of the nature of the enterprise. Form I-526- Immigrant Petition by Alien Entrepreneur, is also required.

The legal definitions and rules for alien investors are complex, and you should seek the advice of a professional if you intend to pursue this category.

12
Immigrant Visas for Foreign Born Orphans

The Immigration and Nationality Act allows for U.S. citizens to apply for immigrant visas for foreign born children who are orphans, and have not yet reached the age of 16.

Two categories of U.S. citizens can file an orphan petition:

1. A married U.S. citizen and spouse (no age requirement). The spouse does not have to be a U.S. citizen, but must be here legally, if living in the U.S.

2. An unmarried U.S. citizen who is at least 25 years old.

A child is an orphan if he or she does not have any parents due to death or disappearance, desertion or abandonment, or separation or loss from both parents. A child can also qualify if a sole surviving parent cannot take proper care of the child, and has issued a written and irrevocable release of the child for adoption and emigration.

Application can be made for advance processing before the U.S. citizen actually locates an orphan to adopt. This allows USCIS to process the part of the application that proves the U.S. citizen's ability to provide a proper home and your suitability as a parent. It is recommended that all prospective adoptive parents do advance processing. The advance processing application is filed with the USCIS office having jurisdiction over where the petitioner lives and consists of:

1. Form I-600A-Application for Advance Processing of Orphan Petition

2. Proof of U.S. citizenship

3. Proof of spouse's U.S. citizenship or lawful immigration status, if living in the U.S.

4. Proof of marriage, and termination of prior marriages

5. Complete home study

6. Proof of compliance with the pre-adoption requirements of the state where you will live with the adopted child

7. Fingerprints for each adult household member

8. Filing fee of $750.00.

Note: The USCIS publishes Document M-249N-The Immigration of Adopted and Prospective Adoptive Children that contains more detailed information.

Approval of the Application for Advance Processing will facilitate the filing of Form I-600-Petition to Classify Orphan as an Immediate Relative. This second application can be processed at an overseas USCIS office or American Embassy or Consulate, once an orphan is located for adoption. The complete application consists of:

1. Form I-600-Petition to Classify Orphan as an Immediate Relative

2. The child's birth certificate or evidence of the child's age and identity

3. Proof that the child is an orphan, as defined above

4. A final adoption decree, if applicable

5. Proof of legal custody of the child for adoption and emigration, if applicable.

6. Proof of compliance with pre-adoption requirements, if applicable

7. Filing fee of $750.00 if not based on an approved I-600A.

The adoption of a foreign born child by a U.S. citizen does not guarantee the child's right to immigrate to the U.S. If the orphan petition is approved, the child becomes an immediate relative of a U.S. citizen, and can apply for an immigrant visa. However, just like any other foreign-born person, the child must qualify for the immigrant visa. Assuming the visa is approved, the orphan will enter the U.S. as a lawful permanent resident, not a U.S. citizen.

A subsequent application for U.S. citizenship must be filed (Form N-643-Application for Certificate of Citizenship on Behalf of an Adopted Child), before the child is 18 years old. If the application is not completed before the child reaches the age of 18, the child will have to apply for citizenship on their own.

13

The Annual Visa Lottery Program

In 1995, the Immigration and Nationality Act established an annual visa lottery. Natives of certain countries, selected by a mathematical formula, are able to compete for visas in this category. The numerical limit on these types of visas is 50,000 per year for people from countries with low rates of immigration to the U.S. The applicant can apply either from within the U.S. or from outside the U.S.

In 1995 the program was known as the DV-1 lottery. In subsequent years the identifying symbol will be "DV" followed by the fiscal year. For example, the 2010 lottery is known as DV-2010. (The government fiscal year begins on October 1 and ends on September 30.) The registration period for DV-2010 began October 2, 2008 and ended on December 1, 2008.

For DV-2010, natives of the following countries were excluded from the lottery: Brazil, Canada, China (mainland-born), Colombia, Dominican Republic, Ecuador, El Salvador, Guatemala, Haiti, India, Jamaica, Mexico, Pakistan, Philippines, Peru, Poland, South Korea, United Kingdom (except Northern Ireland), and Vietnam. People born in Hong Kong SAR, Macau SAR and Taiwan were eligible. For DV-2010, Russia returned to the list and Kosovo has been added.

Special requirements for the DV lottery are as follows:

1. Each applicant must have a high school education or its equivalent

    or

2. Within the past five years, have had two years of work experience in an occupation requiring at least two years of training or experience.

Currently, the Department of State will only accept completed applications (Form E-DV) submitted electronically at www.dvlottery.state.gov during the registration period. All entries by an individual will be disqualified if more than ONE entry for that individual is received, regardless of who submitted the entry. A successfully registered entry will result in the display of a confirmation screen containing your name and a unique confirmation number.

Paper entries will not be accepted.

Please note that the application will be disqualified if the required digital photos are not submitted. A separate digital photo of each family member is required. You do not need to submit a photo for a child who is already a US citizen or Legal Permanent Resident. Photo requirements are very specific and you should follow the instructions on the lottery website carefully.

After the end of the application period, a computer will randomly select cases from among all the applicants from each geographic region. If you are selected, you will receive a letter with instructions on how to complete the process. For DV-2010, selected individuals will be notified by mail between May and July 2009. If you are not selected you will NOT receive any notification. However, starting with DV-2010, as of July 1, 2009, all entrants, including those NOT selected, will be able to check the status of their entry through the E-DV website to find out if the entry was or was not selected. Successful entrants, their spouses and unmarried children under age 21 may also apply for visas to accompany or "follow to join" the principal applicant. DV-2010 visas will be issued between October 1, 2009 and September 30, 2010.

Once you get the acceptance letter it is imperative that you complete all applications, follow the instructions and file the necessary documents immediately. Successful applicants may either apply for an immigrant visa at the American Consulate in their country of residence or, if they are in the United States and are eligible to adjust status, apply at the USCIS office having jurisdiction over their place of residence.

The formal visa application made at the American Consulate consists of:

1. Form DS- 230 I & II- Special Lottery Form

2. Police certificates where applicable

3. Birth certificates

4. Marriage certificate or proof of termination of prior marriages

5. Proof of high school education or equivalent, or required work experience

6. Photographs

7. Completed medical examination

8. Proof of support or job offer for permanent employment.

The application for adjustment of status filed at the USCIS is similar to the application for adjustment of status described in Chapter 8. In addition, the applicant must provide:

1. Copy of the notification letter from the Kentucky Consular Center

2. Proof of high school education or equivalent, or required work experience

3. Proof of support or job offer.

List of Countries by Region Whose Natives Qualify

The lists below show the countries whose natives are QUALIFIED within each geographic region for this diversity program. The determination of countries within each region is based on information provided by the Geographer of the Department of State. The countries whose natives do not qualify for the DV-2010 program were identified by the U.S. Citizenship and Immigration Services (USCIS) according to the formula in Section 203(c) of the Immigration and Nationality Act. Dependent areas overseas are included within the region of the governing country. The countries whose natives do NOT qualify for this diversity program (because they are the principal source countries of Family-Sponsored and Employment-Based immigration, or "high admission" countries) are noted after the respective regional lists.

AFRICA

Algeria	Libya
Angola	Madagascar
Benin	Malawi
Botswana	Mali

Burkina Faso
Burundi
Cameroon
Cape Verde
Central African Republic
Chad
Comoros
Congo
Congo, Democratic Republic of the
Cote D'Ivoire (Ivory Coast)
Djibouti
Egypt
Equatorial Guinea
Eritrea
Ethiopia
Gabon
Gambia, The
Ghana
Guinea
Guinea-Bissau
Kenya
Lesotho
Liberia

Mauritania
Mauritius
Morocco
Mozambique
Namibia
Niger
Nigeria
Rwanda
Sao Tome and Principe
Senegal
Seychelles
Sierra Leone
Somalia
South Africa
Sudan
Swaziland
Tanzania
Togo
Tunisia
Uganda
Zambia
Zimbabwe

List of Countries by Region Whose Natives Qualify

ASIA

Afghanistan
Bahrain
Bangladesh
Bhutan
Brunei
Burma
Cambodia
East Timor
Hong Kong Special Administrative Region
Indonesia
Iran
Iraq

Lebanon
Malaysia
Maldives
Mongolia
Nepal
North Korea
Oman
Qatar
Saudi Arabia
Singapore
Sri Lanka
Syria

Israel
Japan
Jordan
Kuwait
Laos

Taiwan
Thailand
United Arab Emirates
Yemen

Natives of the following Asian countries do not qualify for this year's diversity program: China [mainland-born], India, Pakistan, South Korea, Philippines, and Vietnam. The Hong Kong S.A.R and Taiwan do qualify and are listed above. Macau S.A.R. also qualifies and is listed below.

List of Countries by Region Whose Natives Qualify

EUROPE

Albania
Andorra
Armenia
Austria
Azerbaijan
Belarus
Belgium
Bosnia and Herzegovina
Bulgaria
Croatia
Cyprus
Czech Republic
Denmark (including components
    and dependent areas overseas)
Estonia
Finland
France (including components
    and dependent areas overseas)
Georgia
Germany
Greece
Hungary
Iceland
Ireland

Lithuania
Luxembourg
Macau Special Administrative Region
Macedonia, the Former Yugoslav Republic
Malta
Moldova
Monaco
Montenegro
Netherlands (including components
    and dependent areas overseas)
Northern Ireland
Norway
Portugal (including components and
    dependent areas overseas)
Romania
Russia
San Marino
Serbia
Slovakia
Slovenia
Spain
Sweden
Switzerland
Tajikistan

Italy
Kazakhstan
Kosovo
Kyrgyzstan
Latvia
Liechtenstein

Turkey
Turkmenistan
Ukraine
Uzbekistan
Vatican City

Natives of the following European countries do not qualify for this year's diversity program: Great Britain, and Poland. Great Britain (United Kingdom) includes the following dependent areas: Anguilla, Bermuda, British Virgin Islands, Cayman Islands, Falkland Islands, Gibraltar, Montserrat, Pitcairn, St. Helena, Turks and Caicos Islands. Note that for purposes of the diversity program only, Northern Ireland is treated separately; Northern Ireland does qualify and is listed among the qualifying areas.

List of Countries by Region Whose Natives Qualify

NORTH AMERICA

The Bahamas

In North America, natives of Canada and Mexico do not qualify for this year's diversity program.

OCEANIA

Australia (including components and
    dependent areas overseas)
Fiji
Kiribati
Marshall Islands
Micronesia, Federated States of
Nauru
New Zealand (including components and
    dependent areas overseas)

Palau

Papua New Guinea
Solomon Islands
Tonga
Tuvalu
Vanuatu
Samoa

SOUTH AMERICA, CENTRAL AMERICA, AND THE CARIBBEAN

Antigua and Barbuda
Argentina
Barbados
Belize
Bolivia
Chile
Costa Rica
Cuba
Dominica
Grenada
Guyana

Honduras
Nicaragua
Panama
Paraguay
Saint Kitts and Nevis
Saint Lucia
Saint Vincent and the Grenadines
Suriname
Trinidad and Tobago
Uruguay
Venezuela

Countries in this region whose natives do not qualify for this year's diversity program: Brazil, Colombia, Dominican Republic,Ecuador, El Salvador, Guatemala, Haiti, Jamaica, Mexico and Peru.

14

Renewal of Expiring Green Cards

Since 1989, the USCIS has been issuing Green Cards with a ten-year expiration date on the front of the card. This allowed the agency to update photo identification and implement new card technologies to increase the card's resistance to counterfeiting and tampering.

Procedures are now in place to accommodate Green Card renewal applicants. Application can be made up to six months in advance of the expiration.

Applicants should complete Form I-90 (Application to Replace a Permanent Resident Card). The application can be obtained by calling the toll-free forms request line (1-800-870-3676) or can be completed online at: https://efiling.uscis.dhs.gov/efile/.

Renewal applicants should mail their applications to:

USCIS Citizenship and Immigration Services
PO Box 54870
Los Angeles, CA 90054-0870

Or may send them by courier to:

US Citizenship and Immigration Services
Attention I-90
16420 Valley View Avenue
La Mirada, CA 90638-5821

The application consists of:

1. Form I-90-Application to Replace a Permanent Resident Card

2. Check or money order for $290.00 payable to USCIS

3. $80.00 Biometrics fee

After you apply, USCIS will schedule your biometrics appointment to have your biometrics taken at a USCIS Application Support Center (ASC). You will be receiving a biometrics appointment notice with a specific date, time, and place where you will have your fingerprints and/or photos taken. You MUST wait for your biometrics appointment notice to arrive in the mail prior to going to the ASC for biometrics processing.

Bring the following to your biometrics appointment:

■ Biometrics appointment notice.

■ Photo identification. Acceptable kinds of photo identifications are:

   ■ Passport or national photo identification issued by your country, or

   ■ Driver's license, or

   ■ Military photo identification, or

   ■ State-issued photo identification card.

■ Required initial evidence, including:

   ■ Your prior card, or

   ■ Other evidence of permanent residence or commuter status

■ Supporting documentation, which may include but is not limited to:

   ■ Court ordered name change,

   ■ Marriage certificate,

   ■ Birth certificate, or

   ■ Police report for a stolen or lost card.

If you fail to renew your expiring card, you may have difficulties in obtaining employment, benefits and reentry into the U.S. from abroad.

If your Green Card has already expired, you should apply for a renewal as soon as possible, since you are required by law to carry evidence of your status/registration. You will not be penalized.

15
INFOPASS and the USCIS Website

InfoPass is a free and convenient internet-based system. It eliminates the need to go in person to make an appointment, obtain forms, general information or even specific information about a case pending at one of the Service Centers. The USCIS website is a wonderful resource for immigration information, for obtaining forms and for checking the status of your case filed at a Service Center. The USCIS website can be found at: http://uscis.gov/graphics/index.htm

INFOPASS eliminates the need to stand in line at a USCIS District Office. It is accessible by computer at: http://infopass.uscis.gov/. If you do not have a computer available, the District Offices have kiosks set up and an information officer available to help you. With INFOPASS you can schedule an appointment at a local office by entering your zip code, then choosing one of the following options:

1. You need an immigration form

2. You need to replace your Alien Registration Card

3. You need to file an application for yourself or someone else

4. You have a question about your case

5. You have received an approval letter or Form I-797C from the Service Center or local office instructing you to come into the office for alien identification card processing/passport stamp

6. It has been more than 90 days since you filed an I-765 and you did not receive an Employment Authorization Card

7. You wish to speak to an immigration officer.

Interviews are scheduled two weeks in advance. The best time to access the site is after 5 pm.

The information provided below should help with routine inquiries.

YOU NEED A FORM: All immigration forms are free and can be downloaded from www.uscis.gov. (Select the Immigration Forms box)or by calling the National Customer Service Center (NCSC) at 1-800-375-5283.

YOU WANT TO CHECK THE STATUS OF A CASE: Go to www.uscis.gov and select "Case Status & Processing Dates" under "Hot Topics" on the right side of the home page. You must have your Service Center receipt number.

YOU WANT TO RENEW OR REPLACE A GREEN CARD: You need to file Form I-90 "Application for Replacement of Green Card". Go to www.uscis.gov and select "E-filing" under "Hot Topics" on the right side of the home page.

YOU NEED EMPLOYMENT AUTHORIZATION: To apply or renew employment authorization, you will need Form I-765 "Application for Employment Authorization". This form can be filed online by going to www.uscis.gov and selecting "E-filing" under "Hot Topics" on the right side of the home page.

YOU NEED GENERAL INFORMATION: Before planning a trip to the USCIS, call the NCSC at 1-800-375-5283 to see if they can help you over the phone.

16
Naturalization

Aliens elect to become citizens of the United States in order to reap the benefits, such as the right to vote, the right to obtain a U.S. passport, and the ability to sponsor relatives for permanent residence. This chapter describes the rules and procedures for applying for citizenship or naturalization.

Permanent residents are eligible for naturalization five years after permanent residence is granted. The applicant must have physically resided in the U.S. for at least two and one half years out of the five years and have been a resident of the state where the application for naturalization is filed for at least three months. If the applicant spent more than one full year during the five-year qualifying period outside the U.S., he or she is not eligible for citizenship under the same guidelines.

If the applicant was granted permanent residence based on marriage to a U.S. citizen, he or she can apply for naturalization after three years.

However, the following conditions must be met:

- The spouse must have been a citizen for three years, and

- The couple must have been married for at least three years.

- The applicant must have lived in the U.S. for at least eighteen months out of the three years, and

- The applicant must have been a resident of the state for at least three months.

The application is filed with the USCIS at the Regional Service Center having jurisdiction over the alien's place of residence. It can be filed up to three months in advance of actual eligibility. It consists of:

1. Form N-400-Application for Naturalization

2. Photographs

3. Copy of front and back of your green card

4. Filing fee of $675.00.

The applicant will then be called for an interview at the USCIS. It may take up to eight months to receive the notice. At the interview, the applicant will be asked a series of questions to determine good moral character, the ability to read, write and speak elementary English and the intention to reside in the U.S. permanently. (Aliens over the age of fifty-five who have been living in the U.S. as permanent residents for at least fifteen years can have the English language requirement waived. Aliens who are over the age of fifty and have been permanent residents for at least twenty years can also have this requirement waived.) The applicant will also be tested for a basic understanding of U.S. history and the U.S. government, including their belief in the U.S. constitution. The exam can also be taken as part of a course of study given by an independent organization approved by the USCIS. If the applicant passes, he or she will be given a certificate, valid for one year. The USCIS will accept the certificate in lieu of the written exam.

People who are certified by a physician to have physical or developmental disabilities or mental impairments are exempt from the literacy and government/history knowledge requirements.

The application must be approved or denied within four months of the interview. Assuming it is approved, the final swearing-in ceremony will be held the same day, or at a later date, depending on the current procedure at your local USCIS office. At the time of the swearing-in ceremony, the applicant is required to take the following oath of allegiance to the United States of America, and sign this oath.

I hereby declare, on oath, that I absolutely and entirely renounce and abjure all allegiance and fidelity to any foreign prince, potentate, state or sovereignty of whom or which I have heretofore been a subject or citizen; that I will support and defend the Constitution and laws of the United States of America against all enemies, foreign and domestic; that I will bear true faith and allegiance to the same; * that I will bear arms *on behalf of the United States when required by law; * that I will perform noncombatant service in the Armed Forces of the United States when required by law; that I will perform work of national importance under civilian direction when required by law; and that I take this obligation freely without any mental reservation or purpose of evasion; so help me God.*

* In some cases, the USCIS will allow these clauses to be omitted.

At the end of the ceremony the applicant is granted a Certificate of Naturalization. This can then be presented at a U.S. Passport Agency office to obtain a U.S. passport. During the naturalization process, the applicant retains his or her U.S. permanent resident status.

For more information, please obtain a copy of our book ***Citizenship Made Simple***, an easy to read guide to the U.S. citizenship process. This book can be ordered through your local bookstore, by using the order form provided in the back of this book, or at our web site: www.nextdecade.com.

17

IRCA Employer Obligations and Verification of Employment

In 1986, the Immigration Reform and Control Act (IRCA) was established in the U.S. It was developed, in part, to control the number of illegal aliens coming to the U.S. to work. Since the enactment of the program, there have been many controversial issues and regulatory changes. The Immigration Act of 1990 brought about even further changes.

IRCA requires that employers check the identity and the right to work of all new hires (including U.S. citizens), and complete Form I-9- Employment Eligibility Verification for every employee, regardless of their nationality. These regulations also state that the employer cannot discriminate against potential hires on the basis of their origin or citizenship. Form I-9 must be completed for all employees hired after November 6, 1986. Processing and record keeping of Forms I-9 are as follows:

- The employee completes Section 1 of the form when he or she starts to work.

- The employer reviews the documents that establish the employee's right to work and his or her identity, and completes Section 2 within three business days of hire. (Lists of documents that the employer can accept to prove identity and the right to work are given later in this chapter.) If the employee cannot produce the documents, but can produce an application receipt for them, this should be recorded, and the employee has 90 days to present the actual document. Section 2 of Form I-9 should be amended at that time. Note that special rules apply to the completion of Form I-9 for minors (under age 18) and handicapped employees.

- The employer keeps all Forms I-9 for three years after the employee starts to work or one year after the employee leaves the employer, whichever is later.

■ Employers must again verify employment authorization for those employees who initially produced documents with an expiration date, and complete Section 3 on Form I-9. If updated proof of work authorization cannot be provide, the employer cannot continue to employ that individual.

■ The employer must have all Forms I-9 available to be inspected by an USCIS officer, or related official. Three days notice should be given.

An employer cannot require that the employee present different documents, or more documents, or refuse to accept documents that appear to be genuine. Forms I-9 can be photocopied, or the employer can order several copies from: Superintendent of Documents, U.S. Government Printing Office, Washington, DC 20402. Following are lists of acceptable documents:

List A: Employment Eligibility and Identity

1. U.S. passport (even if it has expired)

2. Permanent Resident Card or Alien Registration Receipt Card. (Form I-551)

3. Valid foreign passport with a valid I-551 stamp

4. An unexpired Employment Authorization Document that contains a photograph

5. An unexpired foreign passport with an unexpired Arrival-Departure Record, Form I-94, bearing the same name as the passport and containing an endorsement of the alien's nonimmigrant status, if that status authorizes the alien to work for the employer.

These five documents establish both employment eligibility and identity. If the employee can produce one of these documents, they have satisfied both the identity and employment eligibility requirement to complete Form I-9:

List B: Identity

1. Driver's license or identification card issued by a state or possession of the U.S., which contains a photo or personal information such as name, birth date, gender, height, eye color and address

2. Identification card issued by a Federal, State or Local government agency, which contains a photo or personal information as indicated above.

3. School identification card with a photo

4. Voter registration card

5. U.S. military card or draft records

6. Military dependent's identification card

7. U.S. Coast Guard Merchant Marine Card

8. Native American Tribal Document

9. Driver's license issued by the Canadian government

For persons under 18 who are unable to present a document listed above:

10. School record or report card

11. Clinic, doctor or hospital record

12. Day-care or nursery school record

The previous twelve documents establish only identity. If the employee can produce one of these documents and one document from List C, he or she has satisfied the identity and employment eligibility requirement for completing Form I-9:

List C: Employment Eligibility

1. U.S. Social Security Card (if it states that it is "not valid for employment", it cannot be accepted)

2. Certification of Birth Abroad that is issued by the U.S. Department of State on Form FS-545 or Form DS-1350

3. Original or certified copy of a birth certificate issued by a state, county, municipal authority or outlying possession of the US bearing an official seal

4. Native American Tribal Document

5. U.S. Citizen identification card (Form I-197)

6. Identification card for use of Resident Citizen in the U.S. (Form I-179)

7. Valid employment authorization document, issued by the DHS (other than those in List A).

The seven documents listed above establish employment eligibility only. As indicated above, one document from List C must be produced with one document from List B.

Note: Certain documents including the U.S. Citizen ID card, Resident Citizen ID card and Native American Tribal Document appear on both List B and List C. These documents can be presented to establish both identity and employment eligibility and should be recorded in both spaces on Form I-9. They are not included in List A, only because Congress has not designated them in the law.

Hiring or continuing to hire aliens who do not have work authorization; failure to complete I-9 forms; and/or unlawful discrimination can result in severe penalties including escalating monetary fines, and in some cases imprisonment.

18
Questions and Answers

Over the years, we have been asked many questions about various aspects of processing visas and related matters involving international relocation. We thought that it would be helpful to include some of these questions so that you may benefit from the answers as well.

Q. Do I need to retain an attorney to assist me in processing my immigration papers and how can I find one to help me?

A. In most cases, you will need an attorney. The U.S. immigration process is extremely complex, and recent changes make it even more so. There are always administrative changes taking place at the USCIS offices. If papers are not prepared and filed properly, the odds for a successful outcome are greatly diminished.

Most aliens have friends who have sought immigration counsel in the past and may be able to provide you with the name of a qualified attorney. The Directory of Immigration Lawyers is in this book to assist you, as well. The local office of the state Bar Association can also be a helpful source of referral, as can the Legal Aid Society. Many attorneys also advertise their services in the Yellow Pages of the Telephone Directory.

One fact to keep in mind is that not every attorney is as qualified as the next to give you advice on immigration matters. Consult with at least two attorneys and choose the one with whom you feel most comfortable. Make sure to find out, before retaining the lawyer, what his or her legal fee will be and exactly what the fee will include - e.g., filing fees, miscellaneous expenses such as copy charges and postage. These disbursements can add up quickly! Ask the attorney about the billing schedule so that you can allocate your money through the various stages of your immigration case.

Never retain the services of a lawyer who promises or guarantees you anything, or who gives you time frames that seem unrealistic. Do not hesitate to change from one lawyer to another during your case, if you are unhappy with the services being provided. Make sure to obtain your complete file to ensure an easy transition from one lawyer to the next.

Q. Will the USCIS be a good source of information on processing my immigration case?

A. In most situations, calling or visiting the USCIS will not be very helpful. The USCIS employees are very busy and usually do not have the time to plan individual immigration strategies. You may also be putting yourself in jeopardy if you are in the U.S. illegally. However, you should visit the USCIS web site (http://uscis.gov/graphics/index.htm)that has quite a bit of valuable information.

Q. What is the difference between a visa and an arrival-departure record?

A. A visa is a permit to enter the U.S. that is normally obtained at an American Consulate outside the U.S. The USCIS creates an arrival-departure record (Form I-94) when the traveler arrives in the U.S. The fact that an individual has a visa does not guarantee their entry into the U.S., nor the amount of time they can remain in the U.S.

Q. Why is my green card case taking so long compared to my friend's?

A. Do not compare your case with those of friends or relatives. In most situations, the facts are not the same, even though they may appear to be. In addition, there are a variety of reasons why identical cases may vary in time frames. Your attorney is interested in completing your case as quickly as possible.

Q. Where can I obtain immigration forms without visiting the USCIS?

A. The easiest way to obtain forms is to call 1-800-870-FORMS. If you have a computer, you can download forms from the USCIS web site at http://uscis.gov/graphics/formsfee/forms/index.htm Many forms can now be completed online.

Q. What if I do not have all of the personal documents that are required to complete my case?

A. The USCIS and the Consular officials are very strict in this matter. It is almost always possible to obtain duplicate originals of any document that was lost or destroyed. Ask your attorney how to do so. For example, some countries do not issue birth certificates. In these cases, the authorities will accept secondary evidence of birth in the form of affidavits from close relatives. However, the USCIS and Consular officials maintain books that list which documents are available from each country. If you go to a visa interview without all of the required documents, there is a good chance that your case will be delayed or denied.

Q. What if a visa appointment is scheduled for me at the USCIS or at the Consular office and I cannot keep it?

A. It is very difficult to reschedule appointments because of the heavy volume of cases that these offices must process, and delays of several months can result if requests for rescheduling are made. Do not attempt to change appointment dates unless you absolutely must. In addition, never ignore a notice to appear for an interview at the USCIS.

Q. If I have filed an Application for Adjustment of Status from a temporary visa to permanent residence through an Immigration office in the U.S., can I travel while the application is pending?

A. Once you have filed for permanent residence, your temporary visa should not be used for travel purposes, with the exception of H & L visas. If you need to travel outside the U.S. during this process for critical business or personal reasons such as a family emergency abroad, you can apply to the USCIS for a travel document known as an Advance Parole. Use Form I-131- Application for Travel Document. This document allows you to leave and reenter the U.S. within a given period of time. You must, however, be prepared to provide the USCIS with ample evidence of the need to travel.

Q. How can I check the status of my case?

A. If you filed your case at an USCIS Service Center you can follow up in two ways:

Online at: https://egov.immigration.gov/cris/jsps/index.jsp

By calling the NCSC at 1-800-375-5283.

If you filed at a local USCIS office, you will need to make an InfoPass appointment.

Q. If I obtain my green card through labor certification, must I always work for the same employer?

A. No. At the time that you are granted permanent residence, the sponsoring employer must intend to have you work for them and you must plan to do so. If the employment relationship does not work out after you have started the job, you can seek other employment.

Q. How can I obtain a work permit?

A. Work permits are only issued if you are eligible under one of the categories authorized by the law, and described in this book.

Q. How can I get a Social Security Number?

A. If you are in the U.S. legally, and have a working visa, Form I-94, or other document authorizing employment in the U.S., you can obtain a number. You must apply in person at the nearest Social Security Administration Office. Bring your passport; Form I-94 and proof of work authorization. You will be asked to complete an application form (Form SS-5). The Social Security Card will be mailed to you within several weeks.

If you are in the U.S. and do not have work authorization, you cannot obtain a Social Security Number. However, if you need an identification number, for example, to open a brokerage account or to purchase investment property in the U.S., you should request Form W-7 from the Internal Revenue Service and apply for a Taxpayer Identification Number.

Q. If I have a Social Security number can I work in the U.S.?

A. The Social Security number is not a work permit. You must also have a visa, Form I-94, or other document that proves you have employment authorization.

Q. Am I eligible to collect Social Security?

A. The following classes of individuals are included in those who may be eligible for Social Security benefits: naturalized citizens; permanent resident aliens; temporary residents through a variety of programs including amnesty; refugees and asylees. This list is not all-inclusive.

Q. Am I eligible for unemployment benefits?

A. If you are a naturalized U.S. citizen or have permanent work authorization, you may be eligible for unemployment benefits.

Q. How can I obtain a U.S. driver's license?

A. In most states you need proof that you are in the U.S. in legal status. If you are in the U.S. illegally, it is very difficult to obtain a driver's license. It is also difficult to obtain a driver's license if you are in the U.S. as a visitor.

Q. If I give birth to a baby in the U.S., what is the baby's status and can the baby grant me an immigration benefit?

A. The baby is a U.S. citizen by having been born in the U.S. A child cannot pass on an immigration benefit to a parent until the child reaches the age of twenty-one.

Q. Should I marry a U.S. citizen solely to obtain a green card?

A. No. Doing so will be considered a fraud by USCIS. The USCIS continues to tighten its policy regarding marriages strictly for immigration purposes, and the penalties can be severe. In fact, you should not get involved in any arrangement that is meant to defraud the USCIS. Remember that the USCIS is a branch of the U.S. Government and should be treated with respect.

Q. What if I am in the United States illegally, can I still adjust my status in the United States?

A. Under certain circumstances you may be allowed to adjust your status. There have been recent changes in the law, however, that may affect your application. Consult a professional before you file any applications.

Q. What do I do if I complete my permanent residence application but do not receive my green card in the mail?

A. This is a common occurrence. If you do not receive your card within ninety days of approval of your application, you should follow up with the NCSC at 1-800-375-5283.

Q. What happens if I lose my green card or if it is stolen?

A. A lost or stolen green card can be replaced. When you first receive your card, record your alien registration number and keep it in a safe place. If your green card is lost and you are in the U.S., you must process an application with USCIS to replace the card. The application consists of Form I-90- Application to Replace Alien Registration Card, photographs and the applicable filing fee. You will need to make an InfoPass appointment. If your green card is stolen, USCIS may ask that you obtain a police report from your local police station. In either event, once the I-90 is filed, USCIS will stamp a new temporary green card in your passport so that you can travel. They will then forward the I-90 application to the Immigration Card Facility for processing of a new card.

If you are outside the U.S. and your card is lost or stolen, go to the nearest American Embassy or Consulate. Your permanent residence will be verified with the Department of State in Washington, DC and you will be issued a document to allow you to return to the U.S. This can sometimes take several days. Once you are back in the U.S., you will need to file an I-90 application as described above.

Q. If I received my green card as a young child do I need to update it?

A. Yes. If your card was issued before the age of fourteen it must be updated to include fingerprints. You will need an InfoPass appointment to file Form I-90 as described above. The USCIS should stamp a temporary green card in your passport so that you can travel outside the U.S. while you are waiting for the new card.

Q. Can I keep my green card if I am not living in the U.S.?

A. If you are temporarily residing outside the U.S. but continue to consider the U.S. your permanent home, and plan to return permanently, it is possible to keep your green card. However, you must comply with several USCIS rules. These rules are complex and you should consult a professional for advice. You can also apply to the USCIS for a Permit to Reenter the United States using Form I-131- Application for Travel Document. The granting of this permit allows you to remain outside the U.S. for up to two years without jeopardizing your permanent resident status. Your absence from the U.S. for more than one year however, can still affect your ability to apply for U.S. citizenship.

Q. Does my green card need to be renewed or does it remain valid forever?

A. In 1989 the Alien Registration Card regulations were revised by the USCIS. The card used to be valid as long as the alien remained a permanent resident. Now the card expires ten years after the date it was issued. The alien will then be required to obtain a new card. In addition, all Alien Registration Cards issued before 1978 as well as those with an expiration date must be replaced with new cards. See Chapter 14-Renewal of Expiring Green Cards.

19
Sample Forms

The following pages contain sample forms that you will need to process applications through the USCIS. The forms in this book are current up to the date of printing. Please check the USCIS website http://www.uscis.gov for more detailed instructions and updated versions as they become available.

OMB No. 1615-0008; Exp. 05/31/09

Department of Homeland Security
U.S. Citizenship and Immigration Services

G-325A, Biographic Information

(Family Name)	(First Name)	(Middle Name)	☐ Male ☐ Female	Birth Date (mm/dd/yyyy)	Citizenship/Nationality	File Number A

All Other Names Used (Including names by previous marriages)	City and Country of Birth	U.S. Social Security # *(If any)*

	Family Name	First Name	Date, City and Country of Birth (If known)	City and Country of Residence
Father				
Mother (Maiden Name)				

Husband or Wife (If none, so state.) Family Name (For wife, give maiden name)	First Name	Birth Date (mm/dd/yyyy)	City and Country of Birth	Date of Marriage	Place of Marriage

Former Husbands or Wives (If none, so state) Family Name (For wife, give maiden name)	First Name	Birth Date (mm/dd/yyyy)	Date and Place of Marriage	Date and Place of Termination of Marriage

Applicant's residence last five years. List present address first.

Street and Number	City	Province or State	Country	From Month	From Year	To Month	To Year
						Present Time	

Applicant's last address outside the United States of more than one year.

Street and Number	City	Province or State	Country	From Month	From Year	To Month	To Year

Applicant's employment last five years. (If none, so state.) List present employment first.

Full Name and Address of Employer	Occupation (Specify)	From Month	From Year	To Month	To Year
				Present Time	

Show below last occupation abroad if not shown above. (Include all information requested above.)

This form is submitted in connection with an application for: ☐ Naturalization ☐ Other (Specify): _____ ☐ Status as Permanent Resident	Signature of Applicant	Date

Submit all copies of this form.	If your native alphabet is in other than Roman letters, write your name in your native alphabet below:

Penalties: Severe penalties are provided by law for knowingly and willfully falsifying or concealing a material fact.

Applicant: Be sure to put your name and Alien Registration Number in the box outlined by heavy border below.

Complete This Box (Family Name)	(Given Name)	(Middle Name)	(Alien Registration Number)

(1) Ident.   See Instructions on **Page 5**   Form G-325A (Rev. 07/14/06)Y

OMB No. 1615-0008; Exp. 05/31/09

Department of Homeland Security
U.S. Citizenship and Immigration Services

G-325A, Biographic Information

(Family Name)	(First Name)	(Middle Name)	☐ Male ☐ Female	Birth Date (mm/dd/yyyy)	Citizenship/Nationality	File Number A

All Other Names Used (Including names by previous marriages)	City and Country of Birth	U.S. Social Security # *(If any)*

	Family Name	First Name	Date, City and Country of Birth (If known)	City and Country of Residence
Father				
Mother (Maiden Name)				

Husband or Wife (If none, so state.) Family Name (For wife, give maiden name)	First Name	Birth Date (mm/dd/yyyy)	City and Country of Birth	Date of Marriage	Place of Marriage

Former Husbands or Wives (If none, so state) Family Name (For wife, give maiden name)	First Name	Birth Date (mm/dd/yyyy)	Date and Place of Marriage	Date and Place of Termination of Marriage

Applicant's residence last five years. List present address first.

Street and Number	City	Province or State	Country	From Month	Year	To Month	Year
						Present Time	

Applicant's last address outside the United States of more than one year.

Street and Number	City	Province or State	Country	From Month	Year	To Month	Year

Applicant's employment last five years. (If none, so state.) List present employment first.

Full Name and Address of Employer	Occupation (Specify)	From Month	Year	To Month	Year
				Present Time	

Show below last occupation abroad if not shown above. (Include all information requested above.)

This form is submitted in connection with an application for: ☐ Naturalization ☐ Other (Specify): ☐ Status as Permanent Resident	Signature of Applicant	Date

Submit all copies of this form.	If your native alphabet is in other than Roman letters, write your name in your native alphabet below:

Penalties: Severe penalties are provided by law for knowingly and willfully falsifying or concealing a material fact.

Applicant: Be sure to put your name and Alien Registration Number in the box outlined by heavy border below.

Complete This Box (Family Name)	(Given Name)	(Middle Name)	(Alien Registration Number)

— Sample Forms ■

OMB No. 1615-0008; Exp. 05/31/09

Department of Homeland Security
U.S. Citizenship and Immigration Services

G-325A, Biographic Information

(Family Name)	(First Name)	(Middle Name)	☐ Male ☐ Female	Birth Date (mm/dd/yyyy)	Citizenship/Nationality	File Number A

All Other Names Used (Including names by previous marriages)	City and Country of Birth	U.S. Social Security # (If any)

	Family Name	First Name	Date, City and Country of Birth (If known)	City and Country of Residence
Father				
Mother (Maiden Name)				

Husband or Wife (If none, so state.) Family Name (For wife, give maiden name)	First Name	Birth Date (mm/dd/yyyy)	City and Country of Birth	Date of Marriage	Place of Marriage

Former Husbands or Wives (If none, so state) Family Name (For wife, give maiden name)	First Name	Birth Date (mm/dd/yyyy)	Date and Place of Marriage	Date and Place of Termination of Marriage

Applicant's residence last five years. List present address first.

Street and Number	City	Province or State	Country	From Month	From Year	To Month	To Year
						Present Time	

Applicant's last address outside the United States of more than one year.

Street and Number	City	Province or State	Country	From Month	From Year	To Month	To Year

Applicant's employment last five years. (If none, so state.) List present employment first.

Full Name and Address of Employer	Occupation (Specify)	From Month	From Year	To Month	To Year
				Present Time	

Show below last occupation abroad if not shown above. (Include all information requested above.)

This form is submitted in connection with an application for: ☐ Naturalization ☐ Other (Specify): _____ ☐ Status as Permanent Resident	Signature of Applicant	Date

Submit all copies of this form.	If your native alphabet is in other than Roman letters, write your name in your native alphabet below:

Penalties: Severe penalties are provided by law for knowingly and willfully falsifying or concealing a material fact.

Applicant: Be sure to put your name and Alien Registration Number in the box outlined by heavy border below.

Complete This Box (Family Name)	(Given Name)	(Middle Name)	(Alien Registration Number)

See Instructions on **Page 5**

Form G-325A (Rev. 07/14/06)Y Page 3

Department of Homeland Security
U.S. Citizenship and Immigration Services

OMB No. 1615-0008; Exp. 05/31/09

G-325A, Biographic Information

(Family Name)	(First Name)	(Middle Name)	☐ Male ☐ Female	Birth Date (mm/dd/yyyy)	Citizenship/Nationality	File Number A

All Other Names Used (Including names by previous marriages)	City and Country of Birth	U.S. Social Security # *(If any)*

	Family Name	First Name	Date, City and Country of Birth (If known)	City and Country of Residence
Father				
Mother (Maiden Name)				

Husband or Wife (If none, so state.) Family Name (For wife, give maiden name)	First Name	Birth Date (mm/dd/yyyy)	City and Country of Birth	Date of Marriage	Place of Marriage

Former Husbands or Wives (If none, so state) Family Name (For wife, give maiden name)	First Name	Birth Date (mm/dd/yyyy)	Date and Place of Marriage	Date and Place of Termination of Marriage

Applicant's residence last five years. List present address first.

Street and Number	City	Province or State	Country	From Month	From Year	To Month	To Year
						Present Time	

Applicant's last address outside the United States of more than one year.

Street and Number	City	Province or State	Country	From Month	From Year	To Month	To Year

Applicant's employment last five years. (If none, so state.) List present employment first.

Full Name and Address of Employer	Occupation (Specify)	From Month	From Year	To Month	To Year
				Present Time	

Show below last occupation abroad if not shown above. (Include all information requested above.)

This form is submitted in connection with an application for: ☐ Naturalization ☐ Other (Specify): _____ ☐ Status as Permanent Resident	Signature of Applicant	Date

Submit all copies of this form.	If your native alphabet is in other than Roman letters, write your name in your native alphabet below:

Penalties: Severe penalties are provided by law for knowingly and willfully falsifying or concealing a material fact.

Applicant: Be sure to put your name and Alien Registration Number in the box outlined by heavy border below.

Complete This Box (Family Name)	(Given Name)	(Middle Name)	(Alien Registration Number)

(4) Consulate

See Instructions on **Page 5**

Form G-325A (Rev. 07/14/06)Y Page 4

Instructions

What Is the Purpose of This Form?

Complete this biographical information form and include it with the application or petition you are submitting to U.S. Citizenship and Immigration Services (USCIS).

USCIS will use the information you provide on this form to process your application or petition. Complete and submit all copies of this form with your petition or application.

If you have any questions on how to complete the form, call our National Customer Service Center at **1-800-375-5283**.

Privacy Act Notice.

We ask for the information on this form and associated evidence to determine if you have established eligibility for the immigration benefit you are seeking. Our legal right to ask for this information is in 8 USC 1101 and 1255. We may provide this information to other Government agencies. Failure to provide this information may delay a final decision or result in denial of your application or petition.

Paperwork Reduction Act Notice.

A person is not required to respond to a collection of information unless it displays a currently valid OMB control number.

We try to create forms and instructions that are accurate, can be easily understood and that impose the least possible burden on you to provide us with information. Often this is difficult because some immigration laws are very complex.

The estimated average time to gather the requested information, complete the form and include it with the appropriate application or petition for filing purposes is 15 minutes. If you have any comments regarding the accuracy of this estimate or suggestions for making this form simpler, write to U.S. Citizenship and Immigration Services, Regulatory Management Division, 111 Massachusetts Avenue, N.W., Washington, D.C. 20529; OMB No. 1615-0008. **Do not send your form to this Washington, D.C. address.**

OMB No. 1615-0047; Expires 06/30/09

Department of Homeland Security
U.S. Citizenship and Immigration Services

Form I-9, Employment Eligibility Verification

Instructions
Please read all instructions carefully before completing this form.

Anti-Discrimination Notice. It is illegal to discriminate against any individual (other than an alien not authorized to work in the U.S.) in hiring, discharging, or recruiting or referring for a fee because of that individual's national origin or citizenship status. It is illegal to discriminate against work eligible individuals. Employers **CANNOT** specify which document(s) they will accept from an employee. The refusal to hire an individual because the documents presented have a future expiration date may also constitute illegal discrimination.

What Is the Purpose of This Form?

The purpose of this form is to document that each new employee (both citizen and non-citizen) hired after November 6, 1986 is authorized to work in the United States.

When Should the Form I-9 Be Used?

All employees, citizens and noncitizens, hired after November 6, 1986 and working in the United States must complete a Form I-9.

Filling Out the Form I-9

Section 1, Employee: This part of the form must be completed at the time of hire, which is the actual beginning of employment. Providing the Social Security number is voluntary, except for employees hired by employers participating in the USCIS Electronic Employment Eligibility Verification Program (E-Verify). **The employer is responsible for ensuring that Section 1 is timely and properly completed.**

Preparer/Translator Certification. The Preparer/Translator Certification must be completed if **Section 1** is prepared by a person other than the employee. A preparer/translator may be used only when the employee is unable to complete **Section 1** on his/her own. However, the employee must still sign **Section 1** personally.

Section 2, Employer: For the purpose of completing this form, the term "employer" means all employers including those recruiters and referrers for a fee who are agricultural associations, agricultural employers or farm labor contractors.

Employers must complete **Section 2** by examining evidence of identity and employment eligibility within three (3) business days of the date employment begins. If employees are authorized to work, but are unable to present the required

document(s) within three business days, they must present a receipt for the application of the document(s) within three business days and the actual document(s) within ninety (90) days. However, if employers hire individuals for a duration of less than three business days, **Section 2** must be completed at the time employment begins. **Employers must record:**

1. Document title;
2. Issuing authority;
3. Document number;
4. Expiration date, if any; and
5. The date employment begins.

Employers must sign and date the certification. Employees must present original documents. Employers may, but are not required to, photocopy the document(s) presented. These photocopies may only be used for the verification process and must be retained with the Form I-9. **However, employers are still responsible for completing and retaining the Form I-9.**

Section 3, Updating and Reverification: Employers must complete **Section 3** when updating and/or reverifying the Form I-9. Employers must reverify employment eligibility of their employees on or before the expiration date recorded in **Section 1**. Employers **CANNOT** specify which document(s) they will accept from an employee.

  A. If an employee's name has changed at the time this form is being updated/reverified, complete Block A.

  B. If an employee is rehired within three (3) years of the date this form was originally completed and the employee is still eligible to be employed on the same basis as previously indicated on this form (updating), complete Block B and the signature block.

  C. If an employee is rehired within three (3) years of the date this form was originally completed and the employee's work authorization has expired **or** if a current employee's work authorization is about to expire (reverification), complete Block B and:

    1. Examine any document that reflects that the employee is authorized to work in the U.S. (see List A **or** C);

    2. Record the document title, document number and expiration date (if any) in Block C, and

    3. Complete the signature block.

What Is the Filing Fee?

There is no associated filing fee for completing the Form I-9. This form is not filed with USCIS or any government agency. The Form I-9 must be retained by the employer and made available for inspection by U.S. Government officials as specified in the Privacy Act Notice below.

USCIS Forms and Information

To order USCIS forms, call our toll-free number at **1-800-870-3676**. Individuals can also get USCIS forms and information on immigration laws, regulations and procedures by telephoning our National Customer Service Center at **1-800-375-5283** or visiting our internet website at **www.uscis.gov**.

Photocopying and Retaining the Form I-9

A blank Form I-9 may be reproduced, provided both sides are copied. The Instructions must be available to all employees completing this form. Employers must retain completed Forms I-9 for three (3) years after the date of hire or one (1) year after the date employment ends, whichever is later.

The Form I-9 may be signed and retained electronically, as authorized in Department of Homeland Security regulations at 8 CFR § 274a.2.

Privacy Act Notice

The authority for collecting this information is the Immigration Reform and Control Act of 1986, Pub. L. 99-603 (8 USC 1324a).

This information is for employers to verify the eligibility of individuals for employment to preclude the unlawful hiring, or recruiting or referring for a fee, of aliens who are not authorized to work in the United States.

This information will be used by employers as a record of their basis for determining eligibility of an employee to work in the United States. The form will be kept by the employer and made available for inspection by officials of U.S. Immigration and Customs Enforcement, Department of Labor and Office of Special Counsel for Immigration Related Unfair Employment Practices.

Submission of the information required in this form is voluntary. However, an individual may not begin employment unless this form is completed, since employers are subject to civil or criminal penalties if they do not comply with the Immigration Reform and Control Act of 1986.

Paperwork Reduction Act

We try to create forms and instructions that are accurate, can be easily understood and which impose the least possible burden on you to provide us with information. Often this is difficult because some immigration laws are very complex. Accordingly, the reporting burden for this collection of information is computed as follows: **1)** learning about this form, and completing the form, 9 minutes; **2)** assembling and filing (recordkeeping) the form, 3 minutes, for an average of 12 minutes per response. If you have comments regarding the accuracy of this burden estimate, or suggestions for making this form simpler, you can write to: U.S. Citizenship and Immigration Services, Regulatory Management Division, 111 Massachusetts Avenue, N.W., 3rd Floor, Suite 3008, Washington, DC 20529. OMB No. 1615-0047.

EMPLOYERS MUST RETAIN COMPLETED FORM I-9
PLEASE DO NOT MAIL COMPLETED FORM I-9 TO ICE OR USCIS

Form I-9 (Rev. 06/05/07) N Page 2

OMB No. 1615-0047; Expires 06/30/09

Department of Homeland Security
U.S. Citizenship and Immigration Services

**Form I-9, Employment
Eligibility Verification**

Please read instructions carefully before completing this form. The instructions must be available during completion of this form.

ANTI-DISCRIMINATION NOTICE: It is illegal to discriminate against work eligible individuals. Employers CANNOT specify which document(s) they will accept from an employee. The refusal to hire an individual because the documents have a future expiration date may also constitute illegal discrimination.

Section 1. Employee Information and Verification. To be completed and signed by employee at the time employment begins.

Print Name: Last	First	Middle Initial	Maiden Name

Address (Street Name and Number)	Apt. #	Date of Birth (month/day/year)

City	State	Zip Code	Social Security #

I am aware that federal law provides for imprisonment and/or fines for false statements or use of false documents in connection with the completion of this form.

I attest, under penalty of perjury, that I am (check one of the following):
- [ ] A citizen or national of the United States
- [ ] A lawful permanent resident (Alien #) A
- [ ] An alien authorized to work until _____
(Alien # or Admission #)

Employee's Signature	Date (month/day/year)

Preparer and/or Translator Certification. *(To be completed and signed if Section 1 is prepared by a person other than the employee.)* I attest, under penalty of perjury, that I have assisted in the completion of this form and that to the best of my knowledge the information is true and correct.

Preparer's/Translator's Signature	Print Name

Address (Street Name and Number, City, State, Zip Code)	Date (month/day/year)

Section 2. Employer Review and Verification. To be completed and signed by employer. Examine one document from List A OR examine one document from List B and one from List C, as listed on the reverse of this form, and record the title, number and expiration date, if any, of the document(s).

List A	OR	List B	AND	List C
Document title:				
Issuing authority:				
Document #:				
Expiration Date (if any):				
Document #:				
Expiration Date (if any):				

CERTIFICATION - I attest, under penalty of perjury, that I have examined the document(s) presented by the above-named employee, that the above-listed document(s) appear to be genuine and to relate to the employee named, that the employee began employment on *(month/day/year)* _____ **and that to the best of my knowledge the employee is eligible to work in the United States. (State employment agencies may omit the date the employee began employment.)**

Signature of Employer or Authorized Representative	Print Name	Title

Business or Organization Name and Address (Street Name and Number, City, State, Zip Code)	Date (month/day/year)

Section 3. Updating and Reverification. To be completed and signed by employer.

A. New Name (if applicable)	B. Date of Rehire (month/day/year) (if applicable)

C. If employee's previous grant of work authorization has expired, provide the information below for the document that establishes current employment eligibility.

Document Title:	Document #:	Expiration Date (if any):

I attest, under penalty of perjury, that to the best of my knowledge, this employee is eligible to work in the United States, and if the employee presented document(s), the document(s) I have examined appear to be genuine and to relate to the individual.

Signature of Employer or Authorized Representative	Date (month/day/year)

Form I-9 (Rev. 06/05/07) N

LISTS OF ACCEPTABLE DOCUMENTS

LIST A	LIST B	LIST C
Documents that Establish Both Identity and Employment Eligibility	**Documents that Establish Identity**	**Documents that Establish Employment Eligibility**
OR		**AND**
1. U.S. Passport (unexpired or expired)	1. Driver's license or ID card issued by a state or outlying possession of the United States provided it contains a photograph or information such as name, date of birth, gender, height, eye color and address	1. U.S. Social Security card issued by the Social Security Administration *(other than a card stating it is not valid for employment)*
2. Permanent Resident Card or Alien Registration Receipt Card (Form I-551)	2. ID card issued by federal, state or local government agencies or entities, provided it contains a photograph or information such as name, date of birth, gender, height, eye color and address	2. Certification of Birth Abroad issued by the Department of State *(Form FS-545 or Form DS-1350)*
3. An unexpired foreign passport with a temporary I-551 stamp	3. School ID card with a photograph	3. Original or certified copy of a birth certificate issued by a state, county, municipal authority or outlying possession of the United States bearing an official seal
4. An unexpired Employment Authorization Document that contains a photograph (Form I-766, I-688, I-688A, I-688B)	4. Voter's registration card	4. Native American tribal document
	5. U.S. Military card or draft record	5. U.S. Citizen ID Card *(Form I-197)*
5. An unexpired foreign passport with an unexpired Arrival-Departure Record, Form I-94, bearing the same name as the passport and containing an endorsement of the alien's nonimmigrant status, if that status authorizes the alien to work for the employer	6. Military dependent's ID card	6. ID Card for use of Resident Citizen in the United States *(Form I-179)*
	7. U.S. Coast Guard Merchant Mariner Card	7. Unexpired employment authorization document issued by DHS *(other than those listed under List A)*
	8. Native American tribal document	
	9. Driver's license issued by a Canadian government authority	
	For persons under age 18 who are unable to present a document listed above:	
	10. School record or report card	
	11. Clinic, doctor or hospital record	
	12. Day-care or nursery school record	

Illustrations of many of these documents appear in Part 8 of the Handbook for Employers (M-274)

OMB No. 1615-0082; Expires 06/30/09

Department of Homeland Security
U.S. Citizenship and Immigration Services

**I-90, Application to Replace
Permanent Resident Card**

START HERE - Please type or print in black ink.

Part 1. Information about you.

Family Name	Given Name	Middle Initial

U.S. Mailing Address - C/O

Street Number and Name	Apt. #

City

State	ZIP Code

Date of Birth(Month/ Day/Year)	Country of Birth

Social Security #	A #

Part 2. Application type.

1. My status is: (check one)

- a. ☐ Permanent Resident - (Not a Commuter)
- b. ☐ Permanent Resident - (Commuter)
- c. ☐ Conditional Permanent Resident

2. Reason for application: (check one)
I am a Permanent Resident or Conditional Permanent Resident and:

- a. ☐ My card was lost, stolen or destroyed.
- b. ☐ My authorized card was never received.
- c. ☐ My card is mutilated.
- d. ☐ My card was issued with incorrect information because of a USCIS administrative error. I have attached the incorrect card and evidence of the correct information.
- e. ☐ My name or other biographic information has changed since the card was issued.

I am a Permanent Resident and:

- f. ☐ My present card has an expiration date and it is expiring.
- g. ☐ I have reached my 14th birthday since my card was issued.
- h. 1. ☐ I have taken up Commuter status.
- h. 2. ☐ I was a Commuter and am now taking up residence in the U.S.
- i. ☐ My status has been automatically converted to permanent resident.
- j. ☐ I have an old edition of the card.

Part 3. Processing information.

Mother's First Name	Father's First Name

City of Residence where you applied for an Immigrant Visa or Adjustment of Status	Consulate where Immigrant Visa was issued or USCIS office where status was Adjusted

City/Town/Village of Birth	Date of Admission as an immigrant or Adjustment of Status

FOR USCIS USE ONLY

Returned	Receipt
Resubmitted	
Reloc Sent	
Reloc Rec'd	
☐ Applicant Interviewed	

Status as _____ Verified by _____
Class _____ Initials _____
FD-258 forwarded on _____
I-89 forwarded on _____
I-551 seen and returned _____
(Initials)
Photocopy of I-551 verified _____
(Initials)
Name _____ Date _____
Sticker # _____
(ten-digit number)

Action Block

**To Be Completed by
Attorney or Representative, if any**
☐ Fill in box if G-28 is attached to represent the applicant

VOLAG#

ATTY State License #

Form I-90 (Rev. 07/30/07)Y

Part 3. Processing information (continued):

If you entered the U.S. with an Immigrant Visa, also complete the following:

Destination in U.S. at
time of Admission

Port of Entry where
Admitted to U.S.

Are you in removal/deportation or recission proceedings? ☐ No ☐ Yes

Since you were granted permanent residence, have you ever filed Form I-407, Abandonment by Alien of Status as Lawful Permanent Resident, or otherwise been judged to have abandoned your status? ☐ No ☐ Yes

If you answer yes to any of the above questions, explain in detail on a separate piece of paper.

Part 4. Signature. *(Read the information on penalties in the instructions before completing this section. You must file this application while in the United States.)*

I certify, under penalty of perjury under the laws of the United States of America, that this application and the evidence submitted with it is all true and correct. I authorize the release of any information from my records that U.S. Citizenship and Immigration Services needs to determine eligibility for the benefit I am seeking.

Signature   Date   Daytime Phone Number

Please Note: *If you do not completely fill out this form or fail to submit required documents listed in the instructions, you cannot be found eligible for the requested document and this application may be denied.*

Part 5. Signature of person preparing form, if other than above. *(Sign below)*

I declare that I prepared this application at the request of the above person and it is based on all information of which I have knowledge.

Signature   Print Your Name   Date   Daytime Phone Number

Name and Address of Business/Organization (if applicable)

U.S Department of Justice
Immigration and Naturalization Service

OMB No. 1115-0077

Admission Number

Welcome to the United States

I-94 Arrival/Departure Record - Instructions

This form must be completed by all persons except U.S.Citizens, returning resident aliens, aliens with immigrant visas, and Canadian Citizens visiting or in transit.

Type or print legibly with pen in ALL CAPITAL LETTERS. Use English. Do not write on the back of this form.

This form is in two parts. Please complete both the Arrival Record (Items 1 through 13) and the Departure Record (Items 14 through 17).

When all items are completed, present this form to the U.S. Immigration and Naturalization Service Inspector.

Item 7 - If you are entering the United States by land, enter **LAND** in this space. If you are entering the United States by ship, enter **SEA** in this space.

Form I-94 (04/06/00)Y

OMB No. 1115-0077

Admission Number

I-94
Arrival Record

1. Family Name

2. First (Given) Name

3. Birth Date (Day/Mo/Yr)

4. Country of Citizenship

5. Sex (Male or Female)

6. Passport Number

7. Airline and Flight Number

8. Country Where You Live

9. City Where You Boarded

10. City Where Visa was Issued

11. Date Issued (Day/Mo/Yr)

12. Address While in the United States (Number and Street)

13. City and State

Authority

The authority to collect this information is contained in Title 8 of the United States Code.

Paperwork Reduction Act Notice. A person is not required to respond to a collection of information unless it displays a currently valid OMB control number. The estimated average time to complete and file this application is 4 minutes per application. If you have comments regarding this form, you can write to the Immigration and Naturalization Service, HQPDI, 425 I Street N.W., Room 4307r, Washington DC 20536; OMB No. 1115-0077. **DO NOT MAIL YOUR COMPLETED APPLICATION TO THIS ADDRESS.**

Departure Number

OMB No. 1115-0077

I-94
Departure Record

14. Family Name

15. First (Given) Name

16. Birth Date (Day/Mo/Yr)

17. Country of Citizenship

See Other Side

STAPLE HERE

Primary Inspection

Applicant's
Name _____
Date
Referred _____ Time _____ Insp. # _____

Reason Referred

☐ 212A ☐☐   ☐ PP ☐ Visa ☐ Parole ☐ SLB ☐ TWOV

☐ Other _____

_____

_____

Secondary Inspection

End Secondary
Time _____ Insp. # _____

Disposition _____

18. Occupation	19. Waivers
20. INS File A-	21. INS FCO
22. Petition Number	23. Program Number
24. ☐ Bond	25. ☐ Prospective Student

26. Itinerary/Comments

_____

_____

_____

_____

_____

27. TWOV Ticket Number

Warning - A nonimmigrant who accepts unauthorized employment is subject to deportation.
Important - Retain this permit in your possession; *you must surrender it when you leave the U.S.* Failure to do so may delay your entry into the U.S. in the future.
You are authorized to stay in the U.S. only until the date written on this form. To remain past this date, without permission from immigration authorities, is a violation of the law.
Surrender this permit when you leave the U.S.
    - By sea or air, to the transportation line;
    - Across the Canadian border, to a Canadian Official;
    - Across the Mexican border, to a U.S. Official.
Students planning to reenter the U.S. within 30 days to return to the same school, see "Arrival-Departure" on page 2 of Form 1-20 **prior to surrendering this permit.**

Record of Change

_____

_____

_____

_____

Port: **Departure Record**

Date:

Carrier:

Flight # / Ship Name: _____

OMB No. 1615-0009; Expires 07/31/10

Department of Homeland Security
U.S. Citizenship and Immigration Services

I-129, Petition for a
Nonimmigrant Worker

START HERE - Please type or print in black ink

For USCIS Use Only

Part 1. Information about the employer filing this petition *If the employer is an individual, complete Number 1. Organizations should complete Number 2.*

1. Family Name *(Last Name)*   Given Name *(First Name)*

Full Middle Name   Telephone No. w/Area Code
( )

2. Company or Organization Name   Telephone No. w/Area Code
( )

Mailing Address: *(Street Number and Name)*   Suite #

C/O: *(In Care Of)*

City   State/Province

Country   Zip/Postal Code   E-Mail Address *(If Any)*

Federal Employer Identification #   U.S. Social Security #   Individual Tax #

Part 2. Information about this petition *(See instructions for fee information.)*

1. Requested Nonimmigrant Classification *(Write classification symbol):*

2. Basis for Classification *(Check one):*
- **a.** ☐ New employment (including new employer filing H-1B extension).
- **b.** ☐ Continuation of previously approved employment without change with the same employer.
- **c.** ☐ Change in previously approved employment.
- **d.** ☐ New concurrent employment.
- **e.** ☐ Change of employer.
- **f.** ☐ Amended petition.

3. If you checked **Box 2b, 2c, 2d, 2e,** or **2f,** give the petition receipt number.

4. Prior Petition If the beneficiary is in the U.S. as a nonimmigrant and is applying to change and/or extend his or her status, give the prior petition or application receipt #:

5. Requested Action *(Check one):*
- **a.** ☐ Notify the office in **Part 4** so the person(s) can obtain a visa or be admitted. (**NOTE:** *a petition is not required for an E-1, E-2 or R visa*).
- **b.** ☐ Change the person(s)' status and extend their stay since the person(s) are all now in the U.S. in another status *(see instructions for limitations)*. This is available only where you check "New Employment" in **Item 2,** above.
- **c.** ☐ Extend the stay of the person(s) since they now hold this status.
- **d.** ☐ Amend the stay of the person(s) since they now hold this status.
- **e.** ☐ Extend the status of a nonimmigrant classification based on a Free Trade Agreement. *(See Free Trade Supplement for TN and H1B1 to Form I-129).*
- **f.** ☐ Change status to a nonimmigrant classification based on a Free Trade Agreement. *(See Free Trade Supplement for TN and H1B1 to Form I-129).*

6. Total number of workers in petition *(See instructions relating to when more than one worker can be included):*

Returned

Date

Date
Resubmitted

Date

Date
Reloc Sent

Date

Date
Reloc Rec'd

Date

Date

☐ Petitioner Interviewed on ____

☐ Beneficiary Interviewed on ____

Class: ____
# of Workers: ____
Priority Number: ____
Validity Dates: ____
From: ____
To: ____

☐ **Classification Approved**
☐ Consulate/POE/PFI Notified At ____
☐ Extension Granted
☐ COS/Extension Granted

Partial Approval *(explain)*

Action Block

To Be Completed by
Attorney or Representative, if any.
☐ Fill in box if G-28 is attached to represent the applicant.

ATTY State License #

Part 3. Information about the person(s) for whom you are filing _Complete the blocks below. Use the continuation sheet to name each person included in this petition._

1. If an Entertainment Group, Give the Group Name

Family Name _(Last Name)_ | Given Name _(First Name)_ | Full Middle Name

All Other Names Used _(include maiden name and names from all previous marriages)_

Date of Birth _(mm/dd/yyyy)_ | U.S. Social Security # _(if any)_ | A # _(if any)_

Country of Birth | Province of Birth | Country of Citizenship

2. If in the United States, Complete the Following:

Date of Last Arrival _(mm/dd/yyyy)_ | I-94 # _(Arrival/Departure Document)_ | Current Nonimmigrant Status

Date Status Expires _(mm/dd/yyyy)_ | Passport Number | Date Passport Issued _(mm/dd/yyyy)_ | Date Passport Expires _(mm/dd/yyyy)_

Current U.S. Address

Part 4. Processing Information

1. If the person named in **Part 3** is outside the United States or a requested extension of stay or change of status cannot be granted, give the U.S. consulate or inspection facility you want notified if this petition is approved.

Type of Office _(Check one)_: ☐ Consulate ☐ Pre-flight inspection ☐ Port of Entry

Office Address _(City)_ | U.S. State or Foreign Country

Person's Foreign Address

2. Does each person in this petition have a valid passport?

☐ Not required to have passport   ☐ No - explain on separate paper   ☐ Yes

3. Are you filing any other petitions with this one? ☐ No ☐ Yes - How many?

4. Are applications for replacement/initial I-94s being filed with this petition? ☐ No ☐ Yes - How many?

5. Are applications by dependents being filed with this petition? ☐ No ☐ Yes - How many?

6. Is any person in this petition in removal proceedings? ☐ No ☐ Yes - explain on separate paper

Form I-129 (Rev. 07/07/08)Y Page 2

Part 4. Processing Information *(Continued)*

7. Have you ever filed an immigrant petition for any person in this petition? ☐ No ☐ Yes - explain on separate paper

8. If you indicated you were filing a new petition in **Part 2**, within the past seven years has any person in this petition:

    a. Ever been given the classification you are now requesting? ☐ No ☐ Yes - explain on separate paper

    b. Ever been denied the classification you are now requesting? ☐ No ☐ Yes - explain on separate paper

9. Have you ever previously filed a petition for this person? ☐ No ☐ Yes - explain on separate paper

10. If you are filing for an entertainment group, has any person in this petition not been with the group for at least one year? ☐ No ☐ Yes - explain on separate paper

Part 5. Basic information about the proposed employment and employer *Attach the supplement relating to the classification you are requesting.*

1. Job Title

2. Nontechnical Job Description

3. LCA Case Number

4. NAICS Code

5. Address where the person(s) will work if different from address in **Part 1**. *(Street number and name, city/town, state, zip code)*

6. Is this a full-time position?

    ☐ No - Hours per week: ☐ Yes - Wages per week or per year:

7. Other Compensation *(Explain)*

8. Dates of intended employment *(mm/dd/yyyy)*: From: To:

9. Type of Petitioner - *Check one*:

    ☐ U.S. citizen or permanent resident ☐ Organization ☐ Other - explain on separate paper

10. Type of Business

11. Year Established

12. Current Number of Employees

13. Gross Annual Income

14. Net Annual Income

Part 6. Signature *Read the information on penalties in the instructions before completing this section.*

I certify, under penalty of perjury under the laws of the United States of America, that this petition and the evidence submitted with it is all true and correct. If filing this on behalf of an organization, I certify that I am empowered to do so by that organization. If this petition is to extend a prior petition, I certify that the proposed employment is under the same terms and conditions as stated in the prior approved petition. I authorize the release of any information from my records, or from the petitioning organization's records that U.S. Citizenship and Immigration Services needs to determine eligibility for the benefit being sought.

Signature

Daytime Phone Number *(Area/Country Code)*

(   )

Print Name

Date *(mm/dd/yyyy)*

NOTE: If you do not completely fill out this form and the required supplement, or fail to submit required documents listed in the instructions, the person(s) filed for may not be found eligible for the requested benefit and this petition may be denied.

Part 7. Signature of person preparing form, if other than above

I declare that I prepared this petition at the request of the above person and it is based on all information of which I have any knowledge.

Signature

Daytime Phone Number *(Area/Country Code)*

(   )

Print Name

Date *(mm/dd/yyyy)*

Firm Name and Address

OMB No. 1615-0009; Expires 07/31/10

Department of Homeland Security
U.S. Citizenship and Immigration Services

E Classification Supplement
to Form I-129

1. Name of person or organization filing petition:

2. Name of person for whom you are filing:

3. Classification sought *(Check one)*:

☐ E-1 Treaty trader ☐ E-2 Treaty investor

4. Name of country signatory to treaty with U.S.:

Section 1. Information about the employer outside the United States (if any)

Employer's Name

Total Number of Employees

Employer's Address *(Street number and name, city/town, state/province, zip/postal code)*

Principal Product, Merchandise or Service

Employee's Position - Title, duties and number of years employed

Section 2. Additional information about the U.S. Employer

1. The U.S. company is to the company outside the United States *(Check one)*.

☐ Parent ☐ Branch ☐ Subsidiary ☐ Affiliate ☐ Joint Venture

2. Date and Place of Incorporation or Establishment in the United States

3. Nationality of Ownership *(Individual or Corporate)*

Name *(First/Middle/Last)*	Nationality	Immigration Status	% Ownership

4. Assets

5. Net Worth

6. Total Annual Income

7. Staff in the United States

  a. How many executive and/or managerial employees does petitioner have who are nationals of the treaty country in either E or L status?

  b. How many specialized qualifications or knowledge persons does the petitioner have who are nationals of the treaty country in either E or L status?

  c. Provide the total number of employees in executive or managerial positions in the United States.

  d. Provide the total number of specialized qualifications or knowledge persons positions in the United States.

8. Total number of employees the alien would supervise; or describe the nature of the specialized skills essential to the U.S. company.

Section 3. Complete if filing for an E-1 Treaty Trader

1. Total Annual Gross Trade/Business of the U.S. company

2. For Year Ending *(yyyy)*

3. Percent of total gross trade between the United States and the country of which the treaty trader organization is a national.

Section 4. Complete if filing for an E-2 Treaty Investor

Total Investment: Cash

Equipment

Other

Inventory

Premises

Total

OMB No.1615-0009; Expires 07/31/10

Nonimmigrant Classification Based on Free Trade Agreement-Supplement to Form I-129

Department of Homeland Security
U.S. Citizenship and Immigration Services

1. Name of person or organization filing petition:

2. Name of person for whom you are filing:

3. Employer is a *(Check one)*:

☐ U.S. Employer ☐ Foreign Employer

4. If Foreign Employer, name the foreign country.

Section 1. Information about requested extension or change *(See instructions attached to this form.)*

1. This is a request for an extension of Free Trade status based on *(Check one)*:

Or

2. This is a request for a change of nonimmigrant status to *(Check one)*:

a. ☐ Free Trade, Canada (TN)

b. ☐ Free Trade, Chile (H1B1)

c. ☐ Free Trade, Mexico (TN)

d. ☐ Free Trade, Singapore (H1B1)

e. ☐ Free Trade, Other

f. ☐ I am an H-1B1 Free Trade Nonimmigrant from Chile or Singapore and this is my sixth consecutive request for an extension.

a. ☐ Free Trade, Canada (TN)

b. ☐ Free Trade, Chile (H1B1)

c. ☐ Free Trade, Mexico (TN)

d. ☐ Free Trade, Singapore (H1B1)

e. ☐ Free Trade, Other

f. ☐ I am an H-1B1 Free Trade Nonimmigrant from Chile or Singapore and this is my first request for a change of status to H-1B1 within the past six years.

Part 2. Signature *Read the information on penalties in the instructions before completing this section.*

I certify, under penalty of perjury under the laws of the United States of America, that this petition and the evidence submitted with it is all true and correct. If filing this on behalf of an organization, I certify that I am empowered to do so by that organization. If this petition is to extend a prior petition, I certify that the proposed employment is under the same terms and conditions as stated in the prior approved petition. I authorize the release of any information from my records, or from the petitioning organization's records, that the U.S. Citizenship and Immigration Services needs to determine eligibility for the benefit being sought.

Signature

Daytime Phone Number *(Area/Country Code)*
( )

Print Name

Date *(mm/dd/yyyy)*

NOTE: If you do not completely fill out this form and the required supplement, or fail to submit required documents listed in the instructions, the person(s) filed for may not be found eligible for the requested benefit and this petition may be denied.

Part 3. Signature of person preparing form, if other than above

I declare that I prepared this petition at the request of the above person and it is based on all information of which I have any knowledge.

Signature

Daytime Phone Number *(Area/Country Code)*
( )

Print Name

Date *(mm/dd/yyyy)*

Firm Name and Address

Form I-129 Supplement FT (Rev. 07/07/08)Y Page 6

OMB No.1615-0009; Expires 07/31/10

Department of Homeland Security
U.S. Citizenship and Immigration Services

**H Classification Supplement
to Form I-129**

1. Name of person or organization filing
petition:

2. Name of person or total number of workers or trainees for
whom you are filing:

3. List the alien's and any dependent family member's prior periods of stay in H classification in the United States for the last six years.
Be sure to list only those periods in which the alien and/or family members were actually in the United States in an H classification.
NOTE: Submit photocopies of Forms I-94, I-797 and/or other USCIS issued documents noting these periods of stay in the H
classification. If more space is needed, attach an additional sheet(s). (If applying for H-2A/H-2B classification skip this item.)

Subject's Name	Period of Stay *(mm/dd/yyyy)*		Subject's Name	Period of Stay *(mm/dd/yyyy)*	
	From:	To:		From:	To:
	From:	To:		From:	To:

4. Classification sought *(Check one)*:

☐ H-1B1   Specialty occupation

☐ H-1B2   Exceptional services relating to a cooperative
research and development project administered by
the U.S. Department of Defense (DOD)

☐ H-1B3   Fashion model of national or international acclaim

☐ H-2A   Agricultural worker

☐ H-2B   Non-agricultural worker

☐ H-3   Trainee

☐ H-3   Special education exchange visitor program

Section 1. Complete this section if filing for H-1B classification

1. Describe the proposed duties

2. Alien's present occupation and summary of prior work experience

Statement for H-1B specialty occupations only:

By filing this petition, I agree to the terms of the labor condition application for the duration of the alien's authorized period of stay
for H-1B employment.

Petitioner's Signature	**Print or Type Name**	**Date** *(mm/dd/yyyy)*

Statement for H-1B specialty occupations and U.S. Department of Defense projects:

As an authorized official of the employer, I certify that the employer will be liable for the reasonable costs of return transportation
of the alien abroad if the alien is dismissed from employment by the employer before the end of the period of authorized stay.

Signature of Authorized Official of Employer	**Print or Type Name**	**Date** *(mm/dd/yyyy)*

Statement for H-1B U.S. Department of Defense projects only:

I certify that the alien will be working on a cooperative research and development project or a co-production project under a
reciprocal government-to-government agreement administered by the U.S. Department of Defense.

DOD Project Manager's Signature	**Print or Type Name**	**Date** *(mm/dd/yyyy)*

Form I-129 Supplement H (Rev. 07/07/08)Y Page 7

Section 2. Complete this section if filing for H-2A or H-2B classification

1. Employment is: *(Check one)*   **2.** Temporary need is: *(Check one)*

  a. ☐ Seasonal   **c.** ☐ Intermittent   **a.** ☐ Unpredictable   **c.** ☐ Recurrent annually

  b. ☐ Peakload   **d.** ☐ One-time occurence   **b.** ☐ Periodic

3. Explain your temporary need for the alien's services *(attach a separate sheet(s) paper if additional space is needed).*

Section 3. Complete this section if filing for H-2A classification

The petitioner and each employer consent to allow government access to the site where the labor is being performed for the purpose of determining compliance with H-2A requirements. The petitioner further agrees to notify USCIS in the manner and within the time frame specified if an H-2A worker absconds, or if the authorized employment ends more than five days before the relating certification document expires, and pay liquidated damages of ten dollars ($10 for each instance where it cannot demonstrate compliance with this notification requirement. The petitioner agrees also to pay liquidated damages of two hundred dollars ($200.00) for each instance where it cannot be demonstrated that the H-2A worker either departed the United States or obtained authorized status during the period of admission or within five days of early termination, whichever comes first.

The petitioner must execute **Part A**. If the petitioner is the employer's agent, the employer must execute **Part B**. If there are joint employers, they must each execute **Part C**.

Part A. Petitioner:

By filing this petition, I agree to the conditions of H-2A employment and agree to the notice requirements and limited liabilities defined in 8 CFR 214.2(h)(3)(vi).

Petitioner's Signature	Print or Type Name	Date *(mm/dd/yyyy)*

Part B. Employer who is not the petitioner:

I certify that I have authorized the party filing this petition to act as my agent in this regard. I assume full responsibility for all representations made by this agent on my behalf and agree to the conditions of H-2A eligibility.

Employer's Signature	Print or Type Name	Date *(mm/dd/yyyy)*

Part C. Joint Employers:

I agree to the conditions of H-2A eligibility.

Joint Employer's Signature(s)	**Print or Type Name**	**Date** *(mm/dd/yyyy)*

Joint Employer's Signature(s)	**Print or Type Name**	**Date** *(mm/dd/yyyy)*

Joint Employer's Signature(s)	**Print or Type Name**	**Date** *(mm/dd/yyyy)*

Joint Employer's Signature(s)	**Print or Type Name**	**Date** *(mm/dd/yyyy)*

Section 4. Complete this section if filing for H-3 classification

1. If you answer "yes" to any of the following questions, attach a full explanation.

   a. Is the training you intend to provide, or similar training, available in the alien's country?   ☐ No   ☐ Yes

   b. Will the training benefit the alien in pursuing a career abroad?   ☐ No   ☐ Yes

   c. Does the training involve productive employment incidental to training?   ☐ No   ☐ Yes

   d. Does the alien already have skills related to the training?   ☐ No   ☐ Yes

   e. Is this training an effort to overcome a labor shortage?   ☐ No   ☐ Yes

   f. Do you intend to employ the alien abroad at the end of this training?   ☐ No   ☐ Yes

2. If you do not intend to employ this person abroad at the end of this training, explain why you wish to incur the cost of providing this training and your expected return from this training.

Form I-129 Supplement H (Rev. 07/07/08)Y Page 9

OMB No.1615-0009; Expires 07/31/10

H-1B Data Collection and
Filing Fee Exemption Supplement

Department of Homeland Security
U.S. Citizenship and Immigration Services

Petitioner's Name [_____]

Part A. General Information

1. **Employer Information** - *(check all items that apply)*

    a. Is the petitioner a dependent employer? ☐ No ☐ Yes

    b. Has the petitioner ever been found to be a willful violator? ☐ No ☐ Yes

    c. Is the beneficiary an exempt H-1B nonimmigrant? ☐ No ☐ Yes

       1. If yes, is it because the beneficiary's annual rate of pay is equal to at least $60,000? ☐ No ☐ Yes

       2. Or is it because the beneficiary has a master's or higher degree in a specialty related to the employment? ☐ No ☐ Yes

2. **Beneficiary's Last Name** [_____] **First Name** [_____] **Middle Name** [_____]

    Attention To or In Care Of [_____] Current Residential Address - Street Number and Name [_____] Apt. # [_____]

    City [_____] State [_____] Zip/Postal Code [_____]

    U.S. Social Security # *(If Any)* [_____] I-94 # *(Arrival/Departure Document)* [_____] Previous Receipt # *(If Any)* [_____]

3. **Beneficiary's Highest Level of Education** Please check one box below.

    ☐ NO DIPLOMA

    ☑ HIGH SCHOOL GRADUATE - high school DIPLOMA or the equivalent (example: GED)

    ☐ Some college credit, but less than one year

    ☐ One or more years of college, no degree

    ☐ Associate's degree *(for example: AA, AS)*

    ☐ Bachelor's degree *(for example: BA, AB, BS)*

    ☑ Master's degree *(for example: MA, MS, MEng, MEd, MSW, MBA)*

    ☐ Professional degree *(for example: MD, DDS, DVM, LLB, JD)*

    ☐ Doctorate degree *(for example: PhD, EdD)*

4. **Major/Primary Field of Study**
    [ ]

5. Has the beneficiary of this petition earned a master's or higher degree from a U.S. institution of higher education as defined in 20 U.S.C. section 1001(a)?

    ☐ No ☑ Yes (If "Yes" provide the following information):

    Name of the U.S. institution of higher education [_____] Date Degree Awarded [_____] Type of U.S. Degree [_____]

    Address of the U.S. institution of higher education [_____]

6. **Rate of Pay Per Year** [_____]   7. **LCA Code** [ ][ ][ ]   8. **NAICS Code** [ ][ ][ ][ ][ ][ ]

Part B. Fee Exemption and/or Determination

In order for USCIS to determine if you must pay the additional $1,500 or $750 fee, please answer all of the following questions:

1. ☐ Yes ☐ No Are you an institution of higher education as defined in the Higher Education Act of 1965, section 101 (a), 20 U.S.C. section 1001(a)?

2. ☐ Yes ☐ No Are you a nonprofit organization or entity related to or affiliated with an institution of higher education, as such institutions of higher education are defined in the Higher Education Act of 1965, section 101 (a), 20 U.S.C. section 1001(a)?

3. ☐ Yes ☐ No Are you a nonprofit research organization or a governmental research organization, as defined in 8 CFR 214.2(h)(19)(iii)(C)?

4. ☐ Yes ☐ No Is this the second or subsequent request for an extension of stay that you have filed for this alien?

5. ☐ Yes ☐ No Is this an amended petition that does not contain any request for extensions of stay?

6. ☐ Yes ☐ No Are you filing this petition in order to correct a USCIS error?

7. ☐ Yes ☐ No Is the petitioner a primary or secondary education institution?

8. ☐ Yes ☐ No Is the petitioner a non-profit entity that engages in an established curriculum-related clinical training of students registered at such an institution?

If you answered "Yes" to any of the questions above, then you are required to submit the fee for your H-1B Form I-129 petition, which is $320. If you answered "No" to all questions, please answer Question 9.

9. ☐ Yes ☐ No Do you currently employ a total of no more than 25 full-time equivalent employees in the United States, including any affiliate or subsidiary of your company?

If you answered "Yes" to Question 9 above, then you are required to pay an additional fee of $750. If you answered "No", then you are required to pay an additional fee of $1,500.

NOTE: On or after March 8, 2005, a U.S. employer seeking initial approval of H-1B or L nonimmigrant status for a beneficiary, or seeking approval to employ an H-1B or L nonimmigrant currently working for another U.S. employer, must submit an additional $500 fee. This additional $500 Fraud Prevention and Detection fee was mandated by the provisions of the H-1B Visa Reform Act of 2004. **There is no exemption from this fee.**

Part C. Numerical Limitation Exemption Information

1. ☐ Yes ☐ No Are you an institution of higher education as defined in the Higher Education Act of 1965, section 101 (a), 20 U.S.C section 1001(a)?

2. ☐ Yes ☐ No Are you a nonprofit organization or entity related to or affiliated with an institution of higher education, as such institutions of higher education as defined in the Higher Education Act of 1965, section 101(a), 20 U.S.C. section 1001(a)?

3. ☐ Yes ☐ No Are you a nonprofit research organization or a governmental research organization, as defined in 8 CFR 214.2(h)(19)(iii)(C)?

4. ☐ Yes ☐ No Is the beneficiary of this petition a J-1 nonimmigrant alien who received a waiver of the two-year foreign residency requirement described in section 214 (l)(1)(B) or (C) of the Act?

5. ☐ Yes ☐ No Has the beneficiary of this petition been previously granted status as an H-1B nonimmigrant in the past 6 years and not left the United States for more than one year after attaining such status?

6. ☐ Yes ☐ No If the petition is to request a change of employer, did the beneficiary previously work as an H-1B for an institution of higher education, an entity related to or affiliated with an institution of higher education, or a nonprofit research organization or governmental research institution defined in questions 1, 2 and 3 of Part C of this form?

7. ☐ Yes ☐ No Has the beneficiary of this petition earned a master's or higher degree from a U.S. institution of higher education, as defined in the Higher Education Act of 1965, section 101(a), 20 U.S.C. section 1001(a)?

I certify under penalty of perjury, under the laws of the United States of America, that this attachment and the evidence submitted with it is true and correct. If filing this on behalf of an organization or entity, I certify that I am empowered to do so by that organization or entity. I authorize the release of any information from my records, or from the petitioning organization or entity's records, that U.S. Citizenship and Immigration Services may need to determine eligibility for the exemption being sought.

Certification

Signature | **Print Name**

Title | **Date** *(mm/dd/yyyy)*

OMB No.1615-0009; Expires 07/31/10

**L Classification Supplement
to Form I-129**

Department of Homeland Security
U.S. Citizenship and Immigration Services

---

1. Name of person or organization filing petition:

2. Name of person for whom you are filing:

3. This petition is *(Check one)*:

     a. ☐ An individual petition   **b.** ☐ A blanket petition

---

Section 1.   **Complete this section if filing for an individual petition**

1. Classification sought *(Check one)*:

     a. ☐ L-1A manager or executive   **b.** ☐ L-1B specialized knowledge

2. List the alien's and any dependent family member's prior periods of stay in an H or L classification in the United States for the last seven years. Be sure to list only those periods in which the alien and/or family members were actually in the U.S. in an H or L classification. **NOTE:** Submit photocopies of Forms I-94, I-797 and/or other USCIS issued documents noting these periods of stay in the H or L classification. If more space is needed, attach an additional sheet(s).

Subject's Name	Period of Stay *(mm/dd/yyyy)*	
	From:	To:
	From:	To:
	From:	To:
	From:	To:
	From:	To:

3. Name of employer abroad

4. Address of employer abroad *(Street number and name, city/town, state/province, zip/postal code)*

5. Dates of alien's employment with this employer *(Explain any interruptions in employment)*

Dates of Employment *(mm/dd/yyyy)*		Explanation of Interruptions
From:	To:	
From:	To:	
From:	To:	

6. Description of the alien's duties for the past three years

7. Description of the alien's proposed duties in the United States

8. Summary of the alien's education and work experience

---

1. Name of person or organization filing petition:

2. Name of person for whom you are filing:

Section 1. Complete this section if filing for an individual petition *(Continued)*

9. The U.S. company is to the company abroad: *(Check one)*

a. ☐ Parent **b.** ☐ Branch **c.** ☐ Subsidiary **d.** ☐ Affiliate **e.** ☐ Joint Venture

10. Describe the stock ownership and managerial control of each company. Provide the U.S. Tax Code Number for each company.

Company stock ownership and managerial control of each company	U.S. Tax Code Number

11. Do the companies currently have the same qualifying relationship as they did during the one-year period of the alien's employment with the company abroad?   ☐ Yes   ☐ No *(Attach explanation)*

12. Is the alien coming to the United States to open a new office?   ☐ Yes *(Attach explanation)* ☐ No

13. If you are seeking L-1B specialized knowledge status for an individual, answer the following question:

Will the beneficiary be stationed primarily offsite (at the worksite of an employer other than the petitioner or its affiliate, subsidiary, or parent)?   ☐ Yes ☐ No

If you answered "Yes" to the preceding question, describe how and by whom the beneficiary's work will be controlled and supervised. Include a description of the amount of time each supervisor is expected to control and supervise the work. Use an attachment if needed.

If you answered "Yes" to the preceding question, also describe the reasons why placement at another worksite outside the petitioner, subsidiary, or parent is needed. Include a description of how the beneficiary's duties at another worksite relate to the need for the specialized knowledge he or she possesses. Use an attachment if needed.

Section 2. Complete this section if filing a blanket petition

List all U.S. and foreign parent, branches, subsidiaries and affiliates included in this petition. *(Attach a separate sheet(s) of paper if additional space is needed.)*

Name and Address	Relationship

Section 3. Fraud Prevention and Detection Fee

As of **March 8, 2005**, a U.S. employer seeking initial approval of L nonimmigrant status for a beneficiary, or seeking approval to employ an L nonimmigrant currently working for another U.S. employer, must submit an additional $500 fee. This additional **$500** Fraud Prevention and Detection fee was mandated by the provisions of the H-1B Visa Reform Act of 2004. **There is no exemption from this fee.** You must include payment of this **$500** fee with your submission of this form. Failure to submit the fee when required will result in rejection or denial of your submission.

OMB No.1615-0009; Expires 07/31/10

Department of Homeland Security
U.S. Citizenship and Immigration Services

O and P Classifications
Supplement to Form I-129

1. **Name of person or organization filing petition:**	2. **Name of person or group or total number of workers for whom you are filing:**

3. **Classification sought** *(Check one)*:

a. ☐ O-1A Alien of extraordinary ability in sciences, education, business, or athletics (not including the arts, motion picture, or television industry.)

b. ☐ O-1B Alien of extraordinary ability in the arts or extraordinary achievement in the motion picture or television industry.

c. ☐ O-2 Accompanying alien who is coming to the U.S. to assist in the performance of the O-1.

d. ☐ P-1 Athletic/Entertainment group.

e. ☐ P-1S Essential Support Personnel for P-1.

f. ☐ P-2 Artist or entertainer for reciprocal exchange program.

g. ☐ P-2S Essential Support Personnel for P-2.

h. ☐ P-3 Artist/Entertainer coming to the United States to perform, teach, or coach under a program that is culturally unique.

i. ☐ P-3S Essential Support Personnel for P-3.

4. Explain the nature of the event

5. Describe the duties to be performed

6. If filing for an O-2 or P support alien, list dates of the alien's prior experience with the O-1 or P alien

7. Have you obtained the required written consultation(s)? ☐ Yes - Attached ☐ No - Copy of request attached
If not, give the following information about the organization(s) to which you have sent a duplicate of this petition.

O-1 Extraordinary Ability

Name of Recognized Peer Group	Daytime Telephone # *(Area/Country Code)* ( )
Complete Address	Date Sent *(mm/dd/yyyy)*

O-1 Extraordinary achievement in motion pictures or television

Name of Labor Organization	Daytime Telephone # *(Area/Country Code)* ( )
Complete Address	Date Sent *(mm/dd/yyyy)*
Name of Management Organization	Daytime Telephone # *(Area/Country Code)* ( )
Complete Address	Date sent *(mm/dd/yyyy)*

O-2 or P alien

Name of Labor Organization	Daytime Telephone # *(Area/Country Code)* ( )
Complete Address	Date Sent *(mm/dd/yyyy)*

OMB No.1615-0009; Expires 07/31/10

Department of Homeland Security
U.S. Citizenship and Immigration Services

**Q-1 and R-1 Classifications
Supplement to Form I-129**

1. Name of person or organization filing petition:

2. Name of person for whom you are filing:

Section 1. Complete this section if you are filing for a Q-1 international cultural exchange alien

I hereby certify that the participant(s) in the international cultural exchange program:

A. Is at least 18 years of age,

B. Is qualified to perform the service or labor or receive the type of training stated in the petition,

C. Has the ability to communicate effectively about the cultural attributes of his or her country of nationality to the American public, and

D. Has resided and been physically present outside the United States for the immediate prior year, if he or she was previously admitted as a Q-1.

I also certify that I will offer the alien(s) the same wages and working conditions comparable to those accorded local domestic workers similarly employed.

Petitioner's signature

Date *(mm/dd/yyyy)*

Section 2. Complete this section if you are filing for an R-1 religious worker

1. List the alien's and any dependent family member's prior periods of stay in R classification in the United States for the last six years. Be sure to list only those periods in which the alien and/or family members were actually in the United States in an R classification. **NOTE:** Submit photocopies of Forms I-94, I-797 and/or other USCIS issued documents noting these periods of stay in the R classification. If more space is needed, attach an additional sheet(s).

Subject's Name	Period of Stay *(mm/dd/yyyy)*		Subject's Name	Period of Stay *(mm/dd/yyyy)*
	From:	To:		From: To:
	From:	To:		From: To:
	From:	To:		From: To:

2. Describe the alien's proposed duties in the United States

3. Describe the alien's qualifications for the vocation or occupation

4. Description of the relationship between the religious organization in the United States and the organization abroad of which the alien was a member

Attachment - 1

Attach to Form I-129 when more than one person is included in the petition. *(List each person separately. Do not include the person you named on the Form I-129.)*

Family Name *(Last Name)*	Given Name *(First Name)*	Full Middle Name	Date of Birth *mm/dd/yyyy*

Country of Birth	Country of Citizenship	U.S. Social Security # *(if any)*	A # *(if any)*

IF IN THE U.S.	Date of Arrival *(mm/dd/yyyy)*	I-94 # (Arrival/Departure Document)	Current Nonimmigrant Status	Date Status Expires *(mm/dd/yyyy)*
	Country Where Passport Issued	Date Passport Expires *(mm/dd/yyyy)*	Date Started With Group *(mm/dd/yyyy)*	

Family Name *(Last Name)*	Given Name *(First Name)*	Full Middle Name	Date of Birth *mm/dd/yyyy*

Country of Birth	Country of Citizenship	U.S. Social Security # *(if any)*	A # *(if any)*

IF IN THE U.S.	Date of Arrival *(mm/dd/yyyy)*	I-94 # (Arrival/Departure Document)	Current Nonimmigrant Status	Date Status Expires *(mm/dd/yyyy)*
	Country Where Passport Issued	Date Passport Expires *(mm/dd/yyyy)*	Date Started With Group *(mm/dd/yyyy)*	

Family Name *(Last Name)*	Given Name *(First Name)*	Full Middle Name	Date of Birth *mm/dd/yyyy*

Country of Birth	Country of Citizenship	U.S. Social Security # *(if any)*	A # *(if any)*

IF IN THE U.S.	Date of Arrival *(mm/dd/yyyy)*	I-94 # (Arrival/Departure Document)	Current Nonimmigrant Status	Date Status Expires *(mm/dd/yyyy)*
	Country Where Passport Issued	Date Passport Expires *(mm/dd/yyyy)*	Date Started With Group *(mm/dd/yyyy)*	

Family Name *(Last Name)*	Given Name *(First Name)*	Full Middle Name	Date of Birth *mm/dd/yyyy*

Country of Birth	Country of Citizenship	U.S. Social Security # *(if any)*	A # *(if any)*

IF IN THE U.S.	Date of Arrival *(mm/dd/yyyy)*	I-94 # (Arrival/Departure Document)	Current Nonimmigrant Status	Date Status Expires *(mm/dd/yyyy)*
	Country Where Passport Issued	Date Passport Expires *(mm/dd/yyyy)*	Date Started With Group *(mm/dd/yyyy)*	

Form I-129 Attachment - 1 (Rev. 07/07/08)Y Page 16

Attachment - 1

Attach to Form I-129 when more than one person is included in the petition. *(List each person separately. Do not include the person you named on the Form I-129.)*

Family Name *(Last Name)*	Given Name *(First Name)*	Full Middle Name	Date of Birth *mm/dd/yyyy*

Country of Birth	Country of Citizenship	U.S. Social Security # *(if any)*	A # *(if any)*

IF IN THE U.S.

Date of Arrival *(mm/dd/yyyy)*	I-94 # (Arrival/Departure Document)	Current Nonimmigrant Status	Date Status Expires *(mm/dd/yyyy)*

Country Where Passport Issued	Date Passport Expires *(mm/dd/yyyy)*	Date Started With Group *(mm/dd/yyyy)*

Family Name *(Last Name)*	Given Name *(First Name)*	Full Middle Name	Date of Birth *mm/dd/yyyy*

Country of Birth	Country of Citizenship	U.S. Social Security # *(if any)*	A # *(if any)*

IF IN THE U.S.

Date of Arrival *(mm/dd/yyyy)*	I-94 # (Arrival/Departure Document)	Current Nonimmigrant Status	Date Status Expires *(mm/dd/yyyy)*

Country Where Passport Issued	Date Passport Expires *(mm/dd/yyyy)*	Date Started With Group *(mm/dd/yyyy)*

Family Name *(Last Name)*	Given Name *(First Name)*	Full Middle Name	Date of Birth *mm/dd/yyyy*

Country of Birth	Country of Citizenship	U.S. Social Security # *(if any)*	A # *(if any)*

IF IN THE U.S.

Date of Arrival *(mm/dd/yyyy)*	I-94 # (Arrival/Departure Document)	Current Nonimmigrant Status	Date Status Expires *(mm/dd/yyyy)*

Country Where Passport Issued	Date Passport Expires *(mm/dd/yyyy)*	Date Started With Group *(mm/dd/yyyy)*

Family Name *(Last Name)*	Given Name *(First Name)*	Full Middle Name	Date of Birth *mm/dd/yyyy*

Country of Birth	Country of Citizenship	U.S. Social Security # *(if any)*	A # *(if any)*

IF IN THE U.S.

Date of Arrival *(mm/dd/yyyy)*	I-94 # (Arrival/Departure Document)	Current Nonimmigrant Status	Date Status Expires *(mm/dd/yyyy)*

Country Where Passport Issued	Date Passport Expires *(mm/dd/yyyy)*	Date Started With Group *(mm/dd/yyyy)*

Form I-129 Attachment - 1 (Rev. 07/07/08)Y Page 17

OMB No. 1615-0001; Expires 01/31/2010

Department of Homeland Security
U.S. Citizenship and Immigration Services

**I-129F, Petition
for Alien Fiancé(e)**

Do not write in these blocks.	**For USCIS Use Only**	
Case ID #	**Action Block**	**Fee Stamp**
A #		
G-28 #		**AMCON:** _____
The petition is approved for status under Section 101(a)(5)(k). It is valid for four months from the date of action. _____		☐ Personal Interview ☐ Previously Forwarded ☐ Document Check ☐ Field Investigation
Remarks:		

Part A.   Start Here. Information about you.

1. Name *(Family name in CAPS)*   *(First)*   *(Middle)*

2. Address *(Number and Street)*   Apt. #

(Town or City)   (State or Country)   (Zip/Postal Code)

3. Place of Birth *(Town or City)*   (State/Country)

4. Date of Birth *(mm/dd/yyyy)*   **5. Gender**
☐ Male   ☐ Female

6. Marital Status
☐ Married   ☐ Single   ☐ Widowed   ☐ Divorced

7. Other Names Used *(including maiden name)*

8a. U.S. Social Security Number   8b. A# *(if any)*

9. Names of Prior Spouses   **Date(s) Marriage(s) Ended**

10. My citizenship was acquired through *(check one)*

☐ Birth in the U.S.   ☐ Naturalization
Give number of certificate, date and place it was issued.

☐ Parents
Have you obtained a certificate of citizenship in your name?
☐ Yes   ☐ No
If "Yes," give certificate number, date and place it was issued.

11. Have you ever filed for this or any other alien fiancé(e) or husband/wife before?
☐ Yes   ☐ No
If "Yes," give name of all aliens, place and date of filing, A# and result. *(Attached additional sheets as necessary.)*

Part B.   Information about your alien fiancé(e).

1. Name *(Family name in CAPS)*   *(First)*   *(Middle)*

2. Address *(Number and Street)*   Apt. #

(Town or City)   (State or Country)   (Zip/Postal Code)

3a. Place of Birth *(Town or City)*   (State/Country)

3b. Country of Citizenship

4. Date of Birth *(mm/dd/yyyy)*   **5. Gender**
☐ Male   ☐ Female

6. Marital Status
☐ Married   ☐ Single   ☐ Widowed   ☐ Divorced

7. Other Names Used *(including maiden name)*

8. U.S. Social Security #   **9. A# *(if any)***

10. Names of Prior Spouses   **Date(s) Marriage(s) Ended**

11. Has your fiancé(e) ever been in the U.S.?
☐ Yes   ☐ No

12. If your fiancé(e) is currently in the U.S., complete the following:

He or she last arrived as a: *(visitor, student, exchange alien, crewman, stowaway, temporary worker, without inspection, etc.)*

Arrival/Departure Record (I-94) Number

☐☐☐☐ — ☐☐☐☐☐☐☐☐

Date of Arrival *(mm/dd/yy)*   **Date authorized stay expired, or will expire as shown on I-94 or I-95**

INITIAL RECEIPT ____   RESUBMITTED ____   RELOCATED: Rec'd ____   Sent ____   COMPLETED: Appv'd ____   Denied ____   Ret'd ____

Form I-129F (Rev. 07/30/07) Y

Part B.   Information about your alien fiancé(e).   *(Continued.)*

13. List all children of your alien fiancé(e) *(if any)*

Name *(First/Middle/Last)*	Date of Birth *(mm/dd/yyyy)*	Country of Birth	Present Address

14. Address in the United States where your fiancé(e) intends to live.

(Number and Street)　　　　　　　　　　　　　　　　(Town or City)　　　　　(State)

15. Your fiancé(e)'s address abroad.

(Number and Street)　　　　　　　　　　　　　　　　(Town or City)　　　　(State or Province)

(Country)　　　　　　　　　　　　　　　(Phone Number; Include Country, City and Area Codes)

16. If your fiancé(e)'s native alphabet uses other than Roman letters, write his or her name and address abroad in the native alphabet.

(Name)　　　　　　　　　　　　　　　　　　(Number and Street)

(Town or City)　　　　　　(State or Province)　　　　　(Country)

17. Is your fiancé(e) related to you?　　　☐ Yes　　☐ No

If you are related, state the nature and degree of relationship, e.g., third cousin or maternal uncle, etc.

18. Has your fiancé(e) met and seen you within the two-year period immediately receding the filing of this petition?

☐ Yes　　☐ No

Describe the circumstances under which you met. If you have not personally met each other, explain how the relationship was established. If you met your fiancé(e) or spouse though an international marriage broker, please explain those circumstances in Question 19 below. Explain also in detail any reasons you may have for requesting that the requirement that you and your fiancé(e) must have met should not apply to you.

19. Did you meet your fiancé(e) or spouse through the services of an international marriage broker?

☐ Yes　　☐ No

If you answered yes, please provide the name and any contact information you may have (including internet or street address) of the international marriage broker and where the international marriage broker is located. Attach additional sheets of paper if necessary.

20. Your fiancé(e) will apply for a visa abroad at the American embassy or consulate at:

(City)　　　　　　　　　　　　　　　　(Country)

NOTE: (Designation of a U.S. embassy or consulate outside the country of your fiancé(e)'s last residence does not guarantee acceptance for processing by that foreign post. Acceptance is at the discretion of the designated embassy or consulate.)

Part C. Other information.

1. If you are serving overseas in the Armed Forces of the United States, please answer the following:

I presently reside or am stationed overseas and my current mailing address is:

2. Have you ever been convicted by a court of law (civil or criminal) or court martialed by a military tribunal for any of the following crimes:

- Domestic violence, sexual assault, child abuse and neglect, dating violence, elder abuse or stalking. (Please refer to page 3 of the instructions for the full definition of the term "domestic violence.)

- Homicide, murder, manslaughter, rape, abusive sexual contact, sexual exploitation, incest, torture, trafficking, peonage, holding hostage, involuntary servitude, slave trade, kidnapping, abduction, unlawful criminal restraint, false imprisonment or an attempt to commit any of these crimes, or

- Three or more convictions for crimes relating to a controlled substance or alcohol not arising from a single act.

☐ Yes   ☐ No

Answering this question is required even if your records were sealed or otherwise cleared or if anyone, including a judge, law enforcement officer, or attorney, told you that you no longer have a record. Using a separate sheet(s) of paper, attach information relating to the conviction(s), such as crime involved, date of conviction and sentence.

3. If you have provided information about a conviction for a crime listed above and you were being battered or subjected to extreme cruelty by your spouse, parent, or adult child at the time of your conviction, check all of the following that apply to you:

☐ I was acting in self-defense.

☐ I violated a protection order issued for my own protection.

☐ I committed, was arrested for, was convicted of, or plead guilty to committing a crime that did not result in serious bodily injury, and there was a connection between the crime committed and my having been battered or subjected to extreme cruelty.

Part D. Penalties, certification and petitioner's signature.

PENALTIES: You may by law be imprisoned for not more than five years, or fined $250,000, or both, for entering into a marriage contract for the purpose of evading any provision of the immigration laws, and you may be fined up to $10,000 or imprisoned up to five years, or both, for knowingly and willfully falsifying or concealing a material fact or using any false document in submitting this petition.

YOUR CERTIFICATION: I am legally able to and intend to marry my alien fiancé(e) within 90 days of his or her arrival in the United States. I certify, under penalty of perjury under the laws of the United States of America, that the foregoing is true and correct. Furthermore, I authorize the release of any information from my records that U.S. Citizenship and Immigration Services needs to determine eligibility for the benefit that I am seeking.

Moreover, I understand that this petition, including any criminal conviction information that I am required to provide with this petition, as well as any related criminal background information pertaining to me that U.S. Citizenship and Immigration Services may discover independently in adjudicating this petition will be disclosed to the beneficiary of this petition.

Signature	**Date** *(mm/dd/yyyy)*	**Daytime Telephone Number** *(with area code)*

E-Mail Address (if any)

Part E. Signature of person preparing form, if other than above. *(Sign below.)*

I declare that I prepared this application at the request of the petitioner and it is based on all information of which I have knowledge.

Signature	Print or Type Your Name	G-28 ID Number	Date *(mm/dd/yyyy)*

Firm Name and Address	Daytime Telephone Number *(with area code)*
	E-Mail Address (if any)

Form I-129F (Rev. 07/30/07) Y Page 3

OMB No. 1615-0010; Expires 12/31/09

Department of Homeland Security
U.S. Citizenship and Immigration Services

**I-129S, Nonimmigrant Petition
Based on Blanket L Petition**

What Is the Purpose of This Form?

This form is for an employer to classify employees as L-1 nonimmigrant intra-company transferees under a blanket L petition approval.

Who May File?

An employer who has already obtained approval of a blanket L-1 petition may file this form to classify employees outside the United States as executives, managers or specialized knowledge professionals. If the employee is in the United States and you are requesting a change of status or extension of stay for that employee, use Form I-129, Petition for a Nonimmigrant Worker.

General Filing Instructions.

Please answer all questions by typing or clearly printing in black ink. Indicate that an item is not applicable with "N/A." If the answer is "none" write "none."

If you need extra space to answer any item, attach a sheet of paper with your name and Alien Registration Number (A#), if any, and indicate the number of the item to which the answer related.

You must file your petition with the required **Initial Evidence.** Your petition must be properly signed. Retain a copy of the form and supporting documents for your records.

Translations. Any foreign language document must be accompanied by a full English translation that a translator has certified as complete and correct. The translator must also certify that he or she is competent to translate the foreign language into English.

Copies. If these instructions state that a copy of a document may be filed with this petition, and you choose to send us the original, we may keep that original for our records.

Initial Evidence.

You must file your petition with:

- A copy of the approval notice for the blanket petition;

- A letter from the alien's foreign qualifying employer detailing his or her dates of employment, job duties, qualifications and salary. The letter must also show that the alien worked for the employer for at least one continuous year in the three-year period preceeding the filing of the petition in an executive, managerial or specialized knowledge professional capacity; and

- If the alien is a specialized knowlege professional, a copy of a U.S. degree, a foreign degree equivalent to a U.S. degree, or evidence establishing that the combination of the beneficiary's education and experience is the equivalent of a U.S. degree.

Where to File.

If the alien requires a visa, he or she should present the completed petition at a U.S. embassy or consulate abroad.

If the alien is not required to obtain a visa, he or she should file this petition at the Service Center of the U.S. Citizenship and Immigration Services (USCIS) that approved the blanket petition.

Fee.

There is no fee for this petition.

Processing Information.

Acceptance. A petition that is not signed will be rejected with a notice that the petition is deficient. You may correct the deficiency and resubmit the petition. However, a petition is not considered properly filed until it is accepted by USCIS.

Initial processing. Once the petition has been accepted, it will be checked for completeness, including submission of the required initial evidence. If you do not completely fill out the form or file it without required initial evidence, you will not establish a basis for eligibility and we may deny your petition.

Requests for more information or interview. We may request more information or evidence or we may request that you appear at a USCIS office for an interview. We may also request that you submit the original of any copy. We will return these originals when they are no longer required.

Decision. You will be notified in writing of the decision on your petition. If you filed the petition at a USCIS service center and it is approved, the approval notice will be sent to you so you can send it to the beneficiary to present at a port of entry when he or she enters the United States.

Penalties.

If you knowingly and willfully falsify or conceal a material fact or submit a false document with this request, we will deny the benefit you are seeking and may deny any other immigration benefit. In addition, you will face severe penalties provided by law and you may be subjected to criminal prosecution.

Privacy Act Notice.

We ask for the information on this form and associated evidence to determine if you have established eligibility for the immigration benefit you are seeking. Our legal right to ask for this information is in 8 USC 1154. We may provide this information to other government agencies. Failure to provide this information and any requested evidence may delay a final decision or result in denial of your application.

Information and USCIS Forms.

For information on immigration laws, regulations, procedures and to order USCIS forms call our toll-free forms line at **1-800-870-3676**. You can also get USCIS forms and information on immigration laws, regulations and procedures by telephoning our **National Customer Service Center** toll-free at **1-800-375-5283** or visiting our internet website at **www.uscis.gov**.

Use InfoPass for Appointments.

As an altenative to waiting in line for assistance at your local USCIS office, you can now schedule an appointment through our internet-based system, **InfoPass**. To access the system, visit our website at **www.uscis.gov**. Use the **InfoPass** appointment scheduler and follow the screen prompts to set up your appointment. **InfoPass** generates an electronic appointment notice that appears on the screen. Print the notice and take it with you to your appointment. The notice gives the time and date of your appointment, along with the address of the USCIS office.

Paperwork Reduction Act Notice.

A person is not required to respond to a collection of information unless it displays a currently valid OMB control number. We try to create forms and instructions that are accurate, can be easily understood and that impose the least possible burden on you to provide us with information. Often this is difficult because some immigration laws are very complex.

The estimated average time to complete and file this application is as follows: (1) 10 minutes to learn about the law and form; (2) 10 minutes to complete the form; and (3) 15 minutes to assemble and file the petition; for a total estimated average of 35 minutes per application.

If you have comments regarding the accuracy of this estimate or suggestions for making this form simpler, you can write to the U.S. Citizenship and Immigration Services, Regulatory Management Division, 111 Massachusetts Avenue, N.W.,3rd Floor, Suite 3008 , Washington, D.C. 20529; OMB No. 1615-0010. **Do not mail your completed application to this address.**

OMB No. 1615-0010; Expires 12/31/09

Department of Homeland Security
U.S. Citizenship and Immigration Services

**I-129S, Nonimmigrant Petition
Based on Blanket L Petition**

START HERE - Please type or print in black ink.

Part 1. Information about employer.

Sponsoring Company of Organization's Name

Address - ATTN:

Street Number and Name   Room/Suite #

City or Town   State or Province   Country   Zip/Postal Code

Part 2. Information about employment.

This alien will be a:

a. ☐ Manager/Executive

b. ☐ Specialized knowledge professional

Blanket petition approval number:

Part 3. Information about employee.

Family Name   Given Name   Middle Name

Foreign Address: Street Number and Name   Room/Suite #

City or Town   State or Province   Country   Zip/Postal Code

Date of Birth *(mm/dd/yyyy)*   Country of Birth   Country of Citizenship/Nationality

Part 4. Additional information about the employment.

Address: Street Number and Name   Room/Suite #

City or Town   State or Province

Country   Zip/Postal Code

For USCIS Use Only	
Returned	**Receipt**
Date	
Date	
Resubmitted	
Date	
Date	
Reloc Sent	
Date	
Date	
Reloc Sent	
Date	
Date	
☐ Petitioner Interviewed on _____	
☐ Beneficiary Interviewed on _____	

Approved as:

☐ Manager/executive

☐ Specialized knowledge

on _____

Validity Dates:

From: _____

To: _____

Denied (Give reason)

Action Block

To Be Completed by

Attorney or Representative, if any.

☐ Fill in box if G-28 is attached to represent the petition.

ATTY State License #

Form I-129S (Rev. 01/16/07)N

Part 4. Additional Information about the employment. *(Continued.)*

Date of intended employment *(mm/dd/yyyy)*

From:

To:

Weekly Wage

$

Hours Per Week

$

Title and detailed description of duties to be performed.

Give the alien's dates of prior periods of stay in the United States in a work authorized capacity and the type of visa.

Give the alien's dates of employment and job duties for the immediate prior three years.

Summarize the alien's education and other work experience.

Form I-129S (Rev. 01/16/07)N Page 2

Part 5. Signature. *Read the information on penalties in the instructions before completing this section.*

I certify, under penalty of perjury under the laws of the United States of America, that this petition and the evidence submitted with it are all true and correct. I am filing this on behalf of an organization, and I certify that I am empowered to do so by that organization. If this petition is to extend a prior petition, I certify that the proposed employment is under the same terms and conditions as in the prior approved petition. I authorize the release of any information from my records, or from the petitioning organizations records that the U.S. Citizenship and Immigration Services needs to determine eligibility for the benefit being sought.

Signature

Date *(mm/dd/yyyy)*

Daytime Telephone Number *(with area code)*

(   )

E-Mail Address *(If any.)*

NOTE: If you do not completely fill out this form or fail to submit required documents listed in the instructions, the person(s) petitioned may not be found eligible for the requested benefit and this petition may be denied.

Part 6. Signature of person preparing form, if other than above. *(Sign below.)*

Signature

Print or Type Your Name

Date *(mm/dd/yyyy)*

Daytime Telephone Number *(with area code)*

(   )

E-Mail Address *(If any.)*

Firm Name and Address

Department of Homeland Security
U.S. Citizenship and Immigration Services

OMB #1615-0012; Expires 01/31/11

I-130, Petition for Alien Relative

DO NOT WRITE IN THIS BLOCK - FOR USCIS OFFICE ONLY

A#	Action Stamp	Fee Stamp

Section of Law/Visa Category
- [ ] 201(b) Spouse - IR-1/CR-1
- [ ] 201(b) Child - IR-2/CR-2
- [ ] 201(b) Parent - IR-5
- [ ] 203(a)(1) Unm. S or D - F1-1
- [ ] 203(a)(2)(A)Spouse - F2-1
- [ ] 203(a)(2)(A) Child - F2-2
- [ ] 203(a)(2)(B) Unm. S or D - F2-4
- [ ] 203(a)(3) Married S or D - F3-1
- [ ] 203(a)(4) Brother/Sister - F4-1

Petition was filed on: _____ (priority date)
- [ ] Personal Interview
- [ ] Pet. [ ] Ben. " A" File Reviewed
- [ ] Field Investigation
- [ ] 203(a)(2)(A) Resolved
- [ ] Previously Forwarded
- [ ] I-485 Filed Simultaneously
- [ ] 204(g) Resolved
- [ ] 203(g) Resolved

Remarks:

A. Relationship   You are the petitioner.   Your relative is the beneficiary.

1. I am filing this petition for my:
[ ] Husband/Wife [ ] Parent [ ] Brother/Sister [ ] Child

2. Are you related by adoption?
[ ] Yes [ ] No

3. Did you gain permanent residence through adoption?
[ ] Yes [ ] No

B. Information about you

1. Name (Family name in CAPS)   (First)   (Middle)

2. Address (Number and Street)   (Apt. No.)

(Town or City)   (State/Country)   (Zip/Postal Code)

3. Place of Birth (Town or City)   (State/Country)

4. Date of Birth

5. Gender
[ ] Male [ ] Female

6. Marital Status
[ ] Married [ ] Single [ ] Widowed [ ] Divorced

7. Other Names Used (including maiden name)

8. Date and Place of Present Marriage (if married)

9. U.S. Social Security Number (If any)

10. Alien Registration Number

11. Name(s) of Prior Husband(s)/Wive(s)

12. Date(s) Marriage(s) Ended

13. If you are a U.S. citizen, complete the following:

My citizenship was acquired through (check one):
[ ] Birth in the U.S.
[ ] Naturalization. Give certificate number and date and place of issuance.

_____

[ ] Parents. Have you obtained a certificate of citizenship in your own name?
[ ] Yes. Give certificate number, date and place of issuance. [ ] No

14. If you are a lawful permanent resident alien, complete the following:

Date and place of admission for or adjustment to lawful permanent residence and class of admission.

14b. Did you gain permanent resident status through marriage to a U.S. citizen or lawful permanent resident?
[ ] Yes [ ] No

C. Information about your relative

1. Name (Family name in CAPS)   (First)   (Middle)

2. Address (Number and Street)   (Apt. No.)

(Town or City)   (State/Country)   (Zip/Postal Code)

3. Place of Birth (Town or City)   (State/Country)

4. Date of Birth

5. Gender
[ ] Male [ ] Female

6. Marital Status
[ ] Married [ ] Single [ ] Widowed [ ] Divorced

7. Other Names Used (including maiden name)

8. Date and Place of Present Marriage (if married)

9. U.S. Social Security Number (If any)

10. Alien Registration Number

11. Name(s) of Prior Husband(s)/Wive(s)

12. Date(s) Marriage(s) Ended

13. Has your relative ever been in the U.S.? [ ] Yes [ ] No

14. If your relative is currently in the U.S., complete the following:
He or she arrived as a:
(visitor, student, stowaway, without inspection, etc.)

Arrival/Departure Record (I-94)   Date arrived

Date authorized stay expired, or will expire, as shown on Form I-94 or I-95

15. Name and address of present employer (if any)

Date this employment began

16. Has your relative ever been under immigration proceedings?
[ ] No [ ] Yes Where _____ When _____
[ ] Removal [ ] Exclusion/Deportation [ ] Rescission [ ] Judicial Proceedings

INITIAL RECEIPT	RESUBMITTED	RELOCATED: Rec'd	Sent	COMPLETED: Appv'd	Denied	Ret'd

Form I-130 (Rev. 05/27/08)Y

C. Information about your alien relative (continued)

17. List husband/wife and all children of your relative.

(Name)   (Relationship)   (Date of Birth)   (Country of Birth)

_____

_____

_____

_____

18. Address in the United States where your relative intends to live.

(Street Address)   (Town or City)   (State)

_____

19. Your relative's address abroad. (Include street, city, province and country)   Phone Number (if any)

_____

20. If your relative's native alphabet is other than Roman letters, write his or her name and foreign address in the native alphabet.

(Name)   Address (Include street, city, province and country):

_____

21. If filing for your husband/wife, give last address at which you lived together. (Include street, city, province, if any, and country):

                                                                                From: To:

22. Complete the information below if your relative is in the United States and will apply for adjustment of status.

Your relative is in the United States and will apply for adjustment of status to that of a lawful permanent resident at the USCIS office in:
                                    If your relative is not eligible for adjustment of status, he or she will apply for a
                                    visa abroad at the American consular post in:

_____   _____
(City)   (State)   (City)   (Country

NOTE: Designation of a U.S. embassy or consulate outside the country of your relative's last residence does not guarantee acceptance for processing by that post. Acceptance is at the discretion of the designated embassy or consulate.

D. Other information

1. If separate petitions are also being submitted for other relatives, give names of each and relationship.

_____

2. Have you ever before filed a petition for this or any other alien? ☐ Yes ☐ No

If "Yes," give name, place and date of filing and result.

_____

WARNING: USCIS investigates claimed relationships and verifies the validity of documents. USCIS seeks criminal prosecutions when family relationships are falsified to obtain visas.

PENALTIES: By law, you may be imprisoned for not more than five years or fined $250,000, or both, for entering into a marriage contract for the purpose of evading any provision of the immigration laws. In addition, you may be fined up to $10,000 and imprisoned for up to five years, or both, for knowingly and willfully falsifying or concealing a material fact or using any false document in submitting this petition.

YOUR CERTIFICATION: I certify, under penalty of perjury under the laws of the United States of America, that the foregoing is true and correct. Furthermore, I authorize the release of any information from my records that U.S. Citizenship and Immigration Services needs to determine eligiblity for the benefit that I am seeking.

E. Signature of petitioner.

                                    Date   Phone Number ( )

F. Signature of person preparing this form, if other than the petitioner.

I declare that I prepared this document at the request of the person above and that it is based on all information of which I have any knowledge.

Print Name _____   Signature _____   Date _____

Address _____   G-28 ID or VOLAG Number, if any. _____

Form I-130 (Rev. 05/27/08)Y Page 2

Department of Homeland Security
U. S. Citizenship and Immigration Services

OMB No. 1615-0013; Expires 02/28/09

I-131, Application for Travel Document

DO NOT WRITE IN THIS BLOCK	FOR USCIS USE ONLY (except G-28 block below)

Document Issued
☐ Reentry Permit
☐ Refugee Travel Document
☐ Single Advance Parole
☐ Multiple Advance Parole
Valid to:

If Reentry Permit or Refugee Travel Document, mail to:
☐ Address in Part 1
☐ American embassy/consulate at:
☐ Overseas DHS office at:

Action Block

Receipt

☐ Document Hand Delivered
On _____ By _____

To be completed by Attorney/Representative, if any.
Attorney State License #
☐ Check box if G-28 is attached.

Part 1.   Information about you. *(Please type or print in black ink.)*

1. A #

2. Date of Birth *(mm/dd/yyyy)*

3. Class of Admission

4. Gender   Male ☐   Female ☐

5. Name *(Family name in capital letters)*   *(First)*   *(Middle)*

6. Address *(Number and Street)*   Apt. #

City   State or Province   Zip/Postal Code   Country

7. Country of Birth   **8.** Country of Citizenship   **9.** Social Security # *(if any.)*

Part 2.   Application type *(check one).*

a. ☐ I am a permanent resident or conditional resident of the United States, and I am applying for a reentry permit.

b. ☐ I now hold U.S. refugee or asylee status and I am applying for a refugee travel document.

c. ☐ I am a permanent resident as a direct result of refugee or asylee status, and I am applying for a refugee travel document.

d. ☐ I am applying for an advance parole document to allow me to return to the United States after temporary foreign travel.

e. ☐ I am outside the United States and I am applying for an advance parole document.

f. ☐ I am applying for an advance parole document for a person who is outside the United States. *If you checked box "f", provide the following information about that person:*

1. Name *(Family name in capital letters)*   *(First)*   *(Middle)*

2. Date of Birth *(mm/dd/yyyy)*   **3.** Country of Birth   **4.** Country of Citizenship

5. Address *(Number and Street)*   Apt. #   Daytime Telephone # *(area/country code)*

City   State or Province   Zip/Postal Code   Country

Form I-131 (Rev. 05/27/08)Y

Part 3. Processing information.

1. Date of Intended Departure *(mm/dd/yyyy)*

2. Expected Length of Trip

3. Are you, or any person included in this application, now in exclusion, deportation, removal, or recission proceedings? ☐ No ☐ Yes *(Name of DHS office)*:

If you are applying for an Advance Parole Document, skip to Part 7.

4. Have you ever before been issued a reentry permit or refugee travel? ☐ No ☐ Yes *(Give the following information for the last document issued to you)*:

Date Issued *(mm/dd/yyyy)*:

Disposition *(attached, lost, etc.)*:

5. Where do you want this travel document sent? *(Check one)*

a. ☐ To the U.S. address shown in **Part 1** on the first page of this form.

b. ☐ To a U.S. Embassy or consulate at: City: Country:

c. ☐ To a DHS office overseas at: City: Country:

d. If you checked "b" or "c", where should the notice to pick up the travel document be sent?

☐ To the address shown in **Part 2** on the first page of this form.

☐ To the address shown below:

Address *(Number and Street)* Apt. # Daytime Telephone # *(area/country code)*

City State or Province Zip/Postal Code Country

Part 4. Information about your proposed travel.

Purpose of trip. *If you need more room, continue on a seperate sheet(s) of paper.*

List the countries you intend to visit.

Part 5. Complete only if applying for a reentry permit.

Since becoming a permanent resident of the United States (or during the past five years, whichever is less) how much total time have you spent outside the United States?

☐ less than six months ☐ two to three years
☐ six months to one year ☐ three to four years
☐ one to two years ☐ more than four years

Since you became a permanent resident of the United States, have you ever filed a federal income tax return as a nonresident, or failed to file a federal income tax return because you considered yourself to be a nonresident? *(If "Yes," give details on a separate sheet(s) of paper.)* ☐ Yes ☐ No

Part 6. Complete only if applying for a refugee travel document.

1. Country from which you are a refugee or asylee:

If you answer "Yes" to any of the following questions, you must explain on a separate sheet(s) of paper.

2. Do you plan to travel to the above named country? ☐ Yes ☐ No

3. Since you were accorded refugee/asylee status, have you ever:
   a. returned to the above named country? ☐ Yes ☐ No
   b. applied for and/or obtained a national passport, passport renewal or entry permit of that country? ☐ Yes ☐ No
   c. applied for and/or received any benefit from such country (for example, health insurance benefits). ☐ Yes ☐ No

4. Since you were accorded refugee/asylee status, have you, by any legal procedure or voluntary act:
   a. reacquired the nationality of the above named country? ☐ Yes ☐ No
   b. acquired a new nationality? ☐ Yes ☐ No
   c. been granted refugee or asylee status in any other country? ☐ Yes ☐ No

Form I-131 (Rev. 05/27/08)Y Page 2

Part 7. Complete only if applying for advance parole.

On a separate sheet(s) of paper, please explain how you qualify for an advance parole document and what circumstances warrant issuance of advance parole. Include copies of any documents you wish considered. *(See instructions.)*

1. For how many trips do you intend to use this document? ☐ One trip ☐ More than one trip

2. If the person intended to receive an advance parole document is outside the United States, provide the location (city and country) of the U.S. Embassy or consulate or the DHS overseas office that you want us to notify.

City

Country

3. If the travel document will be delivered to an overseas office, where should the notice to pick up the document be sent:

☐ To the address shown in **Part 2** on the first page of this form.

☐ To the address shown below:

Address *(Number and Street)* Apt. # Daytime Telephone # *(area/country code)*

City State or Province Zip/Postal Code Country

Part 8. Signature. *Read the information on penalties in the instructions before completing this section. If you are filing for a reentry permit or refugee travel document, you must be in the United States to file this application.*

I certify, under penalty of perjury under the laws of the United States of America, that this application and the evidence submitted with it are all true and correct. I authorize the release of any information from my records that U.S. Citizenship and Immigration Services needs to determine eligibility for the benefit I am seeking.

Signature Date *(mm/dd/yyyy)* **Daytime Telephone Number** *(with area code)*

Please Note: If you do not completely fill out this form or fail to submit required documents listed in the instructions, you may not be found eligible for the requested document and this application may be denied.

Part 9. Signature of person preparing form, if other than the applicant. *(Sign below.)*

I declare that I prepared this application at the request of the applicant, and it is based on all information of which I have knowledge.

Signature Print or Type Your Name

Firm Name and Address Daytime Telephone Number *(with area code)*

Fax Number *(if any.)* Date *(mm/dd/yyyy)*

Department of Homeland Security
U.S. Citizenship and Immigration Services

OMB No. 1615-0014; Exp. 04-30-07

I-134, Affidavit of Support

Instructions

I. Execution of Affidavit.

A separate affidavit must be submitted for each person. As the sponsor, you must sign the affidavit in your full, true and correct name and affirm or make it under oath.

- If you are **in the United States**, the affidavit may be sworn to or affirmed before an officer of U.S. Citizenship and Immigration Services (USCIS) without the payment of fee, or before a notary public or other officers authorized to administer oaths for general purposes, in which case the official seal or certificate of authority to administer oaths must be affixed.

- If you are **outside the United States,** the affidavit must be sworn to or **notice** affirmed before a U.S. consular or immigration officer.

How you submit the form depends on whether the alien you are sponsoring is in or outside the United States and what type of application is being submitted. See the instructions provided with the corresponding application for detailed information on how to submit this affidavit of support form.

II. Supporting Evidence.

As the sponsor, you must show you have sufficient income and/or financial resources to assure that the alien you are sponsoring will not become a public charge while in the United States.

Evidence should consist of copies of any or all of the following documentation listed below that are applicable to your situation.

Failure to provide evidence of sufficient income and/or financial resources may result in the denial of the alien's application for a visa or his or her removal from the United States.

The sponsor must submit in duplicate evidence of income and resources, as appropriate:

A. Statement from an officer of the bank or other financial institutions where you have deposits, identifying the following details regarding your account:

　1. Date account opened;

　2. Total amount deposited for the past year;

　3. Present balance.

B. Statement of your employer on business stationery, revealing:

　1. Date and nature of employment;

　2. Salary paid;

　3. Whether the position is temporary or permanent.

C. If self-employed:

　1. Copy of last income tax return filed; or

　2. Report of commercial rating concern.

D. List containing serial numbers and denominations of bonds and name of record owner(s).

III. Sponsor and Alien Liability.

Effective October 1, 1980, amendments to section 1614(f) of the Social Security Act and Part A of Title XVI of the Social Security Act establish certain requirements for determining the eligibility of aliens who apply for the first time for Supplemental Security Income (SSI) benefits.

Effective October 1, 1981, amendments to section 415 of the Social Security Act established similar requirements for determining the eligibility of aliens who apply for the first time for Aid to Families with Dependent Children (AFDC), currently administered under Temporary Assistance for Needy Families (TANF). Effective December 22, 1981, amendents to the Food Stamp Act of 1977 affect the eligibility of alien participation in the Food Stamp Program.

These amendments require that the income and resources of any person who, as the sponsor of an alien's entry into the United States, executes an affidavit of support or similar agreement on behalf of the alien, and the income and resources of the sponsor's spouse (if living with the sponsor) shall be deemed to be the income and resources of the alien under formulas for determining eligibility for SSI, TANF and Food Stamp benefits during the three years following the alien's entry into the United States.

Documentation on Income and Resources.

An alien applying for SSI must make available to the Social Security Administration documentation concerning his / her income and resources and those of the sponsor, including information that was provided in support of the corresponding application.

Form I-134 (Rev. 02/28/07)Y

An alien applying for TANF or Food Stamps must make similar information available to the State public assistance agency.

The Secretary of Health and Human Services and the Secretary of Agriculture are authorized to obtain copies of any such documentation submitted to USCIS or the U.S. Department of State and to release such documentation to a State public assistance agency.

Joint and Several Liability Issues.

Sections 1621(e) of the Social Security Act and subsection 5(i) of the Food Stamp Act also provide that an alien and his or her sponsor shall be jointly and severally liable to repay any SSI, TANF or Food Stamp benefits that are incorrectly paid because of mis-information provided by a sponsor or because of a sponsor's failure to provide information, except where the sponsor was without fault or where good cause existed.

Incorrect payments that are not repaid will be withheld from any subsequent payments for which the alien or sponsor are otherwise eligible under the Social Security Act or Food Stamp Act.

These provisions do not apply to SSI, TANF or Food Stamp eligibility of aliens admitted as refugees, granted asylum or Cuban/ Haitian entrants as defined in section 501(e) of P.L. 96-422, and to dependent children of the sponsor or sponsor's spouse.

IV. Information and USCIS Forms.

For information on immigration laws, regulations and procedures or to order USCIS forms, call our National Customer Service Center at **1-800-375-5283** or visit our website at **www.uscis.gov.**

V. Use InfoPass for Appointments.

As an alternative to waiting in line for assistance at your local USCIS office, you can now schedule an appointment through our internet-based system, **InfoPass**. To access the system, visit our website at **www.uscis.gov**. Use the **InfoPass** appointment scheduler and follow the screen prompts to set up your appointment. **InfoPass** generates an electronic appointment notice that appears on the screen. Print the notice and take it with you to your appointment. The notice gives the time and date of your appointment, along with the address of the USCIS office.

VI. Privacy Act Notice.

We ask for the information on this form and associated evidence to determine if you have established eligibility for the immigration benefit you are seeking. We may provide this information to other government agencies. Failure to provide this information and any requested evidence may delay a final decision or result in denial of your request.

Authority for the collection of the information requested on this form is contained in 8 U.S.C. 1182(a)(4),1183(a),1184(a) and 1258.

The information will be used principally by USCIS, or by any consular officer to whom it may be furnished, to support an alien's application for benefits under the Immigration and Nationality Act and specifically the assertion that he or she has adequate means of financial support and will not become a public charge. Submission of the information is voluntary.

However, failure to provide the information may result in the denial of the alien's application.

The information may also as a matter of routine use be disclosed to other federal, state, local and foreign law enforcement and regulatory agencies, including the Department of Health and Human Services, Department of Agriculture, Department of State, Department of Defense and any component thereof (if the deponent has served or is serving in the armed forces of the United States), Central Intelligence Agency, and individuals and organizations during the course of any investigation to elicit further information required to carry out USCIS functions.

VII. Paperwork Reduction Act Notice.

You are not required to respond to this form unless it displays a currently valid OMB control number.

We try to create forms and instructions that are accurate, can be easily understood and impose the least possible burden on you to provide us with information. Often this is difficult because some immigration laws are very complex.

The estimated average time to complete and file this notice is 15 minutes.

If you have comments regarding the accuracy of this estimate, or suggestions for making this form simpler, you may write to: U.S. Citizenship and Immigration Services, Regulatory Management Division, 111 Massachusetts Avenue, N.W., 3rd Floor, Suite 3008, Washington, DC 20529. **Do not mail your completed affidavit of support to this addre**ss.

Form I-134 (Rev. 02/28/07)Y Page 2

Department of Homeland Security
U.S. Citizenship and Immigration Services

OMB No. 1615-0014; Exp. 04-30-07

I-134, Affidavit of Support

(Answer all items. Type or print in black ink.)

I, _____ residing at _____
　　　　　　(Name)　　　　　　　　　　　　　　　　　(Street and Number)

_____
　　(City)　　　　　　　(State)　　　　(Zip Code if in U.S.)　　　　(Country)

Being duly sworn depose and say:

1. I was born on _____ at _____
　　　　　　　(Date-mm/dd/yyyy)　　　　　　　(City)　　　　　　　(Country)

If you are **not** a native born U.S. citizen, answer the following as appropriate:

a. If a U.S.citizen through naturalization, give certificate of naturalization number

b. If a U.S. citizen through parent(s) or marriage, give citizenship certificate number

c. If U.S. citizenship was derived by some other method, attach a statement of explanation.

d. If a lawfully admitted permanent resident of the United States, give "A" number

2. I am _____ years of age and have resided in the United States since (date)

3. This affidavit is executed on behalf of the following person:

Name (Family Name)	(First Name)	(Middle Name)	Gender	Age
Citizen of (Country)		Marital Status	Relationship to Sponsor	
Presently resides at (Street and Number)	(City)	(State)	(Country)	

Name of spouse and children accompanying or following to join person

Spouse	Gender	Age	Child	Gender	Age
Child	Gender	Age	Child	Gender	Age
Child	Gender	Age	Child	Gender	Age

4. This affidavit is made by me for the purpose of assuring the U.S. Government that the person(s) named in item (**3**) will not become a public charge in the United States.

5. I am willing and able to receive, maintain and support the person(s) named in item **3**. That I am ready and willing to deposit a bond, if necessary, to guarantee that such person(s) will not become a public charge during his or her stay in the United States, or to guarantee that the above named person(s) will maintain his or her nonimmigrant status, if admitted temporarily and will depart prior to the expiration of his or her authorized stay in the United States.

6. I understand this affidavit will be binding upon me for a period of three (3) years after entry of the person(s) named in item (**3**) and that the information and documentation provided by me may be made available to the Secretary of Health and Human Services and the Secretary of Agriculture, who may make it available to a public assistance agency.

7. I am employed as or engaged in the business of _____ with _____
　　　　　　　　　　　　　　　　　　　　　　　　　(Type of Business)　　　　　　　(Name of Concern)

at _____
　　(Street and Number)　　　　　　(City)　　　　　(State)　　　　(Zip Code)

I derive an annual income of: (*If self-employed, I have attached a copy of my last income tax return or report of commercial rating concern which I certify to be true and correct to the best of my knowledge and belief. See instructions for nature of evidence of net worth to be submitted.*)　　　　　　　　　　$ _____

I have on deposit in savings banks in the United States:　　　　　　$ _____

I have other personal property, the reasonable value of which is:　　$ _____

Form I-134 (Rev. 02/28/07) Y

I have stocks and bonds with the following market value, as indicated on the attached list, which I certify to be true and correct to the best of my knowledge and belief: $ _____

I have life insurance in the sum of: $ _____

With a cash surrender value of: $ _____

I own real estate valued at: $ _____

With mortgage(s) or other encumbrance(s) thereon amounting to: $ _____

Which is located at: _____

| (Street and Number) | (City) | (State) | (Zip Code) |

8. The following persons are dependent upon me for support: *(Place an "x" in the appropriate column to indicate whether the person named is **wholly** or **partially** dependent upon you for support.)*

Name of Person	Wholly Dependent	Partially Dependent	Age	Relationship to Me
	☐	☐		
	☐	☐		
	☐	☐		

9. I have previously submitted affidavit(s) of support for the following person(s). If none, state none.

Name	Date submitted

10. I have submitted a visa petition(s) to U.S. Citizenship and Immigration Services (USCIS) on behalf of the following person(s). If none, state none.

Name	Relationship	Date submitted

11. I ☐ intend ☐ do not intend to make specific contributions to the support of the person(s) named in item **3**. *(If you check "intend," indicate the exact nature and duration of the contributions. For example, if you intend to furnish room and board, state for how long and, if money, state the amount in U.S. dollars and state whether it is to be given in a lump sum, weekly or monthly, and for how long.)*

Oath or Affirmation of Sponsor.

I acknowledge that I have read Part III of the Instructions, Sponsor and Alien Liability, and am aware of my responsibilities as a sponsor under the Social Security Act, as amended, and the Food Stamp Act, as amended.

I swear (affirm) that I know the contents of this affidavit signed by me and that the statements are true and correct.

Signature of sponsor _____

Subscribed and sworn to (affirmed) before me this _____ **day of** _____, _____

at _____. **My commission expires on** _____

Signature of Officer Administering Oath _____ **Title** _____

If the affidavit is prepared by someone other than the sponsor, please complete the following: I declare that this document was prepared by me at the request of the sponsor and is based on all information of which I have knowledge.

| (Signature) | (Address) | (Date) |

OMB No. 1615-0015; Exp. 10/31/08

Department of Homeland Security
U.S. Citizenship and Immigration Services

Form I-140, Immigrant
Petition for Alien Worker

START HERE - Please type or print in black ink.	**For USCIS Use Only**

Part 1. **Information about the person or organization filing this petition.** If an individual is filing, use the top name line. Organizations should use the second line.

For USCIS Use Only	
Returned	Receipt
Date	
Date	
Resubmitted	
Date	
Date	
Reloc Sent	
Date	
Date	
Reloc Rec'd	
Date	
Date	

Family Name (Last Name)   Given Name (First Name)   Full Middle Name

Company or Organization Name

Address: (Street Number and Name)   Suite #

Attn:

City   State/Province

Country   Zip/Postal Code

IRS Tax #   U.S. Social Security # *(if any)*   E-Mail Address *(if any)*

Part 2. Petition type.

This petition is being filed for: *(Check one.)*

a. ☐ An alien of extraordinary ability.
b. ☐ An outstanding professor or researcher.
c. ☐ A multinational executive or manager.
d. ☐ A member of the professions holding an advanced degree or an alien of exceptional ability (who is NOT seeking a National Interest Waiver).
e. ☐ A professional (at a minimum, possessing a bachelor's degree or a foreign degree equivalent to a U.S. bachelor's degree) or a skilled worker (requiring at least two years of specialized training or experience).
f. ☐ (Reserved.)
g. ☐ Any other worker (requiring less than two years of training or experience).
h. ☐ Soviet Scientist.
i. ☐ An alien applying for a National Interest Waiver (who **IS** a member of the professions holding an advanced degree or an alien of exceptional ability).

Classification:
☐ 203(b)(1)(A) Alien of Extraordinary Ability
☐ 203(b)(1)(B) Outstanding Professor or Researcher
☐ 203(b)(1)(C) Multi-National Executive or Manager
☐ 203(b)(2) Member of Professions w/Adv. Degree or Exceptional Ability
☐ 203(b)(3)(A)(i) Skilled Worker
☐ 203(b)(3)(A)(ii) Professional
☐ 203(b)(3)(A)(iii) Other Worker

Certification:
☐ National Interest Waiver (NIW)
☐ Schedule A, Group I
☐ Schedule A, Group II

Priority Date	Consulate

Part 3. Information about the person you are filing for.

Family Name (Last Name)   Given Name (First Name)   Full Middle Name

Address: (Street Number and Name)   Apt. #

C/O: (In Care Of)

City   State/Province

Country   Zip/Postal Code   E-Mail Address *(if any)*

Daytime Phone # *(with area/country codes)*   Date of Birth *(mm/dd/yyyy)*

City/Town/Village of Birth   State/Province of Birth   Country of Birth

Country of Nationality/Citizenship   A # *(if any)*   U.S. Social Security # *(if any)*

Concurrent Filing:
☐ **I-485 filed concurrently.**

Remarks

Action Block

To Be Completed by
Attorney or Representative, if any.
☐ Fill in box if G-28 is attached to represent the applicant.

ATTY State License #

If in the U.S.	Date of Arrival *(mm/dd/yyyy)*	I-94 # *(Arrival/Departure Document)*
	Current Nonimmigrant Status	Date Status Expires *(mm/dd/yyyy)*

Form I-140 (Rev. 05/16/08) Y

Part 4. Processing Information.

1. Please complete the following for the person named in **Part 3**: *(Check one)*

☐ Alien will apply for a visa abroad at the American Embassy or Consulate at:

City

Foreign Country

☐ Alien is in the United States and will apply for adjustment of status to that of lawful permanent resident.

Alien's country of current residence or, if now in the U.S., last permanent residence abroad.

2. If you provided a U.S. address in **Part 3**, print the person's foreign address:

3. If the person's native alphabet is other than Roman letters, write the person's foreign name and address in the native alphabet:

4. Are any other petition(s) or application(s) being filed with this Form I-140?

☐ No ☐ Yes-(check all that apply)

☐ Form I-485 ☐ Form I-765
☐ Form I-131 ☐ Other - Attach an explanation.

5. Is the person you are filing for in removal proceedings? ☐ No ☐ Yes-Attach an explanation.

6. Has any immigrant visa petition ever been filed by or on behalf of this person? ☐ No ☐ Yes-Attach an explanation.

If you answered yes to any of these questions, please provide the case number, office location, date of decision and disposition of the decision on a separate sheet(s) of paper.

Part 5. Additional information about the petitioner.

1. Type of petitioner *(Check one.)*

☐ Employer ☐ Self ☐ Other (Explain, e.g., Permanent Resident, U.S. citizen or any other person filing on behalf of the alien.)

2. If a company, give the following:

Type of Business

Date Established *(mm/dd/yyyy)*

Current Number of Employees

Gross Annual Income

Net Annual Income

NAICS Code

DOL/ETA Case Number

3. If an individual, give the following:

Occupation

Annual Income

Part 6. Basic information about the proposed employment.

1. Job Title

2. SOC Code

3. Nontechnical Description of Job

4. Address where the person will work if different from address in **Part 1**.

5. Is this a full-time position?

☐ Yes ☐ No

6. If the answer to **Number 5** is "No," how many hours per week for the position?

7. Is this a permanent position?

☐ Yes ☐ No

8. Is this a new position?

☐ Yes ☐ No

9. Wages per week

$

Form I-140 (Rev. 05/16/08) Y Page 2

Part 7. Information on spouse and all children of the person for whom you are filing.

List husband/wife and all children related to the individual for whom the petition is being filed. Provide an attachment of additional family members, if needed.

Name *(First/Middle/Last)*	Relationship	Date of Birth *(mm/dd/yyyy)*	Country of Birth

Part 8. Signature.

*Read the information on penalties in the instructions before completing this section. If someone helped you prepare this petition, he or she must complete **Part 9**.*

I certify, under penalty of perjury under the laws of the United States of America, that this petition and the evidence submitted with it are all true and correct. I authorize U.S. Citizenship and Immigration Services to release to other government agencies any information from my USCIS (or former INS) records, if USCIS determines that such action is necessary to determine eligibility for the benefit sought.

Petitioner's Signature   **Daytime Phone Number** *(Area/Country Codes)*   **E-Mail Address**

Print Name   **Date** *(mm/dd/yyyy)*

NOTE: *If you do not fully complete this form or fail to submit the required documents listed in the instructions, a final decision on your petition may be delayed or the petition may be denied.*

Part 9. Signature of person preparing form, if other than above. *(Sign below.)*

I declare that I prepared this petition at the request of the above person and it is based on all information of which I have knowledge.

Attorney or Representative: In the event of a Request for Evidence (RFE), may the USCIS contact you by Fax or E-mail? ☐ Yes ☐ No

Signature   **Print Name**   **Date** *(mm/dd/yyyy)*

Firm Name and Address

Daytime Phone Number *(Area/Country Codes)*   **Fax Number** *(Area/Country Codes)*   **E-Mail Address**

OMB No. 1615-0023; Expires 09/30/08

Department of Homeland Security
U.S. Citizenship and Immigration Services

**I-485, Application to Register
Permanent Residence or Adjust Status**

START HERE - Please type or print in black ink.	For USCIS Use Only	
Part 1. Information about you.	**Returned**	**Receipt**

Family Name	Given Name	Middle Name

Address- C/O

Street Number and Name		Apt. #

City

State		Zip Code

Date of Birth (*mm/dd/yyyy*)	Country of Birth:
	Country of Citizenship/Nationality:

U.S. Social Security #	A # (*if any*)

Date of Last Arrival (*mm/dd/yyyy*)	I-94 #

Current USCIS Status	Expires on (*mm/dd/yyyy*)

For USCIS Use Only

Returned	Receipt
Resubmitted	
Reloc Sent	
Reloc Rec'd	
Applicant Interviewed	

Part 2.   Application Type. (*Check one.*)

I am applying for an adjustment to permanent resident status because:

a. ☐ An immigrant petition giving me an immediately available immigrant visa number has been approved. (Attach a copy of the approval notice, or a relative, special immigrant juvenile, or special immigrant military visa petition filed with this application that will give you an immediately available visa number, if approved.)

b. ☐ My spouse or parent applied for adjustment of status or was granted lawful permanent residence in an immigrant visa category that allows derivative status for spouses and children.

c. ☐ I entered as a K-1 fiancé(e) of a U.S. citizen whom I married within 90 days of entry, or I am the K-2 child of such a fiancé(e). (Attach a copy of the fiancé(e) petition approval notice and the marriage certificate).

d. ☐ I was granted asylum or derivative asylum status as the spouse or child of a person granted asylum and am eligible for adjustment.

e. ☐ I am a native or citizen of Cuba admitted or paroled into the United States after January 1, 1959, and thereafter have been physically present in the United States for at least one year.

f. ☐ I am the husband, wife, or minor unmarried child of a Cuban described above in **(e),** and I am residing with that person, and was admitted or paroled into the United States after January 1, 1959, and thereafter have been physically present in the United States for at least one year.

g. ☐ I have continuously resided in the United States since before January 1, 1972.

h. ☐ Other basis of eligibility. Explain (for example, I was admitted as a refugee, my status has not been terminated, and I have been physically present in the United States for one year after admission). If additional space is needed, use a separate piece of paper.

I am already a permanent resident and am applying to have the date I was granted permanent
residence adjusted to the date I originally arrived in the United States as a nonimmigrant or
parolee, or as of May 2, 1964, whichever date is later, and: (*Check one.*)

i. ☐ I am a native or citizen of Cuba and meet the description in **(e)** above.

j. ☐ I am the husband, wife, or minor unmarried child of a Cuban and meet the description in **(f)** above.

Section of Law

☐ Sec. 209(b), INA
☐ Sec. 13, Act of 9/11/57
☐ Sec. 245, INA
☐ Sec. 249, INA
☐ Sec. 1 Act of 11/2/66
☐ Sec. 2 Act of 11/2/66
☐ Other

Country Chargeable

Eligibility Under Sec. 245

☐ Approved Visa Petition
☐ Dependent of Principal Alien
☐ Special Immigrant
☐ Other

Preference

Action Block

To be Completed by
Attorney or Representative, if any
☐ Fill in box if G-28 is attached to represent the applicant.

VOLAG #

ATTY State License #

Form I-485 (Rev. 05/27/08) Y

Part 3. Processing Information.

A. City/Town/Village of Birth

Current Occupation

Your Mother's First Name

Your Father's First Name

Give your name exactly as it appears on your Arrival/Departure Record (Form I-94)

Place of Last Entry Into the United States *(City/State)*

In what status did you last enter? *(Visitor, student, exchange alien, crewman, temporary worker, without inspection, etc.)*

Were you inspected by a U.S. Immigration Officer? ☐ Yes ☐ No

Nonimmigrant Visa Number

Consulate Where Visa Was Issued

Date Visa Was Issued (mm/dd/yyyy) — Gender: ☐ Male ☐ Female

Marital Status: ☐ Married ☐ Single ☐ Divorced ☐ Widowed

Have you ever before applied for permanent resident status in the U.S.? ☐ No ☐ Yes. If you checked "Yes," give date and place of filing and final disposition.

B. List your present husband/wife, all of your sons and daughters (If you have none, write "none." If additional space is needed, use separate paper).

Family Name	Given Name	Middle Initial	Date of Birth *(mm/dd/yyyy)*
Country of Birth	Relationship	A #	Applying with you? ☐ Yes ☐ No
Family Name	Given Name	Middle Initial	Date of Birth *(mm/dd/yyyy)*
Country of Birth	Relationship	A #	Applying with you? ☐ Yes ☐ No
Family Name	Given Name	Middle Initial	Date of Birth *(mm/dd/yyyy)*
Country of Birth	Relationship	A #	Applying with you? ☐ Yes ☐ No
Family Name	Given Name	Middle Initial	Date of Birth *(mm/dd/yyyy)*
Country of Birth	Relationship	A #	Applying with you? ☐ Yes ☐ No
Family Name	Given Name	Middle Initial	Date of Birth *(mm/dd/yyyy)*
Country of Birth	Relationship	A #	Applying with you? ☐ Yes ☐ No

C. List your present and past membership in or affiliation with every organization, association, fund, foundation, party, club, society, or similar group in the United States or in other places since your 16th birthday. Include any foreign military service in this part. If none, write "none." Include the name(s) of organization(s), location(s), dates of membership from and to, and the nature of the organization(s). If additional space is needed, use a separate piece of paper.

Form I-485 (Rev. 05/27/08) Y Page 2

Part 3. Processing Information. *(Continued)*

Please answer the following questions. (If your answer is **"Yes"** on any one of these questions, explain on a separate piece of paper and refer to "What Are the General Filing Instructions? Initial Evidence" to determine what documentation to include with your application. Answering **"Yes"** does not necessarily mean that you are not entitled to adjust status or register for permanent residence.)

1. Have you ever, in or outside the United States:

   a. Knowingly committed any crime of moral turpitude or a drug-related offense for which you have not been arrested? ☐ Yes ☐ No

   b. Been arrested, cited, charged, indicted, fined, or imprisoned for breaking or violating any law or ordinance, excluding traffic violations? ☐ Yes ☐ No

   c. Been the beneficiary of a pardon, amnesty, rehabilitation decree, other act of clemency, or similar action? ☐ Yes ☐ No

   d. Exercised diplomatic immunity to avoid prosecution for a criminal offense in the United States? ☐ Yes ☐ No

2. Have you received public assistance in the United States from any source, including the U.S.Government or any State, county, city, or municipality (other than emergency medical treatment), or are you likely to receive public assistance in the future? ☐ Yes ☐ No

3. Have you ever:

   a. Within the past ten years been a prostitute or procured anyone for prostitution, or intend to engage in such activities in the future? ☐ Yes ☐ No

   b. Engaged in any unlawful commercialized vice, including, but not limited to, illegal gambling? ☐ Yes ☐ No

   c. Knowingly encouraged, induced, assisted, abetted, or aided any alien to try to enter the United States illegally? ☐ Yes ☐ No

   d. Illicitly trafficked in any controlled substance, or knowingly assisted, abetted, or colluded in the illicit trafficking of any controlled substance? ☐ Yes ☐ No

4. Have you ever engaged in, conspired to engage in, or do you intend to engage in, or have you ever solicited membership or funds for, or have you through any means ever assisted or provided any type of material support to any person or organization that has ever engaged or conspired to engage in sabotage, kidnapping, political assassination, hijacking, or any other form of terrorist activity? ☐ Yes ☐ No

5. Do you intend to engage in the United States in:

   a. Espionage? ☐ Yes ☐ No

   b. Any activity a purpose of which is opposition to, or the control or overthrow of, the Government of the United States, by force, violence, or other unlawful means? ☐ Yes ☐ No

   c. Any activity to violate or evade any law prohibiting the export from the United States of goods, technology, or sensitive information? ☐ Yes ☐ No

6. Have you ever been a member of, or in any way affiliated with, the Communist Party or any other totalitarian party? ☐ Yes ☐ No

7. Did you, during the period from March 23, 1933, to May 8, 1945, in association with either the Nazi Government of Germany or any organization or government associated or allied with the Nazi Government of Germany, ever order, incite, assist, or otherwise participate in the persecution of any person because of race, religion, national origin, or political opinion? ☐ Yes ☐ No

8. Have you ever engaged in genocide, or otherwise ordered, incited, assisted, or otherwise participated in the killing of any person because of race, religion, nationality, ethnic origin, or political opinion? ☐ Yes ☐ No

9. Have you ever been deported from the United States, or removed from the United States at government expense, excluded within the past year, or are you now in exclusion, deportation, removal, or recission proceedings? ☐ Yes ☐ No

10. Are you under a final order of civil penalty for violating section 274C of the Immigration and Nationality Act for use of fraudulent documents or have you, by fraud or willful misrepresentation of a material fact, ever sought to procure, or procured, a visa, other documentation, entry into the United States or any immigration benefit? ☐ Yes ☐ No

11. Have you ever left the United States to avoid being drafted into the U.S. Armed Forces? ☐ Yes ☐ No

12. Have you ever been a J nonimmigrant exchange visitor who was subject to the two-year foreign residence requirement and have not yet complied with that requirement or obtained a waiver? ☐ Yes ☐ No

13. Are you now withholding custody of a U.S. citizen child outside the United States from a person granted custody of the child? ☐ Yes ☐ No

14. Do you plan to practice polygamy in the United States? ☐ Yes ☐ No

Part 4. Signature. *(Read the information on penalties in the instructions before completing this section. You must file this application while in the United States.)*

Your registration with U.S. Citizenship and Immigration Services.

"I understand and acknowledge that, under section 262 of the Immigration and Nationality Act (Act), as an alien who has been or will be in the United States for more than 30 days, I am required to register with U.S. Citizenship and Immigration Services. I understand and acknowledge that, under section 265 of the Act, I am required to provide USCIS with my current address and written notice of any change of address within **ten** days of the change. I understand and acknowledge that USCIS will use the most recent address that I provide to USCIS, on any form containing these acknowledgements, for all purposes, including the service of a Notice to Appear should it be necessary for USCIS to initiate removal proceedings against me. I understand and acknowledge that if I change my address without providing written notice to USCIS, I will be held responsible for any communications sent to me at the most recent address that I provided to USCIS. I further understand and acknowledge that, if removal proceedings are initiated against me and I fail to attend any hearing, including an initial hearing based on service of the Notice to Appear at the most recent address that I provided to USCIS or as otherwise provided by law, I may be ordered removed in my absence, arrested, and removed from the United States."

Selective Service Registration.

The following applies to you if you are a male at least 18 years old, but not yet 26 years old, who is required to register with the Selective Service System: "I understand that my filing this adjustment-of-status application with U.S. Citizenship and Immigration Services authorizes USCIS to provide certain registration information to the Selective Service System in accordance with the Military Selective Service Act. Upon USCIS acceptance of my application, I authorize USCIS to transmit to the Selective Service System my name, current address, Social Security Number, date of birth, and the date I filed the application for the purpose of recording my Selective Service registration as of the filing date. If, however, USCIS does not accept my application, I further understand that, if so required, I am responsible for registering with the Selective Service by other means, provided I have not yet reached age 26."

Applicant's Certification

I certify, under penalty of perjury under the laws of the United States of America, that this application and the evidence submitted with it is all true and correct. I authorize the release of any information from my records that U.S. Citizenship and Immigration Services (USCIS) needs to determine eligibility for the benefit I am seeking.

Signature	Print Your Name	Date	Daytime Phone Number
			( )

NOTE*: If you do not completely fill out this form or fail to submit required documents listed in the instructions, you may not be found eligible for the requested document and this application may be denied.*

Part 5. Signature of person preparing form, if other than above. (sign below)

I declare that I prepared this application at the request of the above person, and it is based on all information of which I have knowledge.

Signature	Print Your Full Name	Date	Phone Number *(Include Area Code)*
			( )

Firm Name
and Address

E-Mail Address (if any)

OMB No. 1615-0026; Exp. 09/30/08

Department of Homeland Security
U.S. Citizenship and Immigration Services

**I-526, Immigrant Petition
by Alien Entrepreneur**

Do Not Write in This Block - For USCIS Use Only (Except G-28 Block Below)		
Classification _____	**Action Block**	Fee Receipt
Priority Date _____		**To be completed by Attorney or Representative, if any** ☐ G-28 is attached Attorney's State License No. _____
Remarks:		

START HERE - Type or print in black ink.

Part 1.   Information about you.

Family Name [ ]   Given Name [ ]   Middle Name [ ]

Address:
In care of [ ]

Number and Street [ ]   Apt. # [ ]

City [ ]   State or Province [ ]   Country [ ]   Zip/Postal Code [ ]

Date of Birth (mm/dd/yyyy) [ ]   Country of Birth [ ]   Social Security # (if any) [ ]   A # (if any) [ ]

If you are in the United States, provide the following information: Date of Arrival (mm/dd/yyyy) [ ]   I-94 # [ ]

Current Nonimmigrant Status [ ]   Date Current Status Expires (mm/dd/yyyy) [ ]   Daytime Phone # with Area Code [ ]

Part 2.   Application type. (Check one)

a. ☐ This petition is based on an investment in a commercial enterprise in a targeted employment area for which the required amount of capital invested has been adjusted downward.

b. ☐ This petition is based on an investment in a commercial enterprise in an area for which the required amount of capital invested has been adjusted upward.

c. ☐ This petition is based on an investment in a commercial enterprise that is not in either a targeted area or in an upward adjustment area.

Part 3.   Information about your investment.

Name of commercial enterprise in which funds are invested [ ]

Street Address [ ]

Phone # with Area Code [ ]   Business organized as (corporation, partnership, etc.) [ ]

Kind of business (e.g. furniture manufacturer) [ ]   Date established (mm/dd/yyyy) [ ]   IRS Tax # [ ]

RECEIVED: _____   RESUBMITTED: _____   RELOCATED: SENT _____   REC'D _____

Form I-526 (Rev. 07/30/07)Y

Part 3.   Information about your investment. (Continued.)

| Date of your initial investment (mm/dd/yyyy) | | Amount of your initial investment | $ | |

| Your total capital investment in the enterprise to date | $ | Percentage of the enterprise you own | |

If you are not the sole investor in the new commercial enterprise, list on separate paper the names of all other parties (natural and non-natural) who hold a percentage share of ownership of the new enterprise and indicate whether any of these parties is seeking classification as an alien entrepreneur. Include the name, percentage of ownership and whether or not the person is seeking classification under section 203(b)(5). **NOTE:** A "natural" party would be an individual person and a "non-natural" party would be an entity such as a corporation, consortium, investment group, partnership, etc.

If you indicated in **Part 2** that the enterprise is in a targeted employment area or in an upward adjustment area, name the county and state: County _____ State _____

Part 4.   Additional information about the enterprise.

Type of Enterprise (check one):

☐ New commercial enterprise resulting from the creation of a new business.

☐ New commercial enterprise resulting from the purchase of an existing business.

☐ New commercial enterprise resulting from a capital investment in an existing business.

Composition of the Petitioner's Investment:

Total amount in U.S. bank account .... $ _____

Total value of all assets purchased for use in the enterprise.................... $ _____

Total value of all property transferred from abroad to the new enterprise.......... $ _____

Total of all debt financing... $ _____

Total stock purchases.. $ _____

Other (explain on separate paper)... $ _____

Total $ _____

Income:

When you made the investment.........   Gross $ _____   Net $ _____

Now...   Gross $ _____   Net $ _____

Net worth:

When you made investment..............   Gross $ _____   Now $ _____

Part 5.   Employment creation information.

Number of full-time employees in the enterprise in U.S. (excluding you, your spouse, sons and daughters)

When you made your initial investment? [ ]   Now [ ]   Difference [ ]

How many of these new jobs were created by your investment? [ ]   How many additional new jobs will be created by your additional investment? [ ]

What is your position, office or title with the new commercial enterprise?

[ ]

Briefly describe your duties, activities and responsibilities.

[ ]

What is your salary? $ [ ]   What is the cost of your benefits? $ [ ]

Part 6.   Processing information.

Check One:

[ ] The person named in **Part 1** is now in the United States and an application to adjust status to permanent resident will be filed if this petition is approved.

[ ] If the petition is approved and the person named in **Part 1** wishes to apply for an immigrant visa abroad, complete the following for that person:

Country of nationality:

Country of current residence or, if now in the United States, last permanent residence abroad:

If you provided a United States address in **Part 1**, print the person's foreign address:

If the person's native alphabet is other than Roman letters, write the foreign address in the native alphabet:

Is a Form I-485, Application for Adjustment of Status, attached to this petition?   [ ] Yes   [ ] No

Are you in deportation or removal proceedings?   [ ] Yes (Explain on separate paper)   [ ] No

Have you ever worked in the United States without permission?   [ ] Yes (Explain on separate paper)   [ ] No

Part 7.   Signature.   *Read the information on penalties in the instructions before completing this section.*

I certify, under penalty of perjury under the laws of the United States of America, that this petition and the evidence submitted with it is all true and correct. I authorize the release of any information from my records that the U.S. Citizenship and Immigration Services needs to determine eligibility for the benefit I am seeking.

Signature [ ]   Date [ ]

NOTE: *If you do not completely fill out this form or fail to the submit the required documents listed in the instructions, you may not be found eligible for the immigration benefit you are seeking and this petition may be denied.*

Part 8.   Signature of person preparing form, if other than above. (Sign below)

I declare that I prepared this application at the request of the above person and it is based on all information of which I have knowledge.

Signature [ ]   Print Your Name [ ]   Date [ ]

Firm Name [ ]

Address [ ]   Daytime phone # with area code [ ]

Form I-526 (Rev. 07/30/07)Y Page 3

OMB No. 1615-0003; Expires 12/31/08

Department of Homeland Security
U.S. Citizenship and Immigration Services

I-539, Application to Extend/ Change Nonimmigrant Status

START HERE - Please type or print in black ink.	For USCIS Use Only	
Part 1. Information about you		

Family Name	Given Name	Middle Name

Address -
In care of -

Street Number and Name		Apt. #

City	State	Zip Code	Daytime Phone #

Country of Birth	Country of Citizenship

Date of Birth (mm/dd/yyyy)	U. S. Social Security # (if any)	A # (if any)

Date of Last Arrival Into the U.S.	I-94 #

Current Nonimmigrant Status	Expires on (mm/dd/yyyy)

For USCIS Use Only

Returned

Date

Resubmitted

Date

Reloc Sent

Date

Reloc Rec'd

Date

☐ Applicant Interviewed on

_____ Date

Receipt

Part 2. Application type *(See instructions for fee.)*

1. I am applying for: *(Check one.)*
   a. ☐ An extension of stay in my current status.
   b. ☐ A change of status. The new status I am requesting is: _____
   c. ☐ Reinstatement to student status

2. Number of people included in this application: *(Check one.)*
   a. ☐ I am the only applicant.
   b. ☐ Members of my family are filing this application with me.
   The total number of people (including me) in the application is: _____
   (Complete the supplement for each co-applicant.)

☐ Extension Granted to (Date):

Change of Status/Extension Granted
New Class: From *(Date)*: _____
_____   To *(Date)*: _____

Part 3. Processing information

1. I/We request that my/our current or requested status be extended until (mm/dd/yyyy): _____

2. Is this application based on an extension or change of status already granted to your spouse, child, or parent?
   ☐ No ☐ Yes USCIS Receipt # _____

3. Is this application based on a separate petition or application to give your spouse, child, or parent an extension or change of status? ☐ No ☐ Yes, filed with this I-539.
   ☐ Yes, filed previously and pending with USCIS. Receipt #: _____

4. If you answered "Yes" to Question 3, give the name of the petitioner or applicant: _____

If the petition or application is pending with USCIS, also give the following data:

Office filed at	Filed on (mm/dd/yyyy)

If Denied:
☐ Still within period of stay
☐ S/D to: _____
☐ Place under docket control

Remarks:

Action Block

Part 4. Additional information

1. For applicant #1, provide passport information: Valid to: (mm/dd/yyyy)
   Country of Issuance

2. Foreign Address: Street Number and Name	Apt. #
City or Town	State or Province
Country	Zip/Postal Code

To Be Completed by
***Attorney or Representative,* if any**

☐ Fill in box if G-28 is attached to represent the applicant.

ATTY State License #

3. **Answer the following questions. If you answer "Yes" to any question, please describe the circumstances in detail and explain on a separate sheet(s) of paper.**   **Yes**   **No**

a.	Are you, or any other person included on the application, an applicant for an immigrant visa?	☐	☐
b.	Has an immigrant petition ever been filed for you or for any other person included in this application?	☐	☐
c.	Has a Form I-485, Application to Register Permanent Residence or Adjust Status, ever been filed by you or by any other person included in this application?	☐	☐
d. 1.	Have you or any other person, included in this application, ever been arrested or convicted of any criminal offense since last entering the United States?	☐	☐

d. 2. Have you EVER ordered, incited, called for, commited, assisted, helped with, or otherwise participated in any of the following:

  (a) Acts involving torture or genocide?

  (b) Killing any person?

  (c) Intentionally and severely injuring any person?

  (d) Engaging in any kind of sexual contact or relations with any person who was being forced or threatened?

  (e) Limiting or denying any person's ability to exercise religious beliefs?   ☐   ☐

d. 3. Have you EVER:

  (a) Served in, been a member of, assisted in, or participated in any military unit, paramilitary unit, police unit, self-defense unit, vigilante unit, rebel group, guerrilla group, militia, or insurgent organization?

  (b) Served in any prison, jail, prison camp, detention facility, labor camp, or any other situation that involved detaining persons?   ☐   ☐

d. 4. Have you EVER been a member of, assisted in, or participated in any group, unit, or organization of any kind in which you or other persons used any type of weapon against any person or threatened to do so?   ☐   ☐

d. 5. Have you EVER assisted or participated in selling or providing weapons to any person who to your knowledge used them against another person, or in transporting weapons to any person who to your knowledge used them against another person?   ☐   ☐

d. 6. Have you EVER received any type of military, paramilitary, or weapons training?   ☐   ☐

e.	Have you, or any other person included in this application, done anything that violated the terms of the nonimmigrant status you now hold?	☐	☐
f.	Are you, or any other person included in this application, now in removal proceedings?	☐	☐
g.	Have you, or any other person included in this application, been employed in the United States since last admitted or granted an extension or change of status?	☐	☐

1. If you answered "Yes" to Question 3f, give the following information concerning the removal proceedings on the attached page entitled "**Part 4. Additional information. Page for answers to 3f and 3g.**" Include the name of the person in removal proceedings and information on jurisdiction, date proceedings began, and status of proceedings.

2. If you answered "No" to Question 3g, fully describe how you are supporting yourself on the attached page entitled "**Part 4. Additional information. Page for answers to 3f and 3g.**" Include the source, amount, and basis for any income.

3. If you answered "Yes" to Question 3g, fully describe the employment on the attached page entitled "**Part 4. Additional information. Page for answers to 3f and 3g.**" Include the name of the person employed, name and address of the employer, weekly income, and whether the employment was specifically authorized by USCIS.

| | | **Yes** | **No** |

h. Are you currently or have you ever been a J-1 exchange visitor or a J-2 dependent of a J-1 exchange visitor? ☐ ☐

If yes, you must provide the dates you maintained status as a J-1 exchange visitor or J-2 dependent. Willful failure to disclose this information (or other relevant information) can result in your application being denied. Also, please provide proof of your J-1 or J-2 status, such as a copy of Form DS-2019, Certificate of Eligibility for Exchange Visitor Status, or a copy of your passport that includes the J visa stamp.

Part 5. Applicant's Statement and Signature *(Read the information on penalties in the instructions before completing this section. You must file this application while in the United States).*

Applicant's Statement (Check One):

☐ I can read and understand English, and have read and understand each and every question and instruction on this form, as well as my answer to each question.

☐ Each and every question and instruction on this form, as well as my answer to each question, has been read to me by the person named below in _____, a language in which I am fluent. I understand each and every question and instruction on this form, as well as my answer to each question.

Applicant's Signature

I certify, under penalty of perjury under the laws of the United States of America, that this application and the evidence submitted with it is all true and correct. I authorize the release of any information from my records that U.S. Citizenship and Immigration Services needs to determine eligibility for the benefit I am seeking.

Signature	Print your Name	Date
Daytime Telephone Number	E-Mail Address	

NOTE: *If you do not completely fill out this form or fail to submit required documents listed in the instructions, you may not be found eligible for the requested benefit and this application may be denied.*

Part 6. Interpreter's Statement

Language used: _____

I certify that I am fluent in English and the above-mentioned language. I further certify that I have read each and every question and instruction on this form, as well as the answer to each question, to this applicant in the above-mentioned language, and the applicant has understood each and every instruction and question on the form, as well as the answer to each question.

Signature	Print Your Name	Date
Firm Name (If Applicable)	Daytime Telephone Number *(Area Code and Number)*	
Address	Fax Number *(Area Code and Number)*	E-Mail Address

Form I-539 (Rev. 12/31/07)Y Page 3

Part 7. Signature of Person Preparing Form, if Other than Above *(Sign Below)*

Signature	Print Your Name	Date
Firm Name (If Applicable)	Daytime Telephone Number *(Area Code and Number)*	
Address	Fax Number *(Area Code and Number)*	E-Mail Address

I declare that I prepared this application at the request of the above person and it is based on all information of which I have knowledge.

Part 4. (Continued) Additional information. Page for answers to 3f and 3g.

If you answered "Yes" to Question 3f in Part 4 on Page 3 of this form, give the following information concerning the removal proceedings. Include the name of the person in removal proceedings and information on jurisdiction, date proceedings began, and status of proceedings.

If you answered "No" to Question 3g in Part 4 on Page 3 of this form, fully describe how you are supporting yourself. Include the source, amount and basis for any income.

If you answered "Yes" to Question 3g in Part 4 on Page 3 of this form, fully describe the employment. Include the name of the person employed, name and address of the employer, weekly income, and whether the employment was specifically authorized by USCIS.

Supplement -1
Attach to Form I-539 when more than one person is included in the petition or application.
(List each person separately. Do not include the person named in the Form I-539.)

Family Name	Given Name	Middle Name	Date of Birth (mm/dd/yyyy)
Country of Birth	Country of Citizenship	U.S. Social Security # (if any)	A # (if any)

Date of Arrival (mm/dd/yyyy) | I-94 #

Current Nonimmigrant Status: | Expires on (mm/dd/yyyy)

Country Where Passport Issued | Expiration Date (mm/dd/yyyy)

Family Name	Given Name	Middle Name	Date of Birth (mm/dd/yyyy)
Country of Birth	Country of Citizenship	U.S. Social Security # (if any)	A # (if any)

Date of Arrival (mm/dd/yyyy) | I-94 #

Current Nonimmigrant Status: | Expires on (mm/dd/yyyy)

Country Where Passport Issued | Expiration Date (mm/dd/yyyy)

Family Name	Given Name	Middle Name	Date of Birth (mm/dd/yyyy)
Country of Birth	Country of Citizenship	U.S. Social Security # (if any)	A # (if any)

Date of Arrival (mm/dd/yyyy) | I-94 #

Current Nonimmigrant Status: | Expires on (mm/dd/yyyy)

Country Where Passport Issued | Expiration Date (mm/dd/yyyy)

Family Name	Given Name	Middle Name	Date of Birth (mm/dd/yyyy)
Country of Birth	Country of Citizenship	U.S. Social Security # (if any)	A # (if any)

Date of Arrival (mm/dd/yyyy) | I-94 #

Current Nonimmigrant Status: | Expires on (mm/dd/yyyy)

Country Where Passport Issued | Expiration Date (mm/dd/yyyy)

Family Name	Given Name	Middle Name	Date of Birth (mm/dd/yyyy)
Country of Birth	Country of Citizenship	U.S. Social Security # (if any)	A # (if any)

Date of Arrival (mm/dd/yyyy) | I-94 #

Current Nonimmigrant Status: | Expires on (mm/dd/yyyy)

Country Where Passport Issued | Expiration Date (mm/dd/yyyy)

If you need additional space, attach a separate sheet(s) of paper.
Place your name, A #, if any, date of birth, form number, and application date at the top of the sheet(s) of paper.

Form I-539 (Rev. 12/31/07)Y Page 5

OMB No. 1615-0028; Expires 08/31/08

Department of Homeland Security
U.S. Citizenship and Immigration Services

I-600, Petition to Classify Orphan as an Immediate Relative

Do not write in this block. **(For USCIS Use Only.)**

TO THE SECRETARY OF STATE:

The petition was filed by:

☐ Married petitioner   ☐ Unmarried petitioner

The petition is approved for orphan:

☐ Adopted abroad   ☐ Coming to U.S. for adoption. Preadoption requirements have been met.

Remarks:

Fee Stamp

File number

DATE OF ACTION
DD
DISTRICT

Type or print legibly in black ink. Complete a separate petition for each child.
Petition is being made to classify the named orphan as an immediate relative

Block I - Information about petitioner

1. My name is: (Last) (First) (Middle)

2. Other names used (including maiden name if appropriate):

3. I reside in the U.S. at: (C/O if appropriate) (Apt. No.)

(Number and Street) (Town or City) (State) (Zip Code)

4. Address Abroad (if any): (Number and Street) (Apt. No.)

(Town or city) (Province) (Country)

5. I was born on *(mm/dd/yyyy)*

In: (Town or City) (State or Province) (Country)

6. My telephone number is: (Include Area Code)

7. My marital status is:
☐ Married
☐ Widowed
☐ Divorced
☐ Single
  ☐ I have never been married.
  ☐ I have been previously married _____ time(s).

8. If you are now married, give the following information:

Date and place of present marriage *(mm/dd/yyyy)*

Name of present spouse (include maiden name of wife)

Date of birth of spouse *(mm/dd/yyyy)* Place of birth of spouse

Number of prior marriages of spouse

My spouse resides ☐ With me ☐ Apart from me (provide address below)

(Apt. No.) (No. and Street) (City) (State) (Country)

9. I am a citizen of the United States through:
☐ Birth ☐ Parents ☐ Naturalization

If acquired through naturalization, give name under which naturalized, number of naturalization certificate, and date and place of naturalization:

If not, submit evidence of citizenship. See Instruction **2.a(2)**.

If acquired through parentage, have you obtained a certificate in your own name based on that acquisition?
☐ No ☐ Yes

Have you or any person through whom you claimed citizenship ever lost U.S. citizenship?
☐ No ☐ Yes (If Yes, attach detailed explanation.)

Received	Trans. In	Ret'd Trans. Out	Completed

Form I-600 (Rev. 07/30/07)Y

Block II - Information about orphan beneficiary.

10. Name at Birth   (First)   (Middle)   (Last)

11. Name at Present   (First)   (Middle)   (Last)

12. Any other names by which orphan is or was known.

13. Gender   ☐ Male   **14.** Date of birth *(mm/dd/yyyy)*
    ☐ Female

15. Place of Birth (City)   (State or Province)   (Country)

16. The beneficiary is an orphan because (check one):
    ☐ He or she has no parents.
    ☐ He or she has only one parent who is the sole or surviving parent.

17. If the orphan has only one parent, answer the following:
    a. State what has become of the other parent:

    b. Is the remaining parent capable of providing for the orphan's
        support?   ☐ Yes ☐ No
    c. Has the remaining parent in writing irrevocably released the
        orphan for emigration and adoption?   ☐ Yes ☐ No

18. Has the orphan been adopted abroad by the petitioner and spouse
    jointly or the unmarried petitioner?   ☐ Yes ☐ No

    If yes, did the petitioner and spouse or unmarried petitioner
    personally see and observe the child prior to or during the
    adoption proceedings?   ☐ Yes ☐ No

    Date of adoption *(mm/dd/yyyy)*

    Place of adoption

19. If either answer in Question **18** is "No" answer the following:
    a. Do petitioner and spouse jointly or does the unmarried petitioner
        intend to adopt the orphan in the United States?
            ☐ Yes   ☐ No
    b. Have the preadoption requirements, if any, of the orphan's
        proposed State of residence been met?   ☐ Yes ☐ No
    c. If **b** is answered "No," will they be met later?
            ☐ Yes   ☐ No

20. To petitioner's knowledge, does the orphan have any physical or mental
    affliction?   ☐ Yes   ☐ No
    If "Yes," name the affliction.

21. Who has legal custody of the child?

22. Name of child welfare agency, if any, assisting in this case:

23. Name of attorney abroad, if any, representing petitioner in this case.

    Address of above.

24. Address in the United States where orphan will reside.

25. Present address of orphan.

25. If orphan is residing in an institution, give full name of institution.

26. If orphan is not residing in an institution, give full name of person with
    with whom residing.

27. Give any additional information necessary to locate orphan, such as
    name of district, section, zone or locality in which orphan resides.

28. Location of American embassy or consulate where application for visa
    will be made.

    (City in Foreign Country)   (Foreign Country)

Certification of petitioner.
I certify, under penalty of perjury under the laws of the United States of
America, that the foregoing is true and correct and that I will care for an
orphan or orphans properly if admitted to the United States.

(Signature of Petitioner)

Executed on (Date)

Certification of married prospective petitioner's spouse.
I certify, under penalty of perjury under the laws of the United States of
America, that the foregoing is true and correct and that my spouse and I
will care for an orphan or orphans properly if admitted to the United States.

(Signature of Petitioner)

Executed on (Date)

Signature of person preparing form, if other than petitioner.

I declare that this document was prepared by me at the request of the petitioner and is
based entirely on information of which I have knowledge.

(Signature)

Street Address and Room or Suite No./City/State/Zip Code

Executed on (Date)

Form I-600 (Rev. 07/30/07)Y Page 2

OMB No. 1615-0028; Expires 08/31/08

Department of Homeland Security
U.S. Citizenship and Immigration Services

**I-600A, Application for Advance
Processing of Orphan Petition**

Do not write in this block.   **For USCIS Use Only.**

It has been determined that the:

☐ Married   ☐ Unmarried

prospective adoptive parent will furnish proper care to
a beneficiary orphan if admitted to the United States.

There:

☐ are   ☐ are not

preadoptive requirements in the State of the child's proposed
residence.

The following is a description of the preadoption requirements, if any,
of the State of the child's proposed residence:

_____

The preadoption requirements, if any,:
☐ have been met.   ☐ have not been met.

Fee Stamp

DATE OF FAVORABLE
DETERMINATION

DD

DISTRICT

File number of applicant, if applicable

Please type or print legibly in black ink.

This application is made by the named prospective adoptive parent for advance processing of an orphan petition.

BLOCK I - Information about the prospective adoptive parent.

1. My name is: (Last)   (First)   (Middle)

2. Other names used (including maiden name if appropriate):

3. I reside in the U.S. at: (C/O if appropriate)   (Apt. No.)

   (Number and Street)   (Town or City)   (State)   (Zip Code)

4. Address abroad (If any):   (Number and Street)   (Apt. No.)

   (Town or City)   (Province)   (Country)

5. I was born on: *(mm/dd/yyyy)*

   In: (Town or City)   (State or Province)   (Country)

6. My telephone number is: (Include Area Code)

7. My marital status is:
   ☐ Married
   ☐ Widowed
   ☐ Divorced
   ☐ Single
     ☐ I have never been married.
     ☐ I have been previously married _____ time(s).

8. If you are now married, give the following information:

Date and place of present marriage *(mm/dd/yyyy)*

Name of present spouse (include maiden name of wife)

Date of birth of spouse *(mm/dd/yyyy)*   Place of birth of spouse

Number of prior marriages of spouse

My spouse resides   ☐ With me   ☐ Apart from me
(provide address below)

(Apt. No.)   (No. and Street)   (City)   (State)   (Country)

9. I am a citizen of the United States through:
   ☐ Birth   ☐ Parents   ☐ Naturalization

If acquired through naturalization, give name under which naturalized,
number of naturalization certificate, and date and place of naturalization.

_____

If not, submit evidence of citizenship. See Instruction 2.a(2).

If acquired through parentage, have you obtained a certificate in your
own name based on that acquisition?
   ☐ No   ☐ Yes

Have you or any person through whom you claimed citizenship ever lost
United States citizenship?
   ☐ No   ☐ Yes (If Yes, attach detailed explanation.)

Received	Trans. In	Ret'd Trans. Out	Completed

Form I-600A (Rev. 07-30-07) Y

BLOCK II - General information.

10. Name and address of organization or individual assisting you in locating or identifying an orphan
    (Name)

    _____

    (Address)

    _____

11. Do you plan to travel abroad to locate or adopt a child?

    ☐ Yes   ☐ No

12. Does your spouse, if any, plan to travel abroad to locate or adopt a child?

    ☐ Yes   ☐ No

13. If the answer to Question **11** or **12** is "Yes," give the following information:

    a. Your date of intended departure   _____

    b. Your spouse's date of intended departure   _____

    c. City, province   _____

14. Will the child come to the United States for adoption after compliance with the preadoption requirements, if any, of the State of proposed residence?

    ☐ Yes   ☐ No

15. If the answer to Question **14** is "No," will the child be adopted abroad after having been personally seen and observed by you and your spouse, if married?

    ☐ Yes   ☐ No

16. Where do you wish to file your orphan petition?

    The USCIS office located at

    _____

    The American Embassy or Consulate at

    _____

17. Do you plan to adopt more than one child?

    ☐ Yes   ☐ No

    If "Yes," how many children do you plan to adopt?

Certification of prospective adoptive parent.

I certify, under penalty of perjury under the laws of the United States of America, that the foregoing is true and correct and that I will care for an orphan/orphans properly if admitted to the United States.

_____
(Signature of Prospective Adoptive Parent)

_____
Executed on (Date)

Certification of married prospective adoptive parent spouse.

I certify, under penalty of perjury under the laws of the United States of America, that the foregoing is true and correct and that my spouse and I will care for an orphan/orphans properly if admitted to the United States.

_____
(Signature of Prospective Adoptive Parent Spouse)

_____
Executed on (Date)

Signature of person preparing form, if other than petitioner.

I declare that this document was prepared by me at the request of the petitioner and is based entirely on information of which I have knowledge.

_____
(Signature)

_____
Street Address and Room or Suite No./City/State/Zip Code

_____
Executed on (Date)

OMB No. 1615-0038; Expires 10/31/09

Department of Homeland Security
U.S. Citizenship and Immigration Services

**I-751, Petition to Remove
Conditions on Residence**

START HERE - Please type or print in black ink.	**For USCIS Use Only**	

Part 1. Information About You

Family Name (Last Name)	Given Name (First Name)	Full Middle Name

Address: (Street number and name)   Apt. #

C/O: (In care of)

City   State/Province

Country   Zip/Postal Code

Mailing Address, if different than above (Street number and name):   Apt. #

C/O: (In care of)

City   State/Province

Country   Zip/Postal Code

Date of Birth *(mm/dd/yyyy)*   Country of Birth   Country of Citizenship

Alien Registration Number (#A)   Social Security # *(If any)*

Conditional Residence Expires on *(mm/dd/yyyy)*   Daytime Phone # *(Area/Country codes)*

For USCIS Use Only

Returned	Receipt
Date	
Date	
Resubmitted	
Date	
Date	
Reloc Sent	
Date	
Date	
Reloc Rec'd	
Date	
Date	

☐ Petitioner
Interviewed
on _____

Remarks

SAMPLE

Part 2. Basis for Petition *(Check one)*

a. ☐ My conditional residence is based on my marriage to a U.S. citizen or permanent resident, and we are filing this petition together.

b. ☐ I am a child who entered as a conditional permanent resident and I am unable to be included in a joint Petition to Remove the Conditions on Residence (Form 1-751) filed by my parent(s)

OR

My conditional residence is based on my marriage to a U.S. citizen or permanent resident, but I am unable to file a joint petition and I request a waiver because: **(Check one)**

c. ☐ My spouse is deceased.

d. ☐ I entered into the marriage in good faith but the marriage was terminated through divorce or annulment.

e. ☐ I am a conditional resident spouse who entered a marriage in good faith, and during the marriage I was battered by or was the subject of extreme cruelty by my U.S. citizen or permanent resident spouse or parent.

f. ☐ I am a conditional resident child who was battered or subjected to extreme cruelty by my U.S. citizen or conditional resident parent(s).

g. ☐ The termination of my status and removal from the United States would result in an extreme hardship.

Action Block

To Be Completed by
Attorney or Representative, if any.

☐ Fill in box if G-28 is attached to represent the applicant.

ATTY State License #

Form I-751 (Rev. 08/25/08)N

Part 3. Additional Information About You

1. Other Names Used *(including maiden name)*:

2. Date of Marriage *(mm/dd/yyyy)* **3.** Place of Marriage **4.** If your spouse is deceased, give the date of death *(mm/dd/yyyy)*

5. Are you in removal, deportation, or rescission proceedings? ☐ Yes ☐ No

6. Was a fee paid to anyone other than an attorney in connection with this petition? ☐ Yes ☐ No

7. Have you ever been arrested, detained, charged, indicted, fined, or imprisoned for breaking or violating any law or ordinance (excluding traffic regulations), or committed any crime which you were not arrested in the United States or abroad? ☐ Yes ☐ No

8. If you are married, is this a different marriage than the one through which conditional residence status was obtained? ☐ Yes ☐ No

9. Have you resided at any other address since you became a permanent resident? *(If yes, attach a list of all addresses and dates.)* ☐ Yes ☐ No

10. Is your spouse currently serving with or employed by the U.S. government and serving outside the United States? ☐ Yes ☐ No

If you answered "Yes" to any of the above, provide a detailed explanation on a separate sheet(s) of paper and refer to "What Initial Evidence Is Required?" to determine what criminal history documentation to include with your petition. Place your name and Alien Registration Number (A#) at the top of each sheet and give the number of the item that refers to your response.

Part 4. Information About the Spouse or Parent Through Whom You Gained Your Conditional Residence

Family Name   First Name   Middle Name

Address

Date of Birth *(mm/dd/yyyy)*   Social Security # *(if any)*   A# *(if any)*

Part 5. Information About Your Children List all your children *(Attach other sheet(s) if necessary)*

Name *(First/Middle/Last)*	Date of Birth *(mm/dd/yyyy)*	A# *(If any)*	If in U.S., give address/immigration status	Living with you?
				☐ Yes ☐ No
				☐ Yes ☐ No
				☐ Yes ☐ No
				☐ Yes ☐ No
				☐ Yes ☐ No

Part 6. Signature.
Read the information on penalties in the instructions before completing this section. If you checked block "a" in Part 2, your spouse must also sign below.

I certify, under penalty of perjury of the laws of the United States of America, that this petition and the evidence submitted with it is all true and correct. If conditional residence was based on a marriage, I further certify that the marriage was entered in accordance with the laws of the place where the marriage took place and was not for the purpose of procuring an immigration benefit. I also authorize the release of any information from my records that the U.S. Citizenship and Immigration Services needs to determine eligibility for the benefit sought.

Signature   **Print Name**   **Date** *(mm/dd/yyyy)*

Signature of Spouse   **Print Name**   **Date** *(mm/dd/yyyy)*

NOTE: If you do not completely fill out this form or fail to submit any required documents listed in the instructions, you may not be found eligible for the requested benefit and this petition may be denied.

Part 7. Signature of Person Preparing Form, If Other than Above

I declare that I prepared this petition at the request of the above person and it is based on all information of which I have knowledge.

Signature   **Print Name**   **Date** *(mm/dd/yyyy)*

Firm Name and Address   **Daytime Phone Number**
(Area/Country codes)

E-Mail Address
(If any)

Form I-751 (Rev.08/25/08) N Page 2

OMB No. 1615-0040; Expires 08/31/08

I-765, Application For
Employment Authorization

Department of Homeland Security
U.S. Citizenship and Immigration Services

Do not write in this block.

Remarks	Action Block	Fee Stamp
A#		

Applicant is filing under §274a.12 _____

☐ Application Approved. Employment Authorized / Extended (*Circle One*)   until _____ (Date).
_____ (Date).

Subject to the following conditions: _____
Application Denied.
☐ Failed to establish eligibility under 8 CFR 274a.12 (a) or (c).
☐ Failed to establish economic necessity as required in 8 CFR 274a.12(c)(14), (18) and 8 CFR 214.2(f)

I am applying for: ☐ Permission to accept employment.
☐ Replacement (*of lost employment authorization document*)
☐ Renewal of my permission to accept employment (*attach previous employment authorization document*).

1. Name (Family Name in CAPS)   (First)   (Middle)

2. Other Names Used (Include Maiden Name)

3. Address in the United States (Number and Street)   (Apt. Number)

(Town or City)   (State/Country)   (ZIP Code)

4. Country of Citizenship/Nationality

5. Place of Birth (Town or City)   (State/Province)   (Country)

6. Date of Birth (mm/dd/yyyy)   **7.** Gender   ☐ Male   ☐ Female

8. Marital Status   ☐ Married   ☐ Single
☐ Widowed   ☐ Divorced

9. Social Security Number (Include all numbers you have ever used) (if any)

10. Alien Registration Number (A-Number) or I-94 Number (if any)

11. Have you ever before applied for employment authorization from USCIS?
☐ Yes (If yes, complete below)   ☐ No

Which USCIS Office?   Date(s)

Results (Granted or Denied - attach all documentation)

12. Date of Last Entry into the U.S.   (mm/dd/yyyy)

13. Place of Last Entry into the U.S.

14. Manner of Last Entry (Visitor, Student, etc.)

15. Current Immigration Status (Visitor, Student, etc.)

16. Go to **Part 2** of the Instructions, Eligibility Categories. In the space below, place the letter and number of the category you selected from the instructions (For example, (a)(8), (c)(17)(iii), etc.).

Eligibility under 8 CFR 274a.12   (___) (___) (___)

17. If you entered the Eligibility Category, (c)(3)(C), in item 16 above, list your degree, your employer's name as listed in E-Verfy, and your employer's E-Verify Company Identification Number or a valid E-Verify Client Company Identification Number in the space below.

Degree: _____
Employer's Name as listed in E-Verify: _____
Employer's E-Verify Company Identification Number or a valid E-Verify Client Company Identification Number _____

Certification

Your Certification: I certify, under penalty of perjury under the laws of the United States of America, that the foregoing is true and correct. Furthermore, I authorize the release of any information that U.S. Citizenship and Immigration Services needs to determine eligibility for the benefit I am seeking. I have read the Instructions in **Part 2** and have identified the appropriate eligibility category in **Block 16**.

Signature   Telephone Number   Date

Signature of person preparing form, if other than above: I declare that this document was prepared by me at the request of the applicant and is based on all information of which I have any knowledge.

Print Name   Address   *Signature*   Date

Remarks	Initial Receipt	Resubmitted	Relocated		Completed		
			Rec'd	Sent	Approved	Denied	Returned

Form I-765 (Rev. 05/27/08) N

OMB No. 1615-0075; Expires 10/31/10

Department of Homeland Security
U.S. Citizenship and Immigration Services

**I-864, Affidavit of Support
Under Section 213A of the Act**

Instructions

How Should I Complete This Form?

- Print clearly or type your answers using CAPITAL letters.

- Use black or blue ink.

- If you need extra space to answer any item:

  -- Attach a separate sheet of paper (or more sheets if necessary);

  -- Write your name, U.S. Social Security number and the words "Form I-864" on the top right corner of the sheet; and

  -- Write the number and subject of each question for which you are providing additional information.

What Is the Purpose of This Form?

This form is required for most family-based immigrants and some employment-based immigrants to show that they have adequate means of financial support and that they are not likely to become a public charge. For more information about Form I-864, or to obtain related forms please contact:

- The USCIS website (www.uscis.gov);

- The National Customer Service Center (NCSC) telephone line at 1-800-375-5283 TTY: 1-800-767-1833); or

- Your local USCIS office by using Infopass.

How Is This Form Used?

This form is a contract between a sponsor and the U.S. Government. Completing and signing this form makes you the sponsor. You must show on this form that you have enough income and/or assets to maintain the intending immigrant(s) and the rest of your household at 125 percent of the Federal Poverty Guidelines. By signing Form I-864, you are agreeing to use your resources to support the intending immigrant(s) named in this form, if it becomes necessary.

The submission of this form may make the sponsored immigrant ineligible for certain Federal, State, or local means-tested public benefits, because an agency that provides means-tested public benefits will consider *your* resources and assets as available to the sponsored immigrant in determining his or her eligibility for the program.

If the immigrant sponsored in this affidavit does receive one of the designated Federal, State or local means-tested public benefits, the agency providing the benefit may request that you repay the cost of those benefits. That agency can sue you if the cost of the benefits provided is not repaid.

Not all benefits are considered to be means-tested public benefits. See Form I-864P, Poverty Guidelines, for more information on which benefits may be covered by this definition, or the contract on **Page 6** of this form for a list of benefits explicitly not considered means-tested public benefits.

Who Needs This Form?

The following immigrants are required by law to submit Form I-864 completed by the petitioner to obtain an immigrant visa overseas or to adjust status to that of a lawful permanent resident in the United States:

- All immediate relatives of U.S. citizens (spouses, unmarried children under age 21, and parents of U.S. citizens age 21 and older);

- All family-based preference immigrants (unmarried sons and daughters of U.S. citizens, spouses and unmarried sons and daughters of permanent resident aliens, married sons and daughters of U.S. citizens, and brothers and sisters of U.S. citizens age 21 and older); and

- Employment-based preference immigrants in cases only when a U.S. citizen or lawful permanent resident relative filed the immigrant visa petition or such relative has a significant ownership interest (five percent or more) in the entity that filed the petition.

Are There Exceptions to Who Needs This Form?

The following types of intending immigrants do not need to file this form:

- Any intending immigrant who has earned or can be credited with 40 qualifying quarters (credits) of work in the United States. In addition to their own work, intending immigrants may be able to secure credit for work performed by a spouse during marriage and by their parent(s) while the immigrants were under 18 years of age. The Social Security Administration (SSA) can provide information on how to count quarters of work earned or credited and how to provide evidence of such. See the SSA website at www.ssa.gov/mystatement/credits for more information;

- Any intending immigrant who will, upon admission, acquire U.S. citizenship under section 320 of the Immigration and Nationality Act, as amended by the Child Citizenship Act of 2000 (CCA);

- Self-petitioning widow/ers who have an approved Petition for Amerasian, Widow(er), or Special Immigrant, Form I-360; and

- Self-petitioning battered spouses and children who have an approved Petition for Amerasian, Widow(er), or Special Immigrant, Form I-360.

NOTE: *If you qualify for one of the exemptions listed above, submit Form I-864W, Intending Immigrant's I-864 Exemption, instead of Form I-864.*

Who Completes and Signs Form I-864?

A sponsor completes and signs Form I-864. A sponsor is required to be at least 18 years old and domiciled in the United States, or its territories or possessions (see Step-by-step Instructions for more information on domicile). The petitioning sponsor must sign and complete Form I-864, even if a joint sponsor also submits an I-864 to meet the income requirement. The list below identifies who must become sponsors by completing and signing a Form I-864.

- The U.S. citizen or lawful permanent resident who filed a Form I-130 for a family member, Form I-129F for a fiance(e), or Form I-600 or I-600A for an orphan.

- The U.S. citizen or permanent resident alien who filed an employment-based immigrant visa petition (Form I-140) for a spouse, parent, son, daughter, or sibling who: **(1)** has a significant ownership interest (five percent or more) in the business which filed the employment-based immigrant visa petition; or **(2)** is related to the intending immigrant as a spouse, parent, son, daughter, or sibling.

What Are the Income Requirements?

To qualify as a sponsor, you must demonstrate that your income is at least 125 percent of the current Federal poverty guideline for your household size. The Federal poverty line, for purposes of this form, is updated annually and can be found on Form I-864P, Poverty Guidelines.

If you are on active duty in the U.S. Armed Forces, including the Army, Navy, Air Force, Marines or Coast Guard, and you are sponsoring your spouse or minor child, you only need to have an income of 100 percent of the Federal poverty line for your household size. This provision does not apply to joint or substitute sponsors.

How Do I Count Household Size?

Your household size includes yourself and the following individuals, no matter where they live: any spouse, any dependent children under the age of 21, any other dependents listed on your most recent Federal income tax return, all persons being sponsored in this affidavit of support, and any immigrants previously sponsored with a Form I-864 or Form I-864 EZ affidavit of support whom you are still obligated to support. If necessary to meet the income requirements to be a sponsor, you may include additional relatives (adult children, parents, or siblings) as part of your household size as long as they have the same principle residence as you and promise to use their income and resources in support of the intending immigrant(s).

What If I Cannot Meet the Income Requirements?

If your income alone is not sufficient to meet the requirement for your household size, the intending immigrant will be ineligible for an immigrant visa or adjustment of status, unless the requirement can be met using any combination of the following:

- Income from any relatives or dependents living in your household or dependents listed on your most recent Federal tax return who signed a Form I-864A;

- Income from the intending immigrant, if that income will continue from the same source after immigration, and if the intending immigrant is currently living in your residence. If the intending immigrant is your spouse, his or her income can be counted regardless of current residence, but it must continue from the same source after he or she becomes a lawful permanent resident.

- The value of your assets, the assets of any household member who has signed a Form I-864A, or the assets of the intending immigrant;

- A joint sponsor whose income and/or assets equal at least 125 percent of the Poverty Guidelines. See question below for more information on joint sponsors.

How Can My Relatives and Dependents Help Me Meet the Income Requirements?

You may use the income of your spouse and/or any other relatives living in your residence if they are willing to be jointly responsible with you for the intending immigrant(s) you are sponsoring. If you have any unrelated dependents listed on your income tax return you may include their income regardless of where they reside.

The income of such household members and dependents can be used to help you meet the income requirements if they complete and sign Form I-864A, Contract Between Sponsor and Household Member, and if they are at least 18 years of age when they sign the form.

Can the Intending Immigrant Help Me Meet the Income Requirements?

If certain conditions are met, the intending immigrant's income can help you meet the income requirement. If the intending immigrant is your spouse, his or her income can be included if it will continue from the same source after he or she obtains lawful permanent resident status. If the intending immigrant is another relative, there are two requirements.

First, the income must be continuing from the same source after he or she obtains lawful permanent resident status, and second, the intending immigrant must currently live with you in your residence. Evidence must be provided to support both requirements.

However, an intending immigrant whose income is being used to meet the income requirement does not need to complete Form I-864A, Contract Between Sponsor and Household Member, unless the intending immigrant has a spouse and/or children immigrating with him or her. In this instance, the contract relates to support for the spouse and/or children.

Does Receipt of Means-Tested Public Benefits Disqualify me From being a Sponsor?

No. Receipt of means-tested public benefits does not disqualify anyone from being a sponsor. However, means-tested public benefits cannot be accepted as income for the purposes of meeting the income requirement.

How Can I Use Assets to Qualify?

Assets may supplement income if the consular or immigration officer is convinced that the monetary value of the asset could reasonably be made available to support the sponsored immigrant and converted to cash within one year without undue harm to the sponsor or his or her family members. You may not include an automobile unless you show that you own at least one working automobile that you have not included.

What Is a Joint Sponsor?

If the person who is seeking the immigration of one or more of his or her relatives cannot meet the income requirements, a "joint sponsor" who can meet the requirements may submit a Form I-864 to sponsor all or some of the family members.

A joint sponsor can be any U.S. citizen, U.S. national, or lawful permanent resident who is at least 18 years old, domiciled in the United States, or its territories or possessions, and willing to be held jointly liable with the petitioner for the support of the intending immigrant. A joint sponsor does not have to be related to the petitioning sponsor or the intending immigrant.

If the first joint sponsor completes Form I-864 for some rather than all the family members, a second qualifying joint sponsor will be required to sponsor the remaining family members. There may be no more than two joint sponsors. A joint sponsor must be able to meet the income requirements for all the persons he or she is sponsoring without combining resources with the petitioning sponsor or a second joint sponsor. Any dependents applying for an immigrant visa or adjustment of status more than six months after immigration of the intending immigrants must be sponsored by the petitioner but may be sponsored by an original joint sponsor or a different joint sponsor.

Even if one or more I-864s are submitted for an intending immigrant, the petitioning sponsor remains legally accountable for the financial support of the sponsored alien along with the joint sponsor(s).

What Is a Substitute Sponsor?

A substitute sponsor is a sponsor who is completing a Form I-864 on behalf of an intending immigrant whose original I-130 petitioner has died after the Form I-130 was approved, but before the intending immigrant obtained permanent residence.

The substitute sponsor must be related to the intending immigrant in one of the following ways: spouse, parent, mother-in-law, father-in-law, sibling, child (at least 18 years of age), son, daughter, son-in-law, daughter-in-law, brother-in-law, sister-in-law, grandparent, grandchild or legal guardian. The substitute sponsor must also be a U.S. citizen or lawful permanent resident.

If you are a substitute sponsor, you must indicate that that you are related to the intending immigrant in one of the ways listed above and include evidence proving that relationship. The beneficiary must also file this form along with a written statement explaining the reasons why the Form I-130 visa petition should be reinstated, having been revoked following the petitioner's death. The beneficiary must also include a copy of the Form I-130 approval notice.

How Long Does My Obligation as a Sponsor Continue?

Your obligation to support the immigrant(s) you are sponsoring in this affidavit of support will continue until the sponsored immigrant becomes a U.S. citizen, or can be credited with 40 qualifying quarters of work in the United States.

Although 40 qualifying quarters of work (credits) generally equate to ten years of work, in certain cases the work of a spouse or parent adds qualifying quarters. The Social Security Administration can provide information on how to count qualifying quarters (credits) of work.

The obligation also ends if you or the sponsored immigrant dies or if the sponsored immigrant ceases to be a lawful permanent resident and departs the United States. Divorce does not end the sponsorship obligation.

Do I Need to Submit a Separate Affidavit for Each Family Member?

You must submit a Form I-864 affidavit of support for each intending immigrant you are sponsoring. You may submit photocopies if you are sponsoring more than one intending immigrant listed on the same affidavit of support.

Separate affidavits of support are required for intending immigrants for whom different Form I-130 family-based petitions were filed. For instance, if you are sponsoring both parents, each will need an original affidavit of support and accompanying documentation since you were required to submit separate Form I-130 visa petitions for each parent.

Often a spouse or minor children obtain visas or adjust status as dependents of a relative, based on the same visa petition. If you are sponsoring such dependents, you only need to provide a photocopy of the original Form I-864, as long as these dependents are immigrating at the same time as the principal immigrant or within six months of the time he or she immigrates to the United States. You do not need to provide copies of the supporting documents for each of the photocopied Forms I-864.

When Do I Complete Form I-864 and Where Do I Send It?

If the intending immigrant will apply for an immigrant visa at a U.S. Embassy or Consulate overseas:

Complete Form I-864 when it is mailed to you from the National Visa Center (NVC). Different instructions apply to some cases so follow the instructions provided by the National Visa Center for your particular case. The instructions on when and where to submit Form I-864 are included in the information packet that is mailed to you with Form I-864. Form I-864 and all accompanying documentation must be submitted to the government within one year of when you sign Form I-864.

If the intending immigrant will adjust status in the United States:

Complete Form I-864 when the intending immigrant is ready to submit his or her Form Application to Register Permanent Residence or Adjust Status. Then give the completed Form I-864 along with any Forms I-864A and all supporting documentation to the intending immigrant to submit with his or her application for adjustment of status. To be valid, Form I-864 and all supporting documentation must be submitted within one year of when you sign Form I-864. For privacy, you may enclose these documents in a sealed envelope marked "Form I-864: To Be Opened Only by a U.S. Government Official." You may be requested to submit updated information if there is a significant delay in processing.

Do I Have to Report My Change of Address If I Move?

Federal law requires that every sponsor report every change of address to the USCIS within 30 days of the change. To do this, send a completed Form I-865, Sponsor's Change of Address, to the Service Center having jurisdiction over your new address.

Do not complete Form I-865 at the same time that you complete the I-864.

You should complete and submit Form I-865 to USCIS only when the address you indicated on the original I-864 Affidavit of Support has changed. Please see Form I-865 for further directions on filing the Sponsor's Change of Address. This requirement does not relieve a sponsor who is a lawful permanent resident from submitting Form AR-11 within ten days of a change of address.

Step-by-Step Instructions
Form I-864 is divided into nine parts. The information below will help you fill out the form.

Part 1. Basis for Filing Affidavit of Support.

- Check **box "a"** if you are the petitioner who is filing or who has already filed Form I-130, Petition for Alien Relative; Form I-600, Petition to Classify Orphan as an Immediate Relative; or Form I-600A, Application for Advance Processing of Orphan Petition. If you are the petitioner, you must sponsor each intending immigrant.

- Check **box "b"** if you are filing or have filed Form I-140, Immigrant Petition for Alien Worker, for your husband, wife, father, mother, child, adult son or daughter, brother, or sister.

- Check **box "c"** if you have an ownership interest of at least five percent in a business, corporation or other entity that filed or is filing a Form I-140 for your husband, wife, father, mother, child, adult son or daughter, brother, or sister.

- Check **box "d"** if you are the only joint sponsor or box "e" if you are either of two joint sponsors. A joint sponsor must be a person, and may not be a corporation, organization, or other entity. A joint sponsor does not have to be related to the intending immigrant. Indicate whether you are the only joint sponsor or one of two joint sponsors. Check with the petitioning sponsor or the intending immigrant if you are not certain.

- Check **box "f"** if you are the substitute sponsor. A substitute sponsor is a sponsor who is completing a Form I-864 on behalf of an intending immigrant whose original Form I-130 petitioner has died after the Form I-130 was approved, but before the intending immigrant obtained permanent residence. The substitute sponsor must be related to the intending immigrant in one of the following ways: spouse, parent, mother-in-law, father-in-law, sibling, child (at least 18 years of age), son, daughter, son-in-law, daughter-in-law, brother-in-law, sister-in-law, grandparent, grandchild or legal guardian. The substitute sponsor must also be a U.S. citizen or lawful permanent resident. If you are a substitute sponsor, you must sponsor each intending immigrant.

Part 2. Information on the Principal Immigrant.
The principal immigrant is the intending immigrant who is the primary beneficiary of the visa petition.

6. Alien Registration Number. An "A-number" is an Alien Registration Number assigned by the former Immigration and Naturalization Service (INS) or U.S. Citizenship and Immigration Services (USCIS). If the intending immigrants you are sponsoring have not previously been in the United States or have only been in the United States as tourists, they probably do not have A-numbers. Persons with A-numbers can locate the number on their INS or USCIS-issued documentation.

8. Indicate whether you are sponsoring the principal immigrant listed in **item 2** in this Form I-864. This only applies to cases with two joint sponsors. Check "No" only if you are sponsoring only intended immigrants listed in **9** (a through e) and not the principal immigrant listed in **item 2**.

Part 3. Information on Immigrants You Are Sponsoring.

9. Accompanying Family Members You are Sponsoring
The immigrant you are sponsoring may be bringing a spouse and/or children to the United States. If the spouse and/or children will be traveling with the immigrant, or within six months of the immigrant's entry to the United States and you are sponsoring them, you should list the names and other requested information on the lines provided. If any dependents are not immigrating, will be immigrating more than 6 months after the sponsored alien arrives in the United States, or you are not sponsoring them, do not list their names here. A separate Form I-864 will be required for them when they apply for their immigrant visas.

Part 4. Information on the Sponsor.

15. Country of Domicile. This question is asking you to indicate the country where you maintain your principal residence and where you plan to reside for the foreseeable future. If your mailing address and/or place of residence is not in the United States, but your country of domicile is the United States, you must attach a written explanation and documentary evidence indicating how you meet the domicile requirement. If you are not currently living in the United States, you may meet the domicile requirement if you can submit evidence to establish that any of the following conditions apply:

A. You are employed by a certain organization.

Some individuals employed overseas are automatically considered to be domiciled in the United States because of the nature of their employment. The qualifying types of employment include employment by:

-- The U.S. government;

-- An American institution of research recognized by the Secretary of Homeland Security (The list of qualifying institutions may be found at 8 CFR 316.20);

-- A U.S. firm or corporation engaged in whole or in part in the development of foreign trade and commerce with the United States, or a subsidiary of such a firm or corporation;

-- A public international organization in which the United States participates by treaty or statute;

-- A religious denomination having a bona fide organization in the United States, if the employment abroad involves the person's performance of priestly or ministerial functions on behalf of the denomination; or

-- A religious denomination or interdenominational missionary organization having a bona fide organization in the United States, if the person is engaged solely as a missionary.

B. You are living abroad temporarily.

If you are not currently living in the United States, you must show that your trip abroad is temporary and that you have maintained your domicile in the United States. You can show this by providing proof of your voting record in the United States, proof of paying U.S. State or local taxes, proof of having property in the United States, proof of maintaining bank or investment accounts in the United States, or proof of having a permanent mailing address in the United States. Other proof could be evidence that you are a student studying abroad or that a foreign government has authorized a temporary stay.

C. You intend in good faith to reestablish your domicile in the United States no later than the date of the intending immigrant's admission or adjustment of status.

You must submit proof that you have taken concrete steps to establish you will be domiciled in the United States at a time no later than the date of the intending immigrant's admission or adjustment of status. Concrete steps might include accepting a job in the United States, signing a lease or purchasing a residence in the United States, or registering children in U.S. schools. Please attach proof of the steps you have taken to establish domicile as described above.

18. U.S. Social Security Number.

Every sponsor's Social Security number is required by law. If you do not currently have a Social Security number you must obtain one before submitting this Form I-864.

19. Citizenship/Residency.

Proof of U.S. citizen, national, or permanent resident status is required for joint and substitute sponsors and for relatives of employment-based immigrants who file this form. Petitioning relatives who have already filed proof of their citizenship or immigration status with Forms I-130, Form I-129F, I-600 and I-600A do not need to submit proof of their status with this form.

Proof of U.S. citizen or national status includes a copy of your birth certificate, certificate of naturalization, certificate of citizenship, consular report of birth abroad to citizen parents, or a copy of the biographic data page of your U.S. passport.

Proof of permanent resident status includes a photocopy of both sides of the "green card," Form I-551, Alien Registration Receipt Card/Permanent Resident Card; or a photocopy of an unexpired temporary I-551 stamp in either a foreign passport or a DHS Form I-94, Arrival/Departure Document.

20. Military Service.

Check "yes" if you are the petitioning sponsor and on active duty in the U.S. Army, Navy, Air Force, Marines, or Coast Guard, other than for training. If you provide evidence that you are currently on active duty in the military and you are petitioning for your spouse or minor child, you will need to demonstrate income at only 100 percent of the poverty level for your household size, instead of at 125 percent of the poverty level. (See Form I-864P for information on the poverty levels.) Check "no" if you are not on active duty in the U.S. military. This provision does not apply to joint and substitute sponsors.

Part 5. Sponsor's Household Size.

This section asks you to add together the number of persons for whom you are financially responsible. Some of these persons may not be residing with you. Make sure you do not count any individual more than once, since in some cases the same person could fit into two categories. For example, your spouse (whom you would enter on **line 21c**) might also be a lawful permanent resident whom you have already sponsored using Form I-864 (**line 21f**). If you included your spouse on line 21c, do not include him or her again on **line 21f**.

21d - Enter the number of unmarried children you have who are under age 21, even if you do not have legal custody of these children. You may exclude any unmarried children under 21, if these children have reached majority under the law of their place of domicile and you do not claim them as dependents on your income tax returns.

21e - Enter the number of any other dependents. You must include each and every person whom you have claimed as a dependent on your most recent Federal income tax return, even if that person is not related to you. Even if you are not *legally obligated* to support that person, you must include the person if in fact you did support that person and claimed the person as a dependent.

21f - Enter the number of lawful permanent residents whom you are currently obligated to support based on your previous submission of Form I-864 as a petitioning, substitute, or joint sponsor, or of Form I-864EZ as a petitioning sponsor. Include only those persons who have already immigrated to the United States. Do not include anyone for whom your obligation to support has ended through the sponsored immigrant's acquisition of U.S. citizenship, death, abandonment of lawful permanent residence in the United States, acquisition of 40 quarters of earned or credited work in the United States, or obtaining a new grant of adjustment of status while in removal proceedings based on a new affidavit of support, if one is required.

21g - This question gives you the option of including certain other non-dependent relatives who are living in your residence as part of your household size. Such relatives may include your mother, father, sister, brother or adult children, if they are living in your residence. However, the only reason to include these family members in your household size is if you need to include their income when you calculate your household income for purposes of meeting the income requirement for this form. To be considered, any relative indicated in this category must sign and submit Form I-864A.

Part 6. Sponsor's Income and Employment.

22. Job Classification.

Check the box (**a through d**) that applies to you.

23. Current Individual Annual Income.

Enter your current individual earned or retirement annual income that you are using to meet the requirements of this form and indicate the total on this line.

You may include evidence supporting your claim about your expected income for the current year if you believe that submitting this evidence will help you establish ability to maintain sufficient income. **You are not required to submit this evidence, however, unless specifically instructed to do so by a Government official.** For example, you may include a recent letter from your employer, showing your employer's address and telephone number, and indicating your annual salary. You may also provide pay stub(s) showing your income for the previous six months. If your claimed income includes alimony, child support, dividend or interest income, or income from any other source, you may also include evidence of that income.

24. Annual Household Income.

This section is used to determine the sponsor's household income. Take your annual individual income from **line 23** and enter it on **line 24a**. If this amount is greater than 125 percent (or 100 percent if you are on active duty in the U.S. military and sponsoring your spouse or child) of the Federal Poverty Guidelines for your household size from **line 21h**, you do not need to include any household member's income. See Form I-864P for reference on the Poverty Guidelines.

To determine the filing requirements for your relatives included in **Item 24b**, follow these instructions:

- If you included the income of your **spouse** listed in **21c**, or any **child** listed in **21d**, or any **dependent** listed in **21e**, or any **other relative** listed in **21g**, each one of these individuals must be over 18 years of age and must complete Form I-864A.

- If you included the income of the intending immigrant who is your spouse (he or she would be counted on line **21a**), evidence that his/her income will continue from the current source after obtaining lawful permanent resident status must be provided. He/she does not need to complete Form I-864A unless he/she has accompanying children.

- If you included the income of the intending immigrant who is not your spouse, (he or she would be counted on line **21a**), evidence that his or her income will continue from the current source after obtaining lawful permanent resident status must be provided **and** the intending immigrant must provide evidence that he/she is living in your residence. He or she does not need to complete Form I-864A, Contract Between Sponsor and Household Member, unless he or she has an accompanying spouse or children.

25. Federal Income Tax Information.

You must provide either an IRS transcript or a photocopy from your own records of your Federal individual income tax return for the most recent tax year. If you believe additional returns may help you to establish your ability to maintain sufficient income, you may submit transcripts or photocopies of your Federal individual income tax returns for the three most recent years.

You are not required to have the IRS certify the transcript or photocopy unless specifically instructed to do so by a Government official; a plain transcript or photocopy is acceptable. Telefile tax records are not acceptable proof of filing.

Do not submit copies of your State income tax returns. **Do not** submit any tax returns that you filed with any foreign government unless you claim that you were not required to file a Federal tax return with the United States government and you wish to rely on the foreign return solely to establish the amount of your income that is not subject to tax in the United States.

If you provide a photocopy of your tax return(s), you must include a copy of each and every Form W-2 and Form 1099 that relates to your return(s). Do not include copies of these Forms if you provide an IRS transcript of your return(s) rather than a photocopy.

If you checked box **22(b)** (self-employed), you should have completed one of the following forms with your Federal income tax return. Schedule C (Profit or Loss from Business), Schedule D (Capital Gains), Schedule E (Supplemental Income or Loss) or Schedule F (Profit or Loss from Farming). You must include each and every Form 1040 Schedule, if any, that you filed with your Federal tax return.

If you were required to file a Federal income tax return during any of the previous three tax years but did not do so, you must file any and all late returns with IRS and attach an IRS-generated tax return transcript documenting your late filing before submitting the I-864 Affidavit of Support. If you were not required to file a Federal income tax return under U.S. tax law because your income was too low, attach a written explanation. If you were not required to file a Federal income tax return under U.S. tax law for any other reason, attach a written explanation including evidence of the exemption and how you are subject to it. Residence outside of the United States does not exempt U.S. citizens or lawful permanent

residents from filing a U.S. Federal income tax return. See "Filing Requirements" in the IRS Form 1040 Filing Instructions to determine whether you were required to file.

For purposes of this affidavit, the line for gross (total) income on IRS Forms 1040 and 1040A will be considered when determining income. For persons filing IRS Form 1040 EZ, the line for adjusted gross income will be considered.

Obtaining Tax Transcripts. You may use Internal Revenue Service (IRS) Form 4506-T to request tax transcripts from the IRS. Complete IRS Form 4506-T with the ending date for each of your three most recent tax years listed on line 9. Follow all instructions for completing and filing Form 4506-T with the IRS.

Part 7. Use of Assets to Supplement Income.

Only complete this Part if you need to use the value of assets to meet the income requirements. If your Total Household Income (indicated on **Line 24c**) is equal to or more than needed to meet the income requirement as shown by the current Poverty Guidelines (Form I-864P) for your household size (indicated on **Line 21h**), you do not need to complete this Part. If your total household income does not meet the requirement, you may submit evidence of the value of your assets, the sponsored immigrant's assets, and/or assets of a household member that can be used, if necessary, for the support of the intending immigrant(s). The value of assets of all of these persons may be combined in order to meet the necessary requirement.

Only assets that can be converted into cash within one year and without considerable hardship or financial loss to the owner may be included. The owner of the asset must include a description of the asset, proof of ownership, and the basis for the owner's claim of its net cash value.

You may include the net value of your home as an asset. The net value of the home is the appraised value of the home, minus the sum of any and all loans secured by a mortgage, trust deed, or other lien on the home. If you wish to include the net value of your home, this, you must include documentation demonstrating that you own it, a recent appraisal by a licensed appraiser, and evidence of the amount of any and all loans secured by a mortgage, trust deed, or other lien on the home. You may not include the net value an automobile unless you show that you have more than one automobile, and at least one automobile is not included as an asset.

26. Assets.

To use your own assets, you must complete lines **26a** through **26d** and submit corresponding evidence with this form. Supporting evidence must be attached to establish location, ownership, date of acquisition, and value of any real estate holding.

27. Household Member's Assets.

To use the assets of a relative (spouse, adult son or daughter, parent or sibling), the relative must reside with you and have completed a Form I-864A, Contract Between Sponsor and Household Member, with accompanying evidence of assets. The Form I-864A and accompanying evidence of assets is submitted with Form I-864. You may use the assets of more than one relative who resides with you so long as you submit a complete Form I-864A with evidence of assets for each such relative.

28. Assets of the Intending Immigrant.

You may use the assets of the intending immigrant regardless of where he or she resides. The intending immigrant must provide evidence of such assets with this form. Form I-864A is not required to document the intending immigrant's assets.

29. Total Value of Assets.

In order to qualify based on the value of your assets, the total value of your assets must equal at least five times the difference between your total household income and the current poverty guidelines for your household size. However, if you are a U.S. citizen and you are sponsoring your spouse or minor child, the total value of your assets must only be equal to at least three times the difference. If the intending immigrant is an alien orphan who will be adopted in the United States after the alien orphan acquires permanent residence, and who will, as a result, acquire citizenship under section 320 of the Act, the total value of your assets need only equal the difference.

Example of How to Use Assets: If you are petitioning for a parent and the poverty line for your household size is $22,062 and your current income is $18,062, the difference between your current income and the poverty line is $4,000. In order for assets to help you qualify, the combination of your assets, plus the assets of any household member who is signing Form I-864A, plus any available assets of the sponsored immigrant, would have to equal five times this difference (5 x $4,000). In this case, you would meet the income requirements if the net value of the assets equaled at least $20,000.

Part 8. Sponsor's Contact.

Read the contract carefully, print your name, and then sign and date the form. **If you do not print your name on line 30 and sign and date the form on line 31, the intending immigrant you are sponsoring cannot be issued a visa or be granted adjustment of status.**

Other Information.

Penalties.

The Government may pursue verification of any information provided on or in support of this form, including employment, income, or assets with the employer, financial or other institutions, the Internal Revenue Service, or the Social Security Administration. If you include in this affidavit of support any information that you know to be false, you may be liable for criminal prosecution under the laws of the United States.

If you fail to give notice of your change of address, as required by 8 U.S.C. 1183a(d) and 8 CFR 213a.3, you may be liable for the civil penalty established by 8 U.S.C. 1183a(d) (2). The amount of the civil penalty will depend on whether you failed to give this notice because you were aware that the immigrant(s) you sponsored had received Federal, State, or local means-tested public benefits.

If the failure to report your change of address occurs with knowledge that the sponsored immigrant received means-tested public benefits (other than benefits described in section 401(b), 403(c)(2), or 4ll(b) of the Personal Responsibility and Work Opportunity Reconciliation Act of 1996, which are summarized in the contract in Part 8) such failure may result in a fine of not less than $2,000 or more than $5,000. Otherwise, the failure to report your change of address may result in a fine not less than $250 or more than $2,000.

Privacy Act Notice.

Authority for the collection of the information requested on this form is contained in 8 U.S.C. 1182a(4), 1183a, 1184(a), and 1258. The information will be used principally by an immigration judge, USCIS or a Consular Officer to support an alien's application for benefits under the Immigration and Nationality Act and specifically the assertion that he or she has adequate means of financial support and will not become a public charge. Submission of the information is voluntary. Failure to provide the information will result in denial of the application for an immigrant visa or adjustment of status.

The information may also, as a matter of routine use, be disclosed to other Federal, State and local agencies providing means-tested public benefits for use in civil action against the sponsor for breach of contract. Social Security numbers may be verified with the Social Security Administration consistant with the consent signed as part of the contract in **Part 8** of the Form I-864. It may also be disclosed as a matter of routine use to other Federal, State, local, and foreign law enforcement and regulatory agencies to enable these entities to carry out their law enforcement responsibilities.

USCIS Forms and Information.

To order USCIS forms, call our toll-free forms line at **1-800-870-3676.** You can also obtain forms and information on immigration laws, regulations and procedures by telephoning our National Customer Service Center at **1-800-375-5283** or visiting our internet website at **www.uscis.gov**.

Use InfoPass for Appointments.

As an alternative to waiting in line for assistance at your local USCIS office, you can now schedule an appointment through our internet-based system, **InfoPass**. To access the system, visit our website at www.uscis.gov. Use the **InfoPass** appointment scheduler and follow the screen prompts to set up your appointment. **InfoPass** generates an electronic appointment notice that appears on the screen. Print the notice and take it with you to your appointment. The notice gives the time and date of your appointment, along with the address of the USCIS office.

Reporting Burden.

A person is not required to respond to a collection of information unless it displays a currently valid OMB control number.

We try to create forms and instructions that are accurate, can be easily understood, and which impose the least burden on you to provide us with information. Often this is difficult because some immigration laws are very complex.

The estimated average time to complete and file this form is as follows: (1) 75 minutes to learn about the law and form; (2) 90 minutes to complete the form; and (3) 3 hour and 15 minutes to assemble and file the form; for a total estimated average of 6 hours per form.

If you have comments regarding the accuracy of this estimate, or suggestions for making this form simpler, write to U.S. Citizenship and Immigration Services, Regulatory Management Division, Attn: OMB No. 1615-0075, 111 Massachusetts Avenue N.W., Washington, D.C. 20529. **Do not mail your completed affidavit of support to this address.**

Check List

The following items must be submitted with Form I-864:

For ALL sponsors:

—— A copy of your individual **Federal income tax return, including W-2s** for the most recent tax year, or a statement and/or evidence describing why you were not required to file. Also include a copy of each and every Form 1099, Schedule, and any other evidence of reported income. You may submit this information for the most recent three tax years , pay stub(s) from the most recent six months, and/or a letter from your employer if you believe any of these items will help you qualify.

For SOME sponsors:

—— **If you are currently self-employed**, a copy of your Schedule C, D, E or F from your most recent Federal Tax Return which establishes your income from your business.

—— If you are sponsoring more than one intending immigrant listed on the same affidavit of support, **photocopies of the original affidavit of support** may be submitted for any additional intending immigrants listed. Copies of supporting documentation are not required for these family members.

—— If you are the petitioning sponsor and on active duty in the U.S. Armed Forces and are sponsoring your spouse or child using 100 percent of governing poverty guideline, **proof of your active military status**.

—— If you are using the income of persons in your household or dependents to qualify,

    —— A separate **Form I-864A** for each person whose income you will use. However, an intending immigrant whose income is being used needs to complete Form I-864A only if his or her spouse and/or children are immigrating with him or her.

    —— Proof of their **residency in your household and relationship** to you if they are not the intending immigrants or are not listed as dependents on your Federal income tax return for the most recent tax year.

    —— Proof that the intending immigrant's current employment **will continue from the same source** if his or her income is being used.

    —— A copy of their individual **Federal income tax return, including W-2s and 1099s,** for the most recent tax year, or evidence that they were not required to file. You may submit this information for the most recent three years if you believe it will help you qualify.

—— If you use your assets or the assets of a household member to qualify,

    —— Documentation of assets establishing location, ownership, date of acquisition and value. Evidence of any liens or liabilities against these assets.

    —— A separate **Form I-864A** for each household member using assets other than for the intending immigrant.

—— If you are a joint sponsor, substitute sponsor, or the relative of an employment-based immigrant requiring an affidavit of support, **proof of your citizenship status, U.S. national status or lawful permanent resident status.**

    —— For U.S. citizens or nationals, a copy of your birth certificate, passport, or certificate of naturalization or citizenship.

    —— For lawful permanent residents, a copy of both sides of your Form I-551, Permanent Resident Card.

OMB No. 1615-0075; Expires 10/31/10

I-864, Affidavit of Support
Under Section 213A of the Act

Department of Homeland Security
U.S. Citizenship and Immigration Services

Part 1. Basis for filing Affidavit of Support.

1. I, _____ ,

am the sponsor submitting this affidavit of support because (Check only one box):

a. ☐ **I am the petitioner. I filed or am filing for the immigration of my relative.**

b. ☐ **I filed an alien worker petition on behalf of the intending immigrant, who is related to me as my** _____

c. ☐ **I have an ownership interest of at least 5 percent in** _____ , **which filed an alien worker petition on behalf of the intending immigrant, who is related to me as my** _____

d. ☐ **I am the only joint sponsor.**

e. ☐ **I am the** ☐ **first** ☐ **second of two joint sponsors.** *(Check appropriate box.)*

f. ☐ **The original petitioner is deceased. I am the substitute sponsor. I am the intending immigrant's** _____ .

Part 2. Information on the principal immigrant.

2. Last Name

First Name | Middle Name

3. Mailing Address Street Number and Name *(Include Apartment Number)*

City | State/Province | Zip/Postal Code | Country

4. Country of Citizenship | **5.** Date of Birth *(mm/dd/yyyy)*

6. Alien Registration Number *(if any)*
A- | **7.** U.S. Social Security Number *(if any)*

For Government Use Only
This I-864 is from:
☐ the Petitioner
☐ a Joint Sponsor #
☐ the Substitute Sponsor
☐ 5% Owner
This I-864:
☐ does not meet the requirements of section 213A.
☐ meets the requirements of section 213A.
Reviewer
Location
Date *(mm/dd/yyyy)*
Number of Affidavits of Support in file:
☐ 1   ☐ 2

Part 3. Information on the immigrant(s) you are sponsoring.

8. ☐ I am sponsoring the principal immigrant named in **Part 2** above.

   ☐ Yes   ☐ No (Applicable only in cases with two joint sponsors)

9. ☐ I am sponsoring the following family members immigrating at the same time or within six months of the principal immigrant named in **Part 2** above. Do not include any relative listed on a separate visa petition.

	Name	Relationship to Sponsored Immigrant	Date of Birth *(mm/dd/yyyy)*	A-Number *(if any)*	U.S. Social Security Number *(if any)*
a.					
b.					
c.					
d.					
e.					

10. Enter the total number of immigrants you are sponsoring on this form from **Part 3**, Items **8** and **9**.   ☐☐

Form I-864 (Rev. 10/18/07)Y

Part 4. Information on the Sponsor.

			For Government Use Only
11. Name	Last Name		
	First Name	Middle Name	
12. Mailing Address	Street Number and Name *(Include Apartment Number)*		
	City	State or Province	
	Country	Zip/Postal Code	
13. Place of Residence *(if different from mailing address)*	Street Number and Name *(Include Apartment Number)*		
	City	State or Province	
	Country	Zip/Postal Code	
14. Telephone Number *(Include Area Code or Country and City Codes)*			
15. Country of Domicile			
16. Date of Birth *(mm/dd/yyyy)*			
17. Place of Birth *(City)*	State or Province	Country	
18. U.S. Social Security Number *(Required)*			

19. Citizenship/Residency

☐ I am a U.S. citizen.

☐ I am a U.S. national (for joint sponsors only).

☐ I am a lawful permanent resident. My alien registration number is A-

If you checked box (b), (c), (d), (e) or (f) in line 1 on Page 1, you must include proof of your citizen, national, or permanent resident status.

20. Military Service (To be completed by petitioner sponsors only.)

I am currently on active duty in the U.S. armed services.　　☐ Yes　　☐ No

Part 5. Sponsor's household size.

	For Government Use Only

21. Your Household Size - <u>DO NOT COUNT ANYONE TWICE</u>

Persons you are sponsoring in this affidavit:

    a. Enter the number you entered on line 10.   ☐☐

Persons NOT sponsored in this affidavit:

    b. Yourself.   **1**

    c. If you are currently married, enter "1" for your spouse.   ☐

    d. If you have dependent children, enter the number here.   ☐☐

    e. If you have any other dependents, enter the number here.   ☐☐

    f. If you have sponsored any other persons on an I-864 or I-864 EZ who are now lawful permanent residents, enter the number here.   ☐☐

    g. OPTIONAL: If you have <u>siblings, parents, or adult children</u> with the same principal residence who are combining their income with yours by submitting Form I-864A, enter the number here.   ☐☐

    h. Add together lines and enter the number here. **Household Size:**   ☐☐

Part 6. Sponsor's income and employment.

22. I am currently:

    a. ☐ Employed as a/an _____ .

         Name of Employer #1 *(if applicable)* _____ .

         Name of Employer #2 *(if applicable)* _____ .

    b. ☐ Self-employed as a/an _____ .

    c. ☐ Retired from _____ since _____ .
                          (Company Name)   *(Date)*

    d. ☐ Unemployed since _____ .
                                (Date)

23. My current individual annual income is: $ _____
                                           (See Step-by-Step Instructions)

SAMPLE

24. My current annual household income:

    a. List your income from line 23 of this form. $ _____

    b. Income you are using from any other person who was counted in your household size, including, in certain conditions, the intending immigrant. (See step-by-step instructions.) Please indicate name, relationship and income.

Name	Relationship	Current Income
_____	_____	$ _____
_____	_____	$ _____
_____	_____	$ _____
_____	_____	$ _____

    c. Total Household Income: $ _____

    (Total all lines from 24a and 24b. Will be Compared to Poverty Guidelines -- See Form I-864P.)

    d. ☐ The persons listed above have completed Form I-864A. I am filing along with this form all necessary Forms I-864A completed by these persons.

    e. ☐ The person listed above, _____ does not need to
                                       (Name)
    complete Form I-864A because he/she is the intending immigrant and has no accompanying dependents.

25. Federal income tax return information.

    ☐ I have filed a Federal tax return for each of the three most recent tax years. I have attached the required photocopy or transcript of my Federal tax return for only the most recent tax year.

    My total income (adjusted gross income on IRS Form 1040EZ) as reported on my Federal tax returns for the most recent three years was:

Tax Year		Total Income
_____	*(most recent)*	$ _____
_____	*(2nd most recent)*	$ _____
_____	*(3rd most recent)*	$ _____

    ☐ *(Optional)* I have attached photocopies or transcripts of my Federal tax returns for my second and third most recent tax years.

For Government Use Only

Household Size = _____

Poverty line for year _____ is:

$ _____

SAMPLE

Part 7. Use of assets to supplement income. *(Optional)*

| | For Government Use Only |

If your income, or the total income for you and your household, from line 24c exceeds the Federal Poverty Guidelines for your household size, YOU ARE NOT REQUIRED to complete this Part. Skip to Part 8.

Household Size =

26. **Your assets** *(Optional)*

    a. Enter the balance of all savings and checking accounts. $ _____

    b. Enter the net cash value of real-estate holdings. (Net means current assessed value minus mortgage debt.) $ _____

    Poverty line for year

    _____ **is:**

    $ _____

    c. Enter the net cash value of all stocks, bonds, certificates of deposit, and any other assets not already included in lines 26 (a) or (b). $ _____

    d. Add together lines 26 a, b and c and enter the number here.   **TOTAL:** $ _____

27. **Your household member's assets from Form I-864A.** *(Optional)*

    Assets from Form I-864A, line 12d for

    $ _____

    (Name of Relative)

28. **Assets of the principal sponsored immigrant.** *(Optional)*

    The principal sponsored immigrant is the person listed in line 2.

    a. Enter the balance of the sponsored immigrant's savings and checking accounts. $ _____

    b. Enter the net cash value of all the sponsored immigrant's real estate holdings. (Net means investment value minus mortgage debt.) $ _____

    c. Enter the current cash value of the sponsored immigrant's stocks, bonds, certificates of deposit, and other assets not included on line a or b. $ _____

    d. Add together lines 28a, b, and c, and enter the number here. $ _____

The total value of all assests, line 29, must equal 5 times (3 times for spouses and children of USCs, or 1 time for orphans to be formally adopted in the U.S.) the difference between the poverty guidelines and the sponsor's household income, line 24c.

29. **Total value of assets.**

    Add together lines 26d, 27 and 28d and enter the number here.   **TOTAL:** $ _____

Part 8. Sponsor's Contract.

Please note that, by signing this Form I-864, you agree to assume certain specific obligations under the Immigration and Nationality Act and other Federal laws. The following paragraphs describe those obligations. Please read the following information carefully before you sign the Form I-864. If you do not understand the obligations, you may wish to consult an attorney or accredited representative.

What is the Legal Effect of My Signing a Form I-864?

If you sign a Form I-864 on behalf of any person (called the "intending immigrant") who is applying for an immigrant visa or for adjustment of status to a permanent resident, and that intending immigrant submits the Form I-864 to the U.S. Government with his or her application for an immigrant visa or adjustment of status, under section 213A of the Immigration and Nationality Act these actions create a contract between you and the U.S. Government. The intending immigrant's becoming a permanent resident is the "consideration" for the contract.

Under this contract, you agree that, in deciding whether the intending immigrant can establish that he or she is not inadmissible to the United States as an alien likely to become a public charge, the U.S. Government can consider your income and assets to be available for the support of the intending immigrant.

What If I choose Not to Sign a Form I-864?

You cannot be made to sign a Form I-864 if you do not want to do so. But if you do not sign the Form I-864, the intending immigrant may not be able to become a permanent resident in the United States.

What Does Signing the Form I-864 Require Me to do?

If an intending immigrant becomes a permanent resident in the United States based on a Form I-864 that you have signed, then, until your obligations under the Form I-864 terminate, you must:

-- Provide the intending immigrant any support necessary to maintain him or her at an income that is at least 125 percent of the Federal Poverty Guidelines for his or her household size (100 percent if you are the petitioning sponsor and are on active duty in the U.S. Armed Forces and the person is your husband, wife, unmarried child under 21 years old.)

-- Notify USCIS of any change in your address, within 30 days of the change, by filing Form I-865.

What Other Consequences Are There?

If an intending immigrant becomes a permanent resident in the United States based on a Form I-864 that you have signed, then until your obligations under the Form I-864 terminate, your income and assets may be considered ("deemed") to be available to that person, in determining whether he or she is eligible for certain Federal means-tested public benefits and also for State or local means-tested public benefits, if the State or local government's rules provide for consideration ("deeming") of your income and assets as available to the person.

This provision does **not** apply to public benefits specified in section 403(c) of the Welfare Reform Act such as, but not limited to, emergency Medicaid, short-term, non-cash emergency relief; services provided under the National School Lunch and Child Nutrition Acts; immunizations and testing and treatment for communicable diseases; and means-tested programs under the Elementary and Secondary Education Act.

Contract continued on following page.

What If I Do Not Fulfill My Obligations?

If you do not provide sufficient support to the person who becomes a permanent resident based on the Form I-864 that you signed, that person may sue you for this support.

If a Federal, State or local agency, or a private agency provides any covered means-tested public benefit to the person who becomes a permanent resident based on the Form I-864 that you signed, the agency may ask you to reimburse them for the amount of the benefits they provided. If you do not make the reimbursement, the agency may sue you for the amount that the agency believes you owe.

If you are sued, and the court enters a judgment against you, the person or agency that sued you may use any legally permitted procedures for enforcing or collecting the judgment. You may also be required to pay the costs of collection, including attorney fees.

If you do not file a properly completed Form I-865 within 30 days of any change of address, USCIS may impose a civil fine for your failing to do so.

When Will These Obligations End?

Your obligations under a Form I-864 will end if the person who becomes a permanent resident based on a Form I-864 that you signed:

- Becomes a U.S. citizen;
- Has worked, or can be credited with, 40 quarters of coverage under the Social Security Act;
- No longer has lawful permanent resident status, and has departed the United States;
- Becomes subject to removal, but applies for and obtains in removal proceedings a new grant of adjustment of status, based on a new affidavit of support, if one is required; or
- Dies.

Note that divorce **does not** terminate your obligations under this Form I-864.

Your obligations under a Form I-864 also end if you die. Therefore, if you die, your Estate will not be required to take responsibility for the person's support after your death. Your Estate may, however, be responsible for any support that you owed before you died.

30. I, _____ ,

(Print Sponsor's Name)

certify under penalty of perjury under the laws of the United States that:

a. I know the contents of this affidavit of support that I signed.

b. All the factual statements in this affidavit of support are true and correct.

c. I have read and I understand each of the obligations described in Part 8, and I agree, freely and without any mental reservation or purpose of evasion, to accept each of those obligations in order to make it possible for the immigrants indicated in Part 3 to become permanent residents of the United States;

d. I agree to submit to the personal jurisdiction of any Federal or State court that has subject matter jurisdiction of a lawsuit against me to enforce my obligations under this Form I-864;

e. Each of the Federal income tax returns submitted in support of this affidavit are true copies, or are unaltered tax transcripts, of the tax returns I filed with the U.S. Internal Revenue Service; and

Sign on following page.

Form I-864 (Rev. 10/18/07)Y Page 7

f. I authorize the Social Security Administration to release information about me in its records to the Department of State and U.S. Citizenship and Immigration Services.

g. Any and all other evidence submitted is true and correct.

31. _____   _____
              (Sponsor's Signature)   *(Date-- mm/dd/yyyy)*

Part 9. Information on Preparer, if prepared by someone other than the sponsor

I certify under penalty of perjury under the laws of the United States that I prepared this affidavit of support at the sponsor's request and that this affidavit of support is based on all information of which I have knowledge.

Signature: _____   **Date:** _____
                                                       (mm/dd/yyyy)

Printed Name: _____

Firm Name: _____

Address: _____

Telephone Number: _____

E-Mail Address : _____

Business State ID # *(if any)* _____

OMB No. 1615-0048; Expires 07/31/09

Department of Homeland Security
U.S. Citizenship and Immigration Services

I-907, Request for
Premium Processing Service

START HERE - Please Type or Print (Use black ink.)

	For USCIS Use Only

Part 1. Information about you. *(Person filing this petition.)*

Individual Named in the Related Case:

Family Name *(Last Name)*	Given Name *(First Name)*	Full Middle Name

If filed on behalf of a company: Company or Business Named in the Related Case

Mailing Address - Street Number and Name / P.O. Box Number

Company Contact Information:

Name of Company Contact	Title/Position

City	State/Province	Zip/Postal Code

IRS Tax # *(if any)*

You (the person submitting this request)

- [ ] Are the petitioner who is filing or has filed a petition eligible for Premium Processing.
- [ ] Are the attorney/accredited representative for the petitioner who is filing or has filed a petition eligible for Premium Processing. *(Complete and submit Form G-28.)*
- [ ] Are the applicant who is filing or has filed an application eligible for Premium Processing.
- [ ] Are the attorney/accredited representative for the applicant who is filing or has filed an application eligible for Premium Processing. *(Complete and submit Form G-28.)*

Phone Number *(Area/Country Code)*	Fax Number *(Area/Country Code)*

For USCIS Use Only

Request Physically Received by USCIS	Receipt
Date	
Date	
Returned	
Date	
Date	
Resubmitted	
Date	
Date	

To Be Completed by
Attorney or Representative, if any.

- [ ] Fill in box if G-28 is attached to represent the applicant.

ATTY State License #

E-Mail Address *(If Any)*

Part 2. Information about request.

1. Form number of related petition/application.	2. Receipt number of related petition/application.	3. Classification/Eligibility Requested.

4. Petitioner/Applicant in the relating case.	5. Beneficiary in the relating case.

Part 3. Original signature. *(This is the same person authorized to sign the petition or application.)*

It is understood that if U.S. Citizenship and Immigration Services (USCIS) does not issue an approval notice, request for evidence, notice of intent to deny, or refer for investigation of suspected fraud or misrepresentation within 15-calendar days after this request has been physically received at the appropriate USCIS office, a refund of the Premium Processing fee will be given to the addressee shown in **Part 1** of this request.

I certify, under penalty of perjury under the laws of the United States of America, that the information provided with this request is all true and correct. I authorize the release of any information from my records that USCIS needs to determine eligibility for the benefit being sought.

Signature	Title *(if applicable)*

Print Your Name	Date *(mm/dd/yyyy)*

Part 4. Original signature of attorney or accredited representative. *(Note if attorney is signing above in Part 3.)*

I declare that I prepared this application at the request of the above person and it is based on all information of which I have knowledge.

- [ ] Same individual as signing above in **Part 3**. *(If this box is checked, provide all the requested information below and a submit a Form G-28.)*

Signature	Print Your Name	Date *(mm/dd/yyyy)*

Firm Name and Address	Daytime Phone Number *(Area Code and Number)*

Form I-907 (Rev. 07/30/07) Y

OMB No. 1615-0052; Expires 10/31/08

Department of Homeland Security
U.S Citizenship and Immigration Services

N-400 Application
for Naturalization

Print clearly or type your answers using CAPITAL letters. Failure to print clearly may delay your application. Use black ink.

Part 1. Your Name.*(The person applying for naturalization.)*

A. Your current legal name.

Family Name *(Last Name)*

Given Name *(First Name)* Full Middle Name *(If applicable)*

B. Your name **exactly** as it appears on your Permanent Resident Card.

Family Name *(Last Name)*

Given Name *(First Name)* Full Middle Name *(If applicable)*

C. If you have ever used other names, provide them below.

Family Name *(Last Name)*	Given Name *(First Name)*	Middle Name

D. Name change *(optional)*

Please read the Instructions before you decide whether to change your name.

1. Would you like to legally change your name? ☐ Yes ☐ No

2. If "Yes," print the new name you would like to use. Do not use initials or abbreviations when writing your new name.

Family Name *(Last Name)*

Given Name *(First Name)* Full Middle Name

Write your USCIS "A"- number here:
A

For USCIS Use Only

Bar Code Date Stamp

Remarks

Action Block

Part 2. Information about your eligibility. *(Check only one.)*

I am at least 18 years old **AND**

A. ☐ I have been a Lawful Permanent Resident of the United States for at least five years.

B. ☐ I have been a Lawful Permanent Resident of the United States for at least three years, **and** I have been married to and living with the same U.S. citizen for the last three years, **and** my spouse has been a U.S. citizen for the last three years.

C. ☐ I am applying on the basis of qualifying military service.

D. ☐ Other *(Please explain)* _____

Part 3. Information about you.	Write your USCIS "A"- number here: A

A. U.S. Social Security Number   **B.** Date of Birth *(mm/dd/yyyy)*   **C.** Date You Became a Permanent Resident *(mm/dd/yyyy)*

D. Country of Birth

E. Country of Nationality

F. Are either of your parents U.S. citizens? *(If yes, see instructions.)*   ☐ Yes   ☐ No

G. What is your current marital status?   ☐ Single, Never Married   ☐ Married   ☐ Divorced   ☐ Widowed

☐ Marriage Annulled or Other *(Explain)*

H. Are you requesting a waiver of the English and/or U.S. History and Government requirements based on a disability or impairment and attaching a Form N-648 with your application?   ☐ Yes   ☐ No

I. Are you requesting an accommodation to the naturalization process because of a disability or impairment? *(See Instructions for some examples of accommodations.)*   ☐ Yes   ☐ No

If you answered "Yes," check the box below that applies:

☐ I am deaf or hearing impaired and need a sign language interpreter who uses the following language: _____

☐ I use a wheelchair.

☐ I am blind or sight impaired.

☐ I will need another type of accommodation. Please explain: _____

_____

_____

Part 4. Addresses and telephone numbers.

A. Home Address - Street Number and Name *(Do **not** write a P.O. Box in this space.)*   Apartment Number

City	County	State	ZIP Code	Country

B. Care of   Mailing Address - Street Number and Name *(If different from home address)*   Apartment Number

City	State	ZIP Code	Country

C. Daytime Phone Number *(If any)*   Evening Phone Number *(If any)*   E-mail Address *(If any)*

(   )   (   )

Part 5. Information for criminal records search.	Write your USCIS "A"- number here: A

NOTE: The categories below are those required by the FBI. See Instructions for more information.

A. Gender

☐ Male ☐ Female

B. Height

Feet	Inches

C. Weight

Pounds

D. Are you Hispanic or Latino? ☐ Yes ☐ No

E. Race *(Select one or more.)*

☐ White ☐ Asian ☐ Black or African American ☐ American Indian or Alaskan Native ☐ Native Hawaiian or Other Pacific Islander

F. Hair color

☐ Black ☐ Brown ☐ Blonde ☐ Gray ☐ White ☐ Red ☐ Sandy ☐ Bald (No Hair)

G. Eye color

☐ Brown ☐ Blue ☐ Green ☐ Hazel ☐ Gray ☐ Black ☐ Pink ☐ Maroon ☐ Other

Part 6. Information about your residence and employment.

A. Where have you lived during the last five years? Begin with where you live now and then list every place you lived for the last five years. If you need more space, use a separate sheet(s) of paper.

Street Number and Name, Apartment Number, City, State, Zip Code and Country	Dates (*mm/dd/yyyy*)	
	From	To
Current Home Address - Same as Part 4\A		Present

B. Where have you worked (or, if you were a student, what schools did you attend) during the last five years? Include military service. Begin with your current or latest employer and then list every place you have worked or studied for the last five years. If you need more space, use a separate sheet of paper.

Employer or School Name	Employer or School Address *(Street, City and State)*	Dates (*mm/dd/yyyy*)		Your Occupation
		From	To	

| Part 7. **Time outside the United States.**
(Including Trips to Canada, Mexico and the Caribbean Islands) | Write your USCIS "A"- number here:
A |

A. How many total days did you spend outside of the United States during the past five years? [   ] days

B. How many trips of 24 hours or more have you taken outside of the United States during the past five years? [   ] trips

C. List below all the trips of 24 hours or more that you have taken outside of the United States since becoming a Lawful Permanent Resident. Begin with your most recent trip. If you need more space, use a separate sheet(s) of paper.

Date You Left the United States *(mm/dd/yyyy)*	Date You Returned to the United States *(mm/dd/yyyy)*	Did Trip Last Six Months or More?	Countries to Which You Traveled	Total Days Out of the United States
		☐ Yes ☐ No		
		☐ Yes ☐ No		
		☐ Yes ☐ No		
		☐ Yes ☐ No		
		☐ Yes ☐ No		
		☐ Yes ☐ No		
		☐ Yes ☐ No		
		☐ Yes ☐ No		
		☐ Yes ☐ No		
		☐ Yes ☐ No		

Part 8. Information about your marital history.

A. How many times have you been married (including annulled marriages)? [   ] If you have **never** been married, go to Part 9.

B. If you are now married, give the following information about your spouse:

1. Spouse's Family Name *(Last Name)*   Given Name *(First Name)*   Full Middle Name *(If applicable)*

[   ]   [   ]   [   ]

2. Date of Birth *(mm/dd/yyyy)*   **3.** Date of Marriage *(mm/dd/yyyy)*   **4.** Spouse's U.S. Social Security #

[   ]   [   ]   [   ]

5. Home Address - Street Number and Name   Apartment Number

[   ]   [   ]

City   State   Zip Code

[   ]   [   ]   [   ]

Part 8. Information about your marital history. *(Continued.)*

Write your USCIS "A"- number here:
A

C. Is your spouse a U.S. citizen? ☐ Yes ☐ No

D. If your spouse is a U.S. citizen, give the following information:

    1. When did your spouse become a U.S. citizen? ☐ At Birth ☐ Other

    If "Other," give the following information:

    2. Date your spouse became a U.S. citizen

    3. Place your spouse became a U.S. citizen *(Please see Instructions.)*

    City and State

E. If your spouse is **not** a U.S. citizen, give the following information :

    1. Spouse's Country of Citizenship

    2. Spouse's USCIS "A" Number *(If applicable)*
    A

    3. Spouse's Immigration Status
    ☐ Lawful Permanent Resident ☐ Other

F. If you were married before, provide the following information about your prior spouse. If you have more than one previous marriage, use a separate sheet(s) of paper to provide the information requested in Questions 1-5 below.

    1. Prior Spouse's Family Name *(Last Name)*   Given Name *(First Name)*   Full Middle Name *(If applicable)*

    2. Prior Spouse's Immigration Status
    ☐ U.S. Citizen
    ☐ Lawful Permanent Resident
    ☐ Other

    3. Date of Marriage *(mm/dd/yyyy)*

    4. Date Marriage Ended *(mm/dd/yyyy)*

    5. How Marriage Ended
    ☐ Divorce ☐ Spouse Died ☐ Other

G. How many times has your current spouse been married (including annulled marriages)?

If your spouse has **ever** been married before, give the following information about **your spouse's** prior marriage.
If your spouse has more than one previous marriage, use a separate sheet(s) of paper to provide the information requested in Questions 1 - 5 below.

    1. Prior Spouse's Family Name *(Last Name)*   Given Name *(First Name)*   Full Middle Name *(If applicable)*

    2. Prior Spouse's Immigration Status
    ☐ U.S. Citizen
    ☐ Lawful Permanent Resident
    ☐ Other

    3. Date of Marriage *(mm/dd/yyyy)*

    4. Date Marriage Ended *(mm/dd/yyyy)*

    5. How Marriage Ended
    ☐ Divorce ☐ Spouse Died ☐ Other

Part 9. Information about your children.	Write your USCIS "A"- number here: A

A. How many sons and daughters have you had? For more information on which sons and daughters you should include and how to complete this section, see the Instructions.

B. Provide the following information about all of your sons and daughters. If you need more space, use a separate sheet(s) of paper.

Full Name of Son or Daughter	Date of Birth *(mm/dd/yyyy)*	USCIS "A"- number *(if child has one)*	Country of Birth	Current Address *(Street, City, State and Country)*
		A		
		A		
		A		
		A		
		A		
		A		
		A		
		A		
		A		

Add Children Go to continuation page

| Part 10. Additional questions. |

Please answer Questions 1 through 14. If you answer "Yes" to any of these questions, include a written explanation with this form. Your written explanation should (1) explain why your answer was "Yes" and (2) provide any additional information that helps to explain your answer.

A. General Questions.

1. Have you **ever** claimed to be a U.S. citizen *(in writing or any other way)*? ☐ Yes ☐ No

2. Have you **ever** registered to vote in any Federal, state or local election in the United States? ☐ Yes ☐ No

3. Have you **ever** voted in any Federal, state or local election in the United States? ☐ Yes ☐ No

4. Since becoming a Lawful Permanent Resident, have you **ever** failed to file a required Federal state or local tax return? ☐ Yes ☐ No

5. Do you owe any Federal, state or local taxes that are overdue? ☐ Yes ☐ No

6. Do you have any title of nobility in any foreign country? ☐ Yes ☐ No

7. Have you ever been declared legally incompetent or been confined to a mental institution within the last five years? ☐ Yes ☐ No

| Part 10. Additional questions. (Continued.) | Write your USCIS "A"- number here: A |

B. Affiliations.

8. a Have you **ever** been a member of or associated with any organization, association, fund foundation, party, club, society or similar group in the United States or in any other place? ☐ Yes ☐ No

    b. If you answered "Yes," list the name of each group below. If you need more space, attach the names of the other group(s) on a separate sheet(s) of paper.

Name of Group	Name of Group
1.	6.
2.	7.
3.	8.
4.	9.
5.	10.

9. Have you **ever** been a member of or in any way associated *(either directly or indirectly)* with:

    a. The Communist Party? ☐ Yes ☐ No

    b. Any other totalitarian party? ☐ Yes ☐ No

    c. A terrorist organization? ☐ Yes ☐ No

10. Have you **ever** advocated *(either directly or indirectly)* the overthrow of any government by force or violence? ☐ Yes ☐ No

11. Have you **ever** persecuted *(either directly or indirectly)* any person because of race, religion, national origin, membership in a particular social group or political opinion? ☐ Yes ☐ No

12. Between March 23, 1933 and May 8, 1945, did you work for or associate in any way *(either directly or indirectly)* with:

    a. The Nazi government of Germany? ☐ Yes ☐ No

    b. Any government in any area (1) occupied by, (2) allied with, or (3) established with the help of the Nazi government of Germany? ☐ Yes ☐ No

    c. Any German, Nazi, or S.S. military unit, paramilitary unit, self-defense unit, vigilante unit, citizen unit, police unit, government agency or office, extermination camp, concentration camp, prisoner of war camp, prison, labor camp or transit camp? ☐ Yes ☐ No

C. Continuous Residence.

Since becoming a Lawful Permanent Resident of the United States:

13. Have you **ever** called yourself a "nonresident" on a Federal, state or local tax return? ☐ Yes ☐ No

14. Have you **ever** failed to file a Federal, state or local tax return because you considered yourself to be a "nonresident"? ☐ Yes ☐ No

Part 10. Additional questions. (Continued.)	Write your USCIS "A"- number here: A

D. Good Moral Character.

For the purposes of this application, you must answer "Yes" to the following questions, if applicable, even if your records were sealed or otherwise cleared or if anyone, including a judge, law enforcement officer or attorney, told you that you no longer have a record.

15. Have you **ever** committed a crime or offense for which you were **not** arrested? ☒ Yes ☐ No

16. Have you **ever** been arrested, cited or detained by any law enforcement officer (including USCIS or former INS and military officers) for any reason? ☒ Yes ☐ No

17. Have you **ever** been charged with committing any crime or offense? ☐ Yes ☐ No

18. Have you **ever** been convicted of a crime or offense? ☐ Yes ☐ No

19. Have you **ever** been placed in an alternative sentencing or a rehabilitative program (for example: diversion, deferred prosecution, withheld adjudication, deferred adjudication)? ☐ Yes ☐ No

20. Have you **ever** received a suspended sentence, been placed on probation or been paroled? ☐ Yes ☐ No

21. Have you **ever** been in jail or prison? ☐ Yes ☐ No

If you answered "Yes" to any of Questions 15 through 21, complete the following table. If you need more space, use a separate sheet (s) of paper to give the same information.

Why were you arrested, cited, detained or charged?	Date arrested, cited, detained or charged? *(mm/dd/yyyy)*	Where were you arrested, cited, detained or charged? *(City, State, Country)*	Outcome or disposition of the arrest, citation, detention or charge *(No charges filed, charges dismissed, jail, probation, etc.)*

Answer Questions 22 through 33. If you answer "Yes" to any of these questions, attach (1) your written explanation why your answer was "Yes" and (2) any additional information or documentation that helps explain your answer.

22. Have you **ever:**

    a. Been a habitual drunkard? ☐ Yes ☐ No

    b. Been a prostitute, or procured anyone for prostitution? ☐ Yes ☐ No

    c. Sold or smuggled controlled substances, illegal drugs or narcotics? ☐ Yes ☐ No

    d. Been married to more than one person at the same time? ☐ Yes ☐ No

    e. Helped anyone enter or try to enter the United States illegally? ☐ Yes ☐ No

    f. Gambled illegally or received income from illegal gambling? ☐ Yes ☐ No

    g. Failed to support your dependents or to pay alimony? ☐ Yes ☐ No

23. Have you **ever** given false or misleading information to any U.S. government official while applying for any immigration benefit or to prevent deportation, exclusion or removal? ☐ Yes ☐ No

24. Have you **ever** lied to any U.S. government official to gain entry or admission into the United States? ☐ Yes ☐ No

Form N-400 (Rev. 10/15/07) Y Page 8

Part 10. Additional questions. (Continued.)	Write your USCIS "A"- number here: A

E. Removal, Exclusion and Deportation Proceedings.

25. Are removal, exclusion, rescission or deportation proceedings pending against you? ☐ Yes ☐ No

26. Have you **ever** been removed, excluded or deported from the United States? ☐ Yes ☐ No

27. Have you **ever** been ordered to be removed, excluded or deported from the United States? ☐ Yes ☐ No

28. Have you **ever** applied for any kind of relief from removal, exclusion or deportation? ☐ Yes ☐ No

F. Military Service.

29. Have you **ever** served in the U.S. Armed Forces? ☐ Yes ☐ No

30. Have you **ever** left the United States to avoid being drafted into the U.S. Armed Forces? ☐ Yes ☐ No

31. Have you **ever** applied for any kind of exemption from military service in the U.S. Armed Forces? ☐ Yes ☐ No

32. Have you **ever** deserted from the U.S. Armed Forces? ☐ Yes ☐ No

G. Selective Service Registration.

33. Are you a male who lived in the United States at any time between your 18th and 26th birthdays in any status except as a lawful nonimmigrant? ☐ Yes ☐ No

   If you answered "NO," go on to question 34.

   If you answered "YES," provide the information below.

   If you answered "YES," but you did not register with the Selective Service System and are still under 26 years of age, you must register before you apply for naturalization, so that you can complete the information below:

   Date Registered (mm/dd/yyyy) [_____]   Selective Service Number [_____]

   If you answered "YES," but you did not register with the Selective Service and you are now 26 years old or older, attach a statement explaining why you did not register.

H. Oath Requirements. *(See Part 14 for the Text of the Oath.)*

Answer Questions 34 through 39. If you answer "No" to any of these questions, attach (1) your written explanation why the answer was "No" and (2) any additional information or documentation that helps to explain your answer.

34. Do you support the Constitution and form of government of the United States? ☐ Yes ☐ No

35. Do you understand the full Oath of Allegiance to the United States? ☐ Yes ☐ No

36. Are you willing to take the full Oath of Allegiance to the United States? ☐ Yes ☐ No

37. If the law requires it, are you willing to bear arms on behalf of the United States? ☐ Yes ☐ No

38. If the law requires it, are you willing to perform noncombatant services in the U.S. Armed Forces? ☐ Yes ☐ No

39. If the law requires it, are you willing to perform work of national importance under civilian direction? ☐ Yes ☐ No

Form N-400 (Rev. 10/15/07) Y Page 9

Part 11. Your signature.

Write your USCIS "A"- number here:
A

I certify, under penalty of perjury under the laws of the United States of America, that this application, and the evidence submitted with it, are all true and correct. I authorize the release of any information that the USCIS needs to determine my eligibility for naturalization.

Your Signature

Date *(mm/dd/yyyy)*

Part 12. Signature of person who prepared this application for you. (*If applicable.*)

I declare under penalty of perjury that I prepared this application at the request of the above person. The answers provided are based on information of which I have personal knowledge and/or were provided to me by the above named person in response to the *exact questions* contained on this form.

Preparer's Printed Name

Preparer's Signature

Date *(mm/dd/yyyy)*

Preparer's Firm or Organization Name *(If applicable)*

Preparer's Daytime Phone Number

Preparer's Address - Street Number and Name

City

State

Zip Code

NOTE: Do not complete Parts 13 and 14 until a USCIS Officer instructs you to do so.

Part 13. Signature at interview.

I swear (affirm) and certify under penalty of perjury under the laws of the United States of America that I know that the contents of this application for naturalization subscribed by me, including corrections numbered 1 through _____ and the evidence submitted by me numbered pages 1 through _____, are true and correct to the best of my knowledge and belief.

Subscribed to and sworn to (affirmed) before me

Officer's Printed Name or Stamp

Date *(mm/dd/yyyy)*

Complete Signature of Applicant

Officer's Signature

Part 14. Oath of Allegiance.

If your application is approved, you will be scheduled for a public oath ceremony at which time you will be required to take the following oath of allegiance immediately prior to becoming a naturalized citizen. By signing, you acknowledge your willingness and ability to take this oath:

I hereby declare, on oath, that I absolutely and entirely renounce and abjure all allegiance and fidelity to any foreign prince, potentate, state, or sovereignty, of whom or which I have heretofore been a subject or citizen;

that I will support and defend the Constitution and laws of the United States of America against all enemies, foreign and domestic;

that I will bear true faith and allegiance to the same;

that I will bear arms on behalf of the United States when required by the law;

that I will perform noncombatant service in the Armed Forces of the United States when required by the law;

that I will perform work of national importance under civilian direction when required by the law; and

that I take this obligation freely, without any mental reservation or purpose of evasion; so help me God.

Printed Name of Applicant

Complete Signature of Applicant

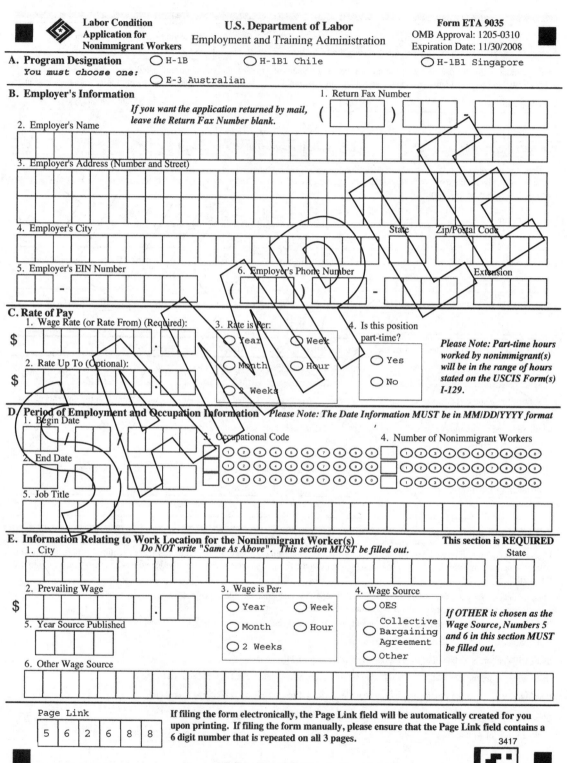

Labor Condition Application for Nonimmigrant Workers

U.S. Department of Labor
Employment and Training Administration

Form ETA 9035
OMB Approval: 1205-0310
Expiration Date: 11/30/2008

A. Program Designation
You must choose one:
○ H-1B   ○ H-1B1 Chile   ○ H-1B1 Singapore
○ E-3 Australian

B. Employer's Information
If you want the application returned by mail, leave the Return Fax Number blank.

1. Return Fax Number
2. Employer's Name
3. Employer's Address (Number and Street)
4. Employer's City   State   Zip/Postal Code
5. Employer's EIN Number   6. Employer's Phone Number   Extension

C. Rate of Pay
1. Wage Rate (or Rate From) (Required): $
2. Rate Up To (Optional): $
3. Rate is Per: ○ Year ○ Week ○ Month ○ Hour ○ 2 Weeks
4. Is this position part-time? ○ Yes ○ No

Please Note: Part-time hours worked by nonimmigrant(s) will be in the range of hours stated on the USCIS Form(s) I-129.

D. Period of Employment and Occupation Information *Please Note: The Date Information MUST be in MM/DD/YYYY format*
1. Begin Date
2. End Date
3. Occupational Code
4. Number of Nonimmigrant Workers
5. Job Title

E. Information Relating to Work Location for the Nonimmigrant Worker(s)   **This section is REQUIRED**
1. City   *Do NOT write "Same As Above". This section MUST be filled out.*   State
2. Prevailing Wage $
3. Wage is Per: ○ Year ○ Week ○ Month ○ Hour ○ 2 Weeks
4. Wage Source ○ OES ○ Collective Bargaining Agreement ○ Other
If OTHER is chosen as the Wage Source, Numbers 5 and 6 in this section MUST be filled out.
5. Year Source Published
6. Other Wage Source

Page Link
5 6 2 6 8 8

If filing the form electronically, the Page Link field will be automatically created for you upon printing. If filing the form manually, please ensure that the Page Link field contains a 6 digit number that is repeated on all 3 pages.

3417

Labor Condition Application for Nonimmigrant Workers	U.S. Department of Labor Employment and Training Administration	Form ETA 9035 OMB Approval: 1205-0310 Expiration Date: 11/30/2008

E. Subsection A Information for Additional or Subsequent Work Location

This Section should be completed only if filing for more than 1 work location.

1. City

State

2. Prevailing Wage

$

3. Wage is Per:
- ○ Year
- ○ Month
- ○ 2 Weeks
- ○ Week
- ○ Hour

4. Wage Source
- ○ OES
- ○ Collective Bargaining Agreement
- ○ Other

If OTHER is chosen as the Wage Source, Numbers 5 and 6 in this section MUST be filled out.

5. Year Source Published

6. Other Wage Source

F. Employer Labor Condition Statements

! **Please Note:** In order for your application to be processed, you MUST read section E of the Labor Condition Application cover pages under the heading "Employer Labor Condition Statements" and agree to all 4 labor condition statements summarized below:

(1) Wages: Pay nonimmigrants at least the local prevailing wage or the employer's actual wage, whichever is higher, and pay for non-productive time. Offer nonimmigrants benefits on the same basis as U.S. workers.

(2) Working Conditions: Provide working conditions for nonimmigrants which will not adversely affect the working conditions of workers similarly employed.

(3) Strike, Lockout, or Work Stoppage: No strike or lockout in the occupational classification at the place of employment.

(4) Notice: Notice to union or to workers at the place of employment. A copy of this form to the nonimmigrant worker(s).

I have read and agree to Employer Labor Condition Statements 1, 2, 3, and 4 as set forth in Section E of the Labor Condition Application Cover Pages.   ○ Yes   ○ No

F-1. Additional Employer Labor Condition Statements - H-1B Employers Only

Please Note: In order for an application regarding H-1B nonimmigrants to be processed, you MUST read Section F-1 - Subsections 1 and 2 of the Labor Condition Application cover pages under the heading "Additional Employer Labor Condition Statements" and choose one of the 3 alternatives (A, B, or C) listed below in Subsection 1. If you mark Alternative B, you MUST read Section F-1 - Subsection 2 of the cover pages under the heading "Additional Employer Labor Condition Statements" and indicate your agreement to all 3 additional statements summarized below in Subsection 2.

1. Subsection 1

Choose ONE of the following 3 alternatives:

A ○ **Employer is not H-1B dependent and is not a willful violator.**

B ○ **Employer is H-1B dependent and/or a willful violator.**

C ○ **Employer is H-1B dependent and/or a willful violator BUT will use this application ONLY to support H-1B petitions for exempt nonimmigrants.**

2. Subsection 2

If Alternative B in Subsection 1 is marked, the following Additional Labor Condition Statements are applicable:

A. **Displacement: Non-displacement of the U.S. workers in employer's work force;**

B. **Secondary Displacement: Non-displacement of U.S. workers in another employer's work force; and**

C. **Recruitment and Hiring: Recruitment of U.S. workers and hiring of U.S. worker applicant(s) who are equally or better qualified than the H-1B nonimmigrant(s).**

I have read and agree to Additional Labor Condition Statements 2 A, B, and C.   ○ Yes   ○ No

Page Link					
5	6	2	6	8	8

If filing the form electronically, the Page Link field will be automatically created for you upon printing. If filing the form manually, please ensure that the Page Link field contains a 6 digit number that is repeated on all 3 pages.

3417

| Labor Condition Application for Nonimmigrant Workers | U.S. Department of Labor
Employment and Training Administration | Form ETA 9035
OMB Approval: 1205-0310
Expiration Date: 11/30/2008 |

G. Public Disclosure Information

You must choose one of the two options listed in this Section.

1. Public disclosure information will be kept at: ○ Employer's principal place of business

○ Place of employment

H. Declaration of Employer

By signing this form, I, on behalf of the employer, attest that the information and labor condition statements provided are true and accurate; that I have read the sections E, F, and F-1 of the cover pages (Form ETA 9035CP), and that I agree to comply with the Labor Condition Statements as set forth in the cover pages and with the Department of Labor regulations (20 CFR part 655, Subparts H and I). I agree to make this application, supporting documentation, and other records available to officials of the Department of Labor upon request during any investigation under the Immigration and Nationality Act.

1. First Name of Hiring or Other Designated Official   MI

2. Last Name of Hiring or Other Designated Official

3. Hiring or Other Designated Official Title

5. Date Signed / /

4. Signature - Do NOT let signature extend beyond the box

Making fraudulent representations on this Form can lead to civil or criminal action under 18 U.S.C. 1001, 18 U.S.C. 1546, or other provisions of law.

I. Contact Information

1. Contact First Name   MI

2. Contact Last Name

3. Contact Phone Number   Extension

( ) -

J. U.S. Government Agency Use Only

By virtue of my signature below, I hereby acknowledge this application certified for

Date Starting _____ and Date Ending _____

_____
Signature and Title of Authorized DOL Official   ETA Case Number   Date

The Department of Labor is not the guarantor of the accuracy, truthfulness, or adequacy of a certified labor condition application.

K. Complaints

Complaints alleging misrepresentation of material facts in the labor condition application and/or failure to comply with the terms of the labor condition application may be filed with any office of the Wage and Hour Division, U.S. Department of Labor. Complaints alleging failure to offer employment to an equally or better qualified U.S. worker, or an employer's misrepresentation regarding such offer(s) of employment, may be filed with: U.S Department of Justice * Office of the Special Counsel for Immigration-Related Unfair Employment Practices* 950 Pennsylvania Ave, NW * Washington, DC * 20530.

Page Link					
5	6	2	6	8	8

If filing the form electronically, the Page Link field will be automatically created for you upon printing. If filing the form manually, please ensure that the Page Link field contains a 6 digit number that is repeated on all 3 pages.

3417

Form ETA 9035 Page 3 of 3

OMB Approval: 1205-0451
Expiration Date: 06/30/2011

Application for Permanent Employment Certification
ETA Form 9089
U.S. Department of Labor

Please read and review the filing instructions before completing this form. A copy of the instructions can be found at http://www.foreignlaborcert.doleta.gov/pdf/9089inst.pdf

Employing or continuing to employ an alien unauthorized to work in the United States is illegal and may subject the employer to criminal prosecution, civil money penalties, or both.

A. Refiling Instructions

1. Are you seeking to utilize the filing date from a previously submitted Application for Alien Employment Certification (ETA 750)?	❏ Yes	❏ No

1-A. If Yes, enter the previous filing date

1-B. Indicate the previous SWA or local office case number OR if not available, specify state where case was originally filed:

B. Schedule A or Sheepherder Information

1. Is this application in support of a Schedule A or Sheepherder Occupation?	❏ Yes	❏ No

If Yes, do NOT send this application to the Department of Labor. All applications in support of Schedule A or Sheepherder Occupations must be sent directly to the appropriate Department of Homeland Security office.

C. Employer Information (Headquarters or Main Office)

1. Employer's name

2. Address 1

   Address 2

3. City	State/Province	Country	Postal code

4. Phone number	Extension

5. Number of employees	6. Year commenced business

7. FEIN (Federal Employer Identification Number)	8. NAICS code

9. Is the employer a closely held corporation, partnership, or sole proprietorship in which the alien has an ownership interest, or is there a familial relationship between the owners, stockholders, partners, corporate officers, incorporators, and the alien?	❏ Yes	❏ No

D. Employer Contact Information (This section must be filled out. This information must be different from the agent or attorney information listed in Section E).

1. Contact's last name	First name	Middle initial

2. Address 1

   Address 2

3. City	State/Province	Country	Postal code

4. Phone number	Extension

5. E-mail address

OMB Approval: 1205-0451
Expiration Date: 06/30/2011

Application for Permanent Employment Certification
ETA Form 9089
U.S. Department of Labor

E. Agent or Attorney Information (If applicable)

1. Agent or attorney's last name	First name	Middle initial

2. Firm name

3. Firm EIN	4. Phone number	Extension

5. Address 1

Address 2

6. City	State/Province	Country	Postal code

7. E-mail address

F. Prevailing Wage Information (as provided by the State Workforce Agency)

1. Prevailing wage tracking number (if applicable)	2. SOC/O*NET(OES) code

3. Occupation Title	4. Skill Level

5. Prevailing wage   Per: (Choose only one)
$ ❏ Hour   ❏ Week   ❏ Bi-Weekly   ❏ Month   ❏ Year

6. Prevailing wage source (Choose only one)
❏ OES   ❏ CBA   ❏ Employer Conducted Survey   ❏ DBA   ❏ SCA   ❏ Other

6-A. If Other is indicated in question 6, specify:

7. Determination date	8. Expiration date

G. Wage Offer Information

1. Offered wage
From: To: (Optional)   Per: (Choose only one)
$ $ ❏ Hour   ❏ Week   ❏ Bi-Weekly   ❏ Month   ❏ Year

H. Job Opportunity Information (Where work will be performed)

1. Primary worksite (where work is to be performed) address 1

Address 2

2. City	State	Postal code

3. Job title

4. Education: minimum level required:
❏ None   ❏ High School   ❏ Associate's   ❏ Bachelor's   ❏ Master's   ❏ Doctorate   ❏ Other

4-A. If Other is indicated in question 4, specify the education required:

4-B. Major field of study

5. Is training required in the job opportunity?   5-A. If Yes, number of months of training required:
❏ Yes   ❏ No

OMB Approval: 1205-0451
Expiration Date: 06/30/2011

Application for Permanent Employment Certification
ETA Form 9089
U.S. Department of Labor

H. Job Opportunity Information Continued

5-B. Indicate the field of training:

6. Is experience in the job offered required for the job? ☐ Yes ☐ No	6-A. If Yes, number of months experience required:

7. Is there an alternate field of study that is acceptable?	☐ Yes ☐ No

7-A. If Yes, specify the major field of study:

8. Is there an alternate combination of education and experience that is acceptable?	☐ Yes ☐ No

8-A. If Yes, specify the alternate level of education required:

☐ None ☐ High School ☐ Associate's ☐ Bachelor's ☐ Master's ☐ Doctorate ☐ Other

8-B. If Other is indicated in question 8-A, indicate the alternate level of education required:

8-C. If applicable, indicate the number of years experience acceptable in question 8:

9. Is a foreign educational equivalent acceptable?	☐ Yes ☐ No

10. Is experience in an alternate occupation acceptable? ☐ Yes ☐ No	10-A. If Yes, number of months experience in alternate occupation required:

10-B. Identify the job title of the acceptable alternate occupation:

11. Job duties – If submitting by mail, add attachment if necessary. Job duties description must begin in this space.

12. Are the job opportunity's requirements normal for the occupation? *If the answer to this question is No, the employer must be prepared to provide documentation demonstrating that the job requirements are supported by business necessity.*	☐ Yes ☐ No
13. Is knowledge of a foreign language required to perform the job duties? *If the answer to this question is Yes, the employer must be prepared to provide documentation demonstrating that the language requirements are supported by business necessity.*	☐ Yes ☐ No

14. Specific skills or other requirements – If submitting by mail, add attachment if necessary. Skills description must begin in this space.

OMB Approval: 1205-0451
Expiration Date: 06/30/2011

Application for Permanent Employment Certification
ETA Form 9089
U.S. Department of Labor

H. Job Opportunity Information Continued

15. Does this application involve a job opportunity that includes a combination of occupations?	❑ Yes ❑ No
16. Is the position identified in this application being offered to the alien identified in Section J?	❑ Yes ❑ No
17. Does the job require the alien to live on the employer's premises?	❑ Yes ❑ No
18. Is the application for a live-in household domestic service worker?	❑ Yes ❑ No
18-A. If Yes, have the employer and the alien executed the required employment contract and has the employer provided a copy of the contract to the alien?	❑ Yes ❑ No ❑ NA

I. Recruitment Information

a. Occupation Type – All must complete this section.

1. Is this application for a **professional occupation**, other than a college or university teacher? Professional occupations are those for which a bachelor's degree (or equivalent) is normally required.	❑ Yes ❑ No
2. Is this application for a college or university teacher? **If Yes, complete questions 2-A and 2-B below.**	❑ Yes ❑ No
2-A. Did you select the candidate using a competitive recruitment and selection process?	❑ Yes ❑ No
2-B. Did you use the basic recruitment process for professional occupations?	❑ Yes ❑ No

b. Special Recruitment and Documentation Procedures for College and University Teachers – Complete only if the answer to question I.a.2-A is Yes.

3. Date alien selected:
4. Name and date of national professional journal in which advertisement was placed:
5. Specify additional recruitment information in this space. Add an attachment if necessary.

c. Professional/Non-Professional Information – Complete this section unless your answer to question B.1 or I.a.2-A is YES.

6. Start date for the SWA job order	7. End date for the SWA job order
8. Is there a Sunday edition of the newspaper in the area of intended employment?	❑ Yes ❑ No
9. Name of newspaper (of general circulation) in which the first advertisement was placed:	
10. Date of first advertisement identified in question 9:	
11. Name of newspaper or professional journal (if applicable) in which second advertisement was placed:	❑ Newspaper ❑ Journal

ETA Form 9089

OMB Approval: 1205-0451
Expiration Date: 06/30/2011

Application for Permanent Employment Certification
ETA Form 9089
U.S. Department of Labor

I. Recruitment Information Continued

12. Date of second newspaper advertisement or date of publication of journal identified in question 11:

d. Professional Recruitment Information – Complete if the answer to question I.a.1 is YES or if the answer to I.a.2-B is YES. Complete at least 3 of the items.

13. Dates advertised at job fair From: To:	14. Dates of on-campus recruiting From: To:
15. Dates posted on employer web site From: To:	16. Dates advertised with trade or professional organization From: To:
17. Dates listed with job search web site From: To:	18. Dates listed with private employment firm From: To:
19. Dates advertised with employee referral program From: To:	20. Dates advertised with campus placement office From: To:
21. Dates advertised with local or ethnic newspaper From: To:	22. Dates advertised with radio or TV ads From: To:

e. General Information – All must complete this section.

23. Has the employer received payment of any kind for the submission of this application?	☐ Yes ☒ No		
23-A. If Yes, describe details of the payment including the amount, date and purpose of the payment :			
24. Has the bargaining representative for workers in the occupation in which the alien will be employed been provided with notice of this filing at least 30 days but not more than 180 days before the date the application is filed?	☐ Yes	☐ No	☐ NA
25. If there is no bargaining representative, has a notice of this filing been posted for 10 business days in a conspicuous location at the place of employment, ending at least 30 days before but not more than 180 days before the date the application is filed?	☐ Yes	☐ No	☐ NA
26. Has the employer had a layoff in the area of intended employment in the occupation involved in this application or in a related occupation within the six months immediately preceding the filing of this application?	☐ Yes	☐ No	
26-A. If Yes, were the laid off U.S. workers notified and considered for the job opportunity for which certification is sought?	☐ Yes	☐ No	☐ NA

J. Alien Information (This section must be filled out. This information must be different from the agent or attorney information listed in Section E).

1. Alien's last name   First name   Full middle name
2. Current address 1   Address 2
3. City   State/Province   Country   Postal code
4. Phone number of current residence
5. Country of citizenship   6. Country of birth
7. Alien's date of birth   8. Class of admission
9. Alien registration number (A#)   10. Alien admission number (I-94)
11. Education: highest level achieved relevant to the requested occupation: ☐ None   ☐ High School   ☐ Associate's   ☐ Bachelor's   ☐ Master's   ☐ Doctorate   ☐ Other

OMB Approval: 1205-0451
Expiration Date: 06/30/2011

Application for Permanent Employment Certification
ETA Form 9089
U.S. Department of Labor

J. Alien Information Continued

11-A. If Other indicated in question 11, specify	
12. Specify major field(s) of study	
13. Year relevant education completed	
14. Institution where relevant education specified in question 11 was received	
15. Address 1 of conferring institution	
Address 2	

16. City	State/Province	Country	Postal code

17. Did the alien complete the training required for the requested job opportunity, as indicated in question H.5?	❑ Yes ❑ No ❑ NA
18. Does the alien have the experience as required for the requested job opportunity indicated in question H.6?	❑ Yes ❑ No ❑ NA
19. Does the alien possess the alternate combination of education and experience as indicated in question H.8?	❑ Yes ❑ No ❑ NA
20. Does the alien have the experience in an alternate occupation specified in question H.10?	❑ Yes ❑ No ❑ NA
21. Did the alien gain any of the qualifying experience with the employer in a position substantially comparable to the job opportunity requested?	❑ Yes ❑ No ❑ NA
22. Did the employer pay for any of the alien's education or training necessary to satisfy any of the employer's job requirements for this position?	❑ Yes ❑ No
23. Is the alien currently employed by the petitioning employer?	❑ Yes ❑ No

K. Alien Work Experience

List all jobs the alien has held during the past 3 years. Also list any other experience that qualifies the alien for the job opportunity for which the employer is seeking certification.

a. Job 1

1. Employer name			
2. Address 1			
Address 2			

3. City	State/Province	Country	Postal code

4. Type of business		5. Job title
6. Start date	7. End date	8. Number of hours worked per week

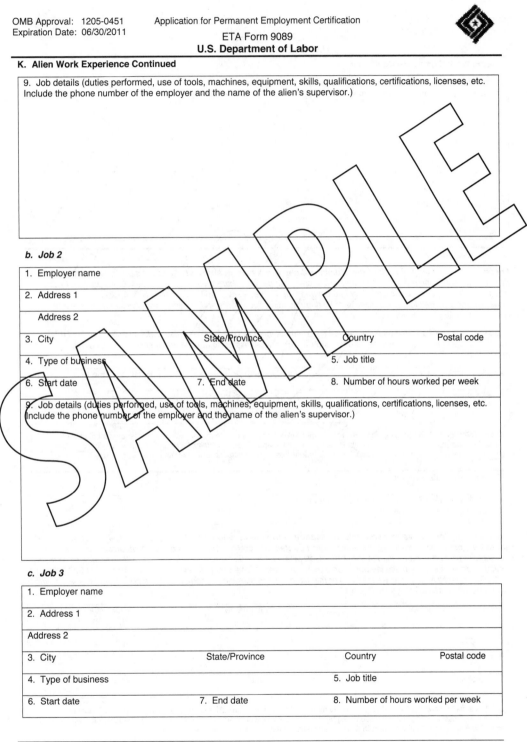

OMB Approval: 1205-0451
Expiration Date: 06/30/2011

Application for Permanent Employment Certification
ETA Form 9089
U.S. Department of Labor

K. Alien Work Experience Continued

9. Job details (duties performed, use of tools, machines, equipment, skills, qualifications, certifications, licenses, etc. Include the phone number of the employer and the name of the alien's supervisor.)

b. Job 2

1. Employer name			
2. Address 1			
Address 2			
3. City	State/Province	Country	Postal code
4. Type of business		5. Job title	
6. Start date	7. End date	8. Number of hours worked per week	

9. Job details (duties performed, use of tools, machines, equipment, skills, qualifications, certifications, licenses, etc. Include the phone number of the employer and the name of the alien's supervisor.)

c. Job 3

1. Employer name			
2. Address 1			
Address 2			
3. City	State/Province	Country	Postal code
4. Type of business		5. Job title	
6. Start date	7. End date	8. Number of hours worked per week	

ETA Form 9089

OMB Approval: 1205-0451
Expiration Date: 06/30/2011

Application for Permanent Employment Certification
ETA Form 9089
U.S. Department of Labor

K. Alien Work Experience Continued

> 9. Job details (duties performed, use of tools, machines, equipment, skills, qualifications, certifications, licenses, etc. Include the phone number of the employer and the name of the alien's supervisor.)

L. Alien Declaration

I declare under penalty of perjury that Sections J and K are true and correct. I understand that to knowingly furnish false information in the preparation of this form and any supplement thereto or to aid, abet, or counsel another to do so is a federal offense punishable by a fine or imprisonment up to five years or both under 18 U.S.C. §§ 2 and 1001. Other penalties apply as well to fraud or misuse of ETA immigration documents and to perjury with respect to such documents under 18 U.S.C. §§ 1546 and 1621.

*In addition, I **further declare** under penalty of perjury that I intend to accept the position offered in Section H of this application if a labor certification is approved and I am granted a visa or an adjustment of status based on this application.*

1. Alien's last name	First name	Full middle name
2. Signature	Date signed	

Note – The signature and date signed do not have to be filled out when electronically submitting to the Department of Labor for processing, but must be complete when submitting by mail. If the application is submitted electronically, any resulting certification MUST be signed *immediately upon receipt* from DOL before it can be submitted to USCIS for final processing.

M. Declaration of Preparer

1. Was the application completed by the employer? If No, you must complete this section.	☐ Yes	☐ No

I hereby certify that I have prepared this application at the direct request of the employer listed in Section C and that to the best of my knowledge the information contained herein is true and correct. I understand that to knowingly furnish false information in the preparation of this form and any supplement thereto or to aid, abet, or counsel another to do so is a federal offense punishable by a fine, imprisonment up to five years or both under 18 U.S.C. §§ 2 and 1001. Other penalties apply as well to fraud or misuse of ETA immigration documents and to perjury with respect to such documents under 18 U.S.C. §§ 1546 and 1621.

2. Preparer's last name	First name	Middle initial
3. Title		
4. E-mail address		
5. Signature	Date signed	

Note – The signature and date signed do not have to be filled out when electronically submitting to the Department of Labor for processing, but must be complete when submitting by mail. If the application is submitted electronically, any resulting certification MUST be signed *immediately upon receipt* from DOL before it can be submitted to USCIS for final processing.

OMB Approval: 1205-0451
Expiration Date: 06/30/2011

Application for Permanent Employment Certification
ETA Form 9089
U.S. Department of Labor

N. Employer Declaration

*By virtue of my signature below, **I HEREBY CERTIFY** the following conditions of employment:*

1. The offered wage equals or exceeds the prevailing wage and I will pay at least the prevailing wage.
2. The wage is not based on commissions, bonuses or other incentives, unless I guarantees a wage paid on a weekly, bi-weekly, or monthly basis that equals or exceeds the prevailing wage.
3. I have enough funds available to pay the wage or salary offered the alien.
4. I will be able to place the alien on the payroll on or before the date of the alien's proposed entrance into the United States.
5. The job opportunity does not involve unlawful discrimination by race, creed, color, national origin, age, sex, religion, handicap, or citizenship.
6. The job opportunity is not:
   a. Vacant because the former occupant is on strike or is being locked out in the course of a labor dispute involving a work stoppage; or
   b. At issue in a labor dispute involving a work stoppage.
7. The job opportunity's terms, conditions, and occupational environment are not contrary to Federal, state or local law.
8. The job opportunity has been and is clearly open to any U.S. worker.
9. The U.S. workers who applied for the job opportunity were rejected for lawful job-related reasons.
10. The job opportunity is for full-time, permanent employment for an employer other than the alien.

I hereby designate the agent or attorney identified in section E (if any) to represent me for the purpose of labor certification and, by virtue of my signature in Block 3 below, **I take full responsibility** for the accuracy of any representations made by my agent or attorney.

I declare under penalty of perjury that I have read and reviewed this application and that to the best of my knowledge the information contained herein is true and accurate. I understand that to knowingly furnish false information in the preparation of this form and any supplement thereto or to aid, abet, or counsel another to do so is a federal offense punishable by a fine or imprisonment up to five years or both under 18 U.S.C. §§ 2 and 1001. Other penalties apply as well to fraud or misuse of ETA immigration documents and to perjury with respect to such documents under 18 U.S.C. §§ 1546 and 1621.

1. Last name	First name	Middle initial
2. Title		
3. Signature	Date signed	

Note – The signature and date signed do not have to be filled out when electronically submitting to the Department of Labor for processing, but must be complete when submitting by mail. If the application is submitted electronically, any resulting certification MUST be signed *immediately upon receipt* from DOL before it can be submitted to USCIS for final processing.

O. U.S. Government Agency Use Only

Pursuant to the provisions of Section 212 (a)(5)(A) of the Immigration and Nationality Act, as amended, I hereby certify that there are not sufficient U.S. workers available and the employment of the above will not adversely affect the wages and working conditions of workers in the U.S. similarly employed.

_____
Signature of Certifying Officer

_____
Date Signed

_____
Case Number

_____
Filing Date

ETA Form 9089

Page 9 of 10

OMB Approval: 1205-0451
Expiration Date: 06/30/2011

Application for Permanent Employment Certification
ETA Form 9089
U.S. Department of Labor

P. OMB Information   *Paperwork Reduction Act Information Control Number 1205-0451*

Persons are not required to respond to this collection of information unless it displays a currently valid OMB control number.

Respondent's reply to these reporting requirements is required to obtain the benefits of permanent employment certification (Immigration and Nationality Act, Section 212(a)(5)). Public reporting burden for this collection of information is estimated to average 1¼ hours per response, including the time for reviewing instructions, searching existing data sources, gathering and maintaining the data needed, and completing and reviewing the collection of information. Send comments regarding this burden estimate to the Division of Foreign Labor Certification * U.S. Department of Labor * Room C4312 * 200 Constitution Ave., NW * Washington, DC * 20210.
Do NOT send the completed application to this address.

Q. Privacy Statement Information

In accordance with the Privacy Act of 1974, as amended (5 U.S.C. 552a), you are hereby notified that the information provided herein is protected under the Privacy Act. The Department of Labor (Department or DOL) maintains a System of Records titled Employer Application and Attestation File for Permanent and Temporary Alien Workers (DOL/ETA-7) that includes this record.

Under routine uses for this system of records, case files developed in processing labor certification applications, labor condition applications, or labor attestations may be released as follows: in connection with appeals of denials before the DOL Office of Administrative Law Judges and Federal courts, records may be released to the employers that filed such applications, their representatives, to named alien beneficiaries or their representatives, and to the DOL Office of Administrative Law Judges and Federal courts; and in connection with administering and enforcing immigration laws and regulations, records may be released to such agencies as the DOL Office of Inspector General, Employment Standards Administration, the Department of Homeland Security, and the Department of State.

Further relevant disclosures may be made in accordance with the Privacy Act and under the following circumstances: in connection with federal litigation; for law enforcement purposes; to authorized parent locator persons under Pub. L. 93-647; to an information source or public authority in connection with personnel, security clearance, procurement, or benefit-related matters; to a contractor or their employees, grantees or their employees, consultants, or volunteers who have been engaged to assist the agency in the performance of Federal activities; for Federal debt collection purposes; to the Office of Management and Budget in connection with its legislative review, coordination, and clearance activities; to a Member of Congress or their staff in response to an inquiry of the Congressional office made at the written request of the subject of the record; in connection with records management; and to the news media and the public when a matter under investigation becomes public knowledge, the Solicitor of Labor determines the disclosure is necessary to preserve confidence in the integrity of the Department, or the Solicitor of Labor determines that a legitimate public interest exists in the disclosure of information, unless the Solicitor of Labor determines that disclosure would constitute an unwarranted invasion of personal privacy.

ETA Form 9089   Page 10 of 10

USCIS Color Photograph Specifications

From Immigration and Naturalization Service Form M-378 (6-92)

Ideal Photograph

The picture at left is ideal size, color, background, and pose. The image should be 30mm (1³/₁₆in) from the hair to just below the chin, and 26mm (1 in) from left cheek to right ear. The image must fit in the box at right.

Image must fit inside this box

The Photograph

- The overall size of the picture, including the background, must be at least 40mm (1⁹/₁₆ in) in height by 35mm (1³/₈ in) in width.

- Photos must be free of shadows and contain no marks, splotches, or discoloration.

- Photos should be high quality, with good back lighting or wrap around lighting, and must have a white or off-white background.

- Photos must be a glossy or matte finish and un-retouched.

- Polaroid film hybrid #5 is acceptable; however SX-70 type film or any other instant processing type film is unacceptable. Non-peel apart films are easily recognized because the back of the film is black. Acceptable instant color film has a gray-toned backing.

The Image of the Person

- The dimensions of the image should be 30mm (1³/₁₆ in) from the hair to the neck just below the chin, and 26mm (1in) from the right ear to the left cheek. Image cannot exceed 32mm by 28mm (1¹/₄ in X 1¹/₁₆ in).

- If the image area on the photograph is too large or too small, the photo cannot be used.

- Facial features **MUST BE IDENTIFIABLE.**

- Contrast between the image and background is essential. Photos for very light skinned people should be slightly under-exposed. Photos for very dark skinned people should be slightly over-exposed.

Samples of Unacceptable Photographs

Incorrect Pose **Image Too Large** **Image Too Small** **Image Too Dark**
Under-Exposed

Image Too Light **Dark Background** **Over-Exposed** **Shadows on Picture**

20

Directory of Immigration Lawyers and Service Providers

The next several pages contain names of attorneys and service providers specializing in U.S. Immigration matters. Next Decade, Inc. has no affiliation with these organizations, other than Mr. Lubiner. However, if you choose to contact them, please let them know that you obtained their name from this book.

California

Adam Green
Law Offices of Adam Green
6300 Wilshire Boulevard, Suite 1020
Los Angeles, CA 90048
(323) 852-6135
(323) 966-4980 (fax)
adamgreen@earthlink.net

Law Office Loretta Nelms Reyes
3130 Bonita Rd., Suite 102
Chula Vista, CA 91910
(619) 427-5113
(619) 427-6113 (fax)
reyesgreencard@yahoo.com

Indu Liladhar-Hathi
1754 Technology Drive, Suite 143
San Jose, CA 95110
(408) 453-5335
(408) 453-5334
indu@indulaw.com

Michael W. Schoenleber, Attorney at Law
Schoenleber & Waltermire, P.C.
911 22nd Street
Sacramento, CA 95816
(916) 441-5327
(916) 669-1046 (fax)
info@mwslaw.com

Connecticut

Andrew L. Wizner, Partner
Leete & Kosto & Wizner LLP
999 Asylum Avenue, Suite 202
Hartford, CT 06105
(860) 249-8100
(860) 727-9184 (fax)
Awizner@lkwvisa.com

Elizabeth Leete, Partner
Leete & Kosto & Wizner LLP
999 Asylum Avenue, Suite 202
Hartford, CT 06105
(860) 249-8100
(860) 727-9184 (fax)
Eleete@lkwvisa.com

Eric Fleischmann, Partner
Leete & Kosto & Wizner LLP
999 Asylum Avenue, Suite 202
Hartford, CT 06105
(860) 249-8100
(860) 727-9184 (fax)
Ericf@lkwvisa.com

Florida

James R. LaVigne, President
LaVigne, Coton & Associates, P.A.
7087 Grand National Drive, Suite 100
Orlando, FL 32819
(407) 316-9988
(407) 316-8820 (fax)
attylavign@aol.com

Hawaii

Carmen Diamore-Siah
Law Office of Carmen Diamore
735 Bishop St., Suite #201
Honolulu, HI 96813
(808) 531-2277
(808) 531-2220 (fax)
carmen@immigrateus.com
http://www.immigrateus.com

Illinois

Scott D. Pollock, Attorney at Law
Scott D. Pollock & Associates, P.C.
105 W. Madison Street, Suite 2200
Chicago,IL 60602
(312) 444-1940
(312) 444-1950 (fax)
spollock@lawfirm1.com

Maryland

Michael L. Kabik
Shulman, Rogers, Gandal,
        Pordy & Ecker, P.A.
11921 Rockville Pike
Rockville, MD 20852
(301) 231-0937
(301) 230-2891 (fax)
mkabik@srgpe.com

Michigan

Michael E. Wooley, Esquire
Braun Kendrick Finkbeiner P.L.C.
4301 Fashion Square Boulevard
Saginaw, MI 48603
(989) 498-2100
(989) 799-4666 (fax)
MIKWOO@BKF-LAW.COM

Mississippi

Thomas J. Rosser, Attorney at Law
Baker, Donelson, Bearman,
        Caldwell & Berkowitz, PC
Suite 250, 2094 Old Taylor Road
Oxford, MS 38655
(662) 234-0350
(662) 234-0360 (fax)
trosser@bakerdonelson.com

Montana

James P. Sites, Attorney
Crowley, Haughey, Hanson, Toole &
Dietrich, P.L.L.P.
490 N. 31st Street, Suite 500
Billings, MT 59101
(406) 252-3441
(406) 256-8526 (fax)
jsites@crowleylaw.com

New Jersey

Alan M. Lubiner, Esq.
Lubiner & Schmidt, L.L.C.
216 North Avenue East
Cranford, NJ 07016
(908) 709-0500
(908) 709-9447 (fax)
alubiner@lslawyers.com
www.lslawyers.com

Anthony F. Siliato, Esq.
Meyner and Landis LLP
One Gateway Center-Suite 2500
Newark, NJ 07102
(973) 624-2800
(973) 624-0356 (fax)
asiliato@meyner.com

David H. Nachman, Esq.
Nachman & Associates, P.C.
Visaserve Plaza
487 Goffle Road
Ridgewood, NJ 07450
(201) 670-0006
(201) 670-0009 (fax)
David_Nachman@visaserve.com

New York

Margaret W. Wong
401 Broadway, Suite 1620
New York, NY 10013
(212)-226-7011
(212) 226-7708

North Carolina

Penni Pearson Bradshaw
Constangy, Brooks & Smith
100 North Cherry Street, Suite 300
Winston-Salem, NC 27101
(336) 721-6842
(336) 748-9112 (fax)
pbradshaw@constangy.com

Ohio

Margaret W. Wong
Margaret W. Wong & Assoc.
3150 Chester Ave.
Cleveland, OH 44114
(216) 566-9908
(216) 566-1125 (fax)
wong@imwong.com

Washington

Bonnie Stern Wasser
Law Office of Bonnie Stern Wasser
320 W. Galen St., #201
(206) 282-2279
(206) 428-7159 (fax)
bonnie@bswasserlaw.com
www.bswasserlaw.com

Canada

Gary E. Hansen
Hansen & Company
538 9th Ave. SE
Calgary, AB
CanadaT2G 0S1
403-261-6890,
 1-800-523-6162 (toll free)
403-263-1632 (fax)
1-877-586-9325 (toll free fax)
info@hansen-company.com

SERVICE PROVIDERS

Foundation for International Services, Inc.
Brian Bosse, Vice President of Operations
14926-35th Avenue West, Suite 210
Lynnwood, WA 98087
425-248-2255
425-248-2262 (fax)
info@fis-web.com

FIS has been providing industry leading
and widely respected credential evaluation
reports of education obtained outside the
United States since 1978. These reports are
used for immigration matters, continuing
education, teacher certification, licensing
and employment. In addition, FIS offers
document translation services from most
foreign languages into English, as well as
English into other languages.

Global Credential Evaluators, Inc.
Jean B. Ringer, President
PO Box 9203
College Station, TX 77842-9203
1-800-707-0971
512-528-9293 (fax)
gce@gceus.com
www.gceus.com

GCE evaluates international academic
credentials for immigration, employment,
school admission, etc. Member of National
Association of Collegiate Evaluation Services, NACES®.

APPENDIX A
Filing Fees for Freqently Used Immigration Forms

Form		Fee
I-90	Application to Replace Permanent Residence Card	.$370
I-102	Application by Nonimmigrant Alien for	
	Replacement of Arrival Document	.$320
I-129	Petition for a Nonimmigrant Worker	.$320
I-129F	Petition for Alien Fiance	.$455
I-130	Petition for Alien Relative.	.$355
I-131	Application for Travel Document.	.$305
I-140	Immigrant Petition for Alien Worker	.$475
I-360	Petition for Widow(er), or Special Immigrant	.$375
I-485	Application to Register Permanent Residence or Adjust Status	.$1010
	Child under 14 accompanying	.$600
	Over 79 years of age.	.$930
I-526	Immigrant Petition by Alien Entrepreneur.	.$1435
I-539	Application to Extend/Change Nonimmigrant Status	.$300
I-751	Petition to Remove Conditions on Residence	.$545
I-765	Application for Employment Authorization	.$340
N-400	Application for Naturalization	.$675

Biometrics fee (for those applications that require fingerprinting) $80

APPENDIX B
USCIS Service Office Addresses

There are four Regional Service Centers in the U.S. that process most nonimmigrant and immigrant visa petitions, as well as all naturalization applications.

Vermont Service Center (VSC)

(direct mailing address)(this address for N-400 Naturalization
U.S. Department of Homeland Securityapplications)
75 Lower Welden StreetU.S. Department of Homeland Security
St. Albans, VT 05479-000175 Lower Welden Street
St. Albans, VT 05479-9400

Service Area: The VSC accepts and processes certain applications and petitions from individuals residing in the following states: Connecticut, Delaware, Maine, Maryland, Massachusetts, New Hampshire, New Jersey, New York, Pennsylvania, Puerto Rico, Rhode Island, Vermont, Virginia, Virgin Islands, West Virginia, and the District of Columbia.

Nebraska Service Center (NSC)
(this address for general correspondence)
P.O Box 82521
Lincoln, NE 68501-2521

Service Area: The NSC accepts and processes certain applications and petitions from individuals residing in the following states: Alaska, Colorado, Idaho, Illinois, Indiana, Iowa, Kansas, Michigan, Minnesota, Missouri, Montana, Nebraska, North Dakota, Ohio, Oregon, South Dakota, Utah, Washington, Wisconsin and Wyoming.

Texas Service Center (TSC)

(this address for general correspondence)(courier delivery)
USCIS TSCUSCIS TSC
PO Box 8514884141 N. St. Augustine Road
Mesquite, TX 75185-1488Dallas, TX 75227

Service Area: The TSC accepts and processes certain applications and petitions from individuals residing in the following states: Alabama, Arkansas, Florida, Georgia, Kentucky, Louisiana, Mississippi, New Mexico, North Carolina, South Carolina, Oklahoma, Tennessee, and Texas.

California Service Center (CSC)

(this address for mail)
U.S. Department of Homeland Security
USCIS
California Service Center
P.O. Box 30111
Laguna Niguel, CA 92607-0111

Service Area: The CSC accepts and processes certain applications and petitions from people residing in the following states: California, Nevada, Arizona, Hawaii, and the Territory of Guam.

IMPORTANT NOTE: There are constantly changes to the addresses to which forms are to be sent. Please check online at: http://www.uscis.gov/portal/site/uscis and go to the tab marked "immigration forms" for instructions on where to file.

District Office addresses are found below. All telephone inquiries should be made to USCIS Customer Service at 1-800-375-5283.

ALASKA	New Federal Building	
	620 East 10th Ave, Rm. 102	
	Anchorage, AK 99501-3701	
ARIZONA	Federal BuildingFederal Building	
	2035 North Central Ave.	6431 S. Country Club Rd.
	Phoenix, AZ 85004	Tucson, AZ 85706

ARKANSAS   4977 Old Greenwood Road
                    Fort Smith, AR 72903

CALIFORNIA   Federal BuildingFederal Building
                    1177 Fulton Mall   300 North Los Angeles St.
                    Fresno, CA 93721   Los Angeles, CA 90012

                    650 Capitol MallU.S. Federal Building
                    Sacramento, CA

                    95814880 Front St., Rm. 1234
                    San Diego, CA 92101-8834

                    444 Washington Street   1887 Monterey Road
                    San Francisco, CA 94111   San Jose, CA 95112

                    34 Civic Center Plaza   655 W. Rialto Avenue
                    Santa Ana, CA 92701   San Bernardino, CA
                                                    92410-3327

                    1261 3rd Avenue, Suite A   509 Industrial Way
                    Chula Vista, CA 91911   Imperial, CA 92251

COLORADO   Albrecht Center
                    4730 Paris St.
                    Denver, CO 80239

CONNECTICUT   Abraham Ribicoff Federal Building
                    450 Main St., 1st Floor
                    Hartford, CT06103-3060

DELAWARE   1305 McD Drive
                    Dover, DE 19901

DISTRICT OF   Washington District Office
COLUMBIA   2675 Prosperity Avenue
                    Fairfax, VA 22031

FLORIDA	4121 Southpoint Blvd. Jacksonville, FL 32216	7880 Biscayne Blvd. Miami, FL 33138
	9403 Tradeport Drive Orlando, FL 32827	5524 W. Cypress Tampa, FL 33607
	West Palm Beach Office 920 Banyan Blvd West Palm Beach, FL 33401	
GEORGIA	2150 Parklake Drive Atlanta, GA 30345	
GUAM	Sirena Plaza, Suite 801 108 Hernan Cortez Ave. Agana, Guam 96910	
HAWAII	595 Ala Moana Blvd. Honolulu, HI 96813	
IDAHO	1185 South Vinnell Way Boise, ID 83709	
ILLINOIS	10 West Congress Parkway Chicago, IL 60605	
INDIANA	Gateway Plaza, Suite 400 950 North Meridian St. Indianapolis, IN 46204	
IOWA	Des Moines Sub-Office 210 Walnut Street, Room 369 Federal Building Des Moines, IA 50309	
KANSAS	271 West 3rd St. North, suite 1050 Wichita, KS 67202-1212	

KENTUCKY	Gene Snyder US Custom House 601 West Broadway, Rm. 601 Louisville, KY 40202
LOUISIANA	Metairie Center Suite 300 2424 Edenborn Avenue Metairie, LA 70001
MAINE	176 Gannett Drive Portland, ME 04106
MARYLAND	Fallon Federal Building 31 Hopkins Plaza Baltimore, MD 21201
MASSACHUSETTS	John F. Kennedy Federal Office Building Government Center, Rm. E-160 Boston, MA 02203
MICHIGAN	Federal Building 333 Mount Elliott St. Detroit, MI 48207-4381
MINNESOTA	2901 Metro Drive, Suite 100 Bloomington, MN 55425
MISSISSIPPI	Dr. McCoy Federal Building 100 West Capitol Street, Suite 727 Jackson, MS 39269
MISSOURI	9747 Northwest Conant Ave. Kansas City, MO 64153 1222 Spruce Street St. Louis, MO 63103
MONTANA	2800 Skyway Drive Helena, MT 59602

NEBRASKA	1717 Avenue H. Omaha, NE 68110	
NEVADA	3373 Pepper Lane Las Vegas, NV 89120	1351 Corporate Boulevard Reno, NV 89502-7102
NEW HAMPSHIRE	803 Canal Street Manchester, NH 03101	
NEW JERSEY	Federal Building 970 Broad St. Newark, NJ 07102	530 Fellowship Road Mount Laurel, NJ 08054
NEW MEXICO	1720 Randolph Rd., SE Albuquerque, NM 87106	
NEW YORK	1086 Troy-Schenecdady Rd. Latham, NY 12110	130 Delaware Ave Buffalo, NY 14202
	Jacob Javits Federal Building 26 Federal Plaza New York, NY 10278	711 Stewart Ave. Garden City, NY 11530
	Federal Building 100 State Street, Room 418 Rochester, NY 14614	412 South Warren Street Syracuse, NY 13202
NORTH CAROLINA	301 Roycroft Drive Durham, NC 27703	6139 Tyvola Centre Drive Charlotte, NC 28217
OHIO	J.W. Peck Federal Bldg. 550 Main St., Rm. 400 Cincinnati, OH 45202	A.J. Celebreeze Federal Office Bldg. 11240 E. 9th St., Rm. 501 Cleveland, OH 44199
	50 W. Broad Street Leveque Tower Columbus, OH 43215	

OKLAHOMA	4400 SW 44ᵗʰ Street, Suite "A" Oklahoma City, OK 73119-2800	
OREGON	Federal Office Building 511 N.W. Broadway Portland, OR 97209	
PENNSYLVANIA	1600 Callowhill St. Philadelphia, PA 19130	3000 Sidney St., Suite 200 Pittsburgh, PA 15203
PUERTO RICO	San Patricio Office Center 7 Tabonuco St., Suite 100 Guaynabo, PR 00968	
RHODE ISLAND	200 Dyer Street Providence, RI 02903	
SOUTH CAROLINA	1 Poston Road, Suite 130 Parkshore Center Charleston, SC 29407	142-D West Phillips Road Greer, SC 29650
TENNESSEE	842 Virginia Run Cove Memphis, TN 38122	
TEXAS	Federal Building 8101 N. Stemmons Freeway Dallas, TX 75247	1545 Hawkins Blvd., Suite 167 El Paso, TX 79925
	1717 Zoy Street Harlingen, TX 78552	126 North Point Drive Houston, TX 77060
	US Federal Building 8940 Four Winds Drive San Antonio, TX 78239	
U.S.VIRGIN ISLANDS	8000 Nisky Center Suite 1A, 1ˢᵗ Floor Charlotte Amalie, St. Thomas, U.S.V.I. 00802	

Sunny Isle Shopping Center
Suite 5A
Christiansted, St. Croix, USVI 00823

UTAH

5272 S. College Dr., Suite 100
Salt Lake City, UT 84123

VERMONT

64 Gricebrook Rd
St. Albans, VT 05478

VIRGINIA

Norfolk Commerce Park
5280 Henneman Drive
Norfolk, VA 23513

WASHINGTON

12500 Tukwila International Blvd
Seattle, WA 98168

U.S. Courthouse
920 W. Riverside, Room 691
Spokane, WA 98201

415 North 3rd Street
Yakima, WA 98901

WEST VIRGINIA

210 Kanawha Boulevard West
Charleston, WV 25302

WISCONSIN

310 East Knapp Street
Milwaukee, WI 53202

There are no USCIS offices in the following states. Contact the USCIS office in parentheses for further information.

ALABAMA (Atlanta, Georgia)
NORTH DAKOTA (Bloomington, Minnesota)
SOUTH DAKOTA (Bloomington, Minnesota
WYOMING (Denver, Colorado)

USCIS Headquarters
425 "I" Street, NW
Washington, DC 20536

Overseas Offices

There are also three overseas District Offices that have jurisdiction for U.S. immigration matters outside the U.S. They are located in Bangkok, Thailand; Mexico City, Mexico; and Rome, Italy. Each of these offices has suboffices as follows:

Bangkok- Beijing, Guangzhou, Ho Chi Minh City, Hong Kong, Manila, New Delhi, Seoul

Mexico City-Ciudad Juarez, Guatemala City, Havana, Kingston, Lima, Monterrey, Panama City, Port-au-Prince, San Salvador, Santo Domingo, Tegucigalpa, Tijuana

Rome-Accra, Athens, Frankfurt, Johannesburg, London, Moscow, Nairobi, Vienna

APPENDIX C
U.S. Department of Labor Office Addresses

Most employers will choose to file their PERM cases electronically. Cases filed electronically will be processed more expeditiously than those filed by mail. Cases may be filed electronically at: http://www.plc.doleta.gov

Beginning June 16, 2008, applications filed by mail for PERM cases must be filed at the Atlanta National Processing Center. Applications for temporary labor certification in connection with H-2B applications must be filed at the Chicago National Processing Center

Atlanta NPC:
US Department of Labor
Employment and Training Administration
Atlanta National Processing Center
Harris Tower
233 Peachtree Street, NE, Suite 410
Atlanta, GA 30303
Phone: 404-893-0101
Fax: 404-893-4642
Help desk email: plc.atlanta@dol.gov

Chicago NPC:
US Department of Labor
Employment and Training Administration
Chicago National Processing Center
844 North Rush Street, 12th Floor
Chicago, Illinois 60611
Phone: 312-886-8000
Fax: 312-353-3352
Help desk email: plc.chicago@dol.gov

APPENDIX D
U.S. Passport Agencies

These offices serve customers who are traveling within 2 weeks (14 days), or who need foreign visas to travel.

Most offices open between 8:00 and 9:00 a.m. and close between 3:00 and 4:00 p.m., Monday through Friday, excluding Federal holidays

Boston, Massachusetts
Thomas P. O'Neill Federal Building
10 Causeway Street, Suite 247
Boston, MA 02222-1094
Automated Appointment Number: (877) 487-2778

Chicago, Illinois
Kluczynski Federal Office Building
230 S. Dearborn, 18th Floor
Chicago, IL 60604-1564
Automated Appointment Number: (877) 487-2778

Aurora, Colorado
Cherry Creek III
3151 South Vaughn Way, Suite 600
Aurora, CO 80014
Automated Appointment Number: (877) 487-2778

Norwalk, Connecticut
50 Washington Street
Norwalk, CT 06854
Automated Appointment Number: (877) 487-2778

Honolulu, Hawaii
Prince Kuhio Federal Building
300 Ala Moana Blvd.-Suite 1-330
Honolulu, HI 96850
Automated Appointment Number: (877) 487-2778

Houston, Texas
Mickey Leland Federal Building
1919 Smith Street, Suite 1400
Houston, TX 77002-8049
Automated Appointment Number: (877) 487-2778

Los Angeles, California
Federal Building
11000 Wilshire Blvd.-Suite 1000
Los Angeles, CA 90024-3615
Automated Appointment Number: (877) 487-2778

Miami, Florida
Claude Pepper Federal Office Building
51 SW First Ave.-3rd Floor
Miami, FL 33130-1680
Automated Appointment Number: (877) 487-2778

New Orleans, Louisiana
One Canal Place
(corner of Canal and North Peters Street)
365 Canal Street, Suite 1300
New Orleans, LA 70130-6508
Automated Appointment Number: (877) 487-2778

New York City, New York
376 Hudson Street
New York, NY 10014
Automated Appointment Number: (877) 487-2778
Note: This office is no longer able to accept walk-in customers who do not have an appointment.

Philadelphia, Pennsylvania
U.S. Custom House
200 Chestnut Street, Room 103
Philadelphia, PA 19106-2970
Automated Appointment Number: (877) 487-2778

San Francisco, California
95 Hawthorne Street, 5th Floor
San Francisco, CA 94105-3901
Automated Appointment Number: (877) 487-2778

Seattle, Washington
Henry Jackson Federal Building
915 Second Ave.-Suite 992
Seattle, WA 98174-1091
Automated Appointment Number: (877) 487-2778

Washington, DC
1111 19th Street, N.W.
Washington, DC 20524
Automated Appointment Number: (877) 487-2778

Special Issuance Agency
1111 19th Street, NW, Suite 200
Washington, DC 20036
Note: Applications for Diplomatic, Official,
and No-Fee Passports

Index

S

BOOK ORDER FORM
Two easy ordering methods:

Credit Card Orders
Call the publisher, Next Decade, Inc.
Telephone: 800-595-5440.

Check or money order
Complete this form, attach your payment, and mail to:
Next Decade, Inc.,
39 Old Farmstead Road, Chester, NJ 07930

If you have any questions, call us:
Telephone: 908-879-6625
Email: info@nextdecade.com

YOUR NAME AND TITLE: _____

NAME OF ORGANIZATION (if applicable): _____

STREET ADDRESS: _____

CITY: _____ STATE: _____ ZIP: _____

TELEPHONE: _____ FAX: _____

E-MAIL: _____

Please ship _____ copy/copies of Citizenship Made Simple at $16.95 per copy $ _____

Please ship _____ copy/copies of Immigration Made Simple at $24.95 per copy $ _____

I've enclosed $ _____

NJ orders ONLY add 6% sales tax if required $ _____

Shipping: Add $5.00 for the first copy and $1.00 for each additional copy $ _____

TOTAL $ _____

A check/money order made payable to Next Decade, Inc. for $ _____ is enclosed.

Please charge my ❏ Visa   ❏ Mastercard

Card Number (16 digits) _____ Expiration _____

Name as it appears on card _____

Signature _____